The Strange Death of
British Birdsong

Michael Waterhouse

Landmark Countryside Collection

Dedication

For my mother and father,
Caroline and Hugo Waterhouse

The Strange Death of
British Birdsong

Michael Waterhouse

Introduction by: Rob Hume – Editor of RSPB *Birds Magazine*
Postscript by: Rt. Hon. Lord Lamont of Lerwick

Contents

Contents

Published by

Ashbourne Hall, Cokayne Ave
Ashbourne, Derbyshire DE6 1EJ England
Tel: (01335) 347349 Fax: (01335) 347303
e-mail: landmark@clara.net
web site: www.landmarkpublishing.co.uk

1st edition

ISBN 1-84306-126-0

Printed by Gutenburg Press Ltd, Malta

Design & reproduction by James Allsopp

Front cover: Whinchat
Page 3 & back cover: Yellowhammer

Foreword

This book is not intended to have any scientific value; keen ornithologists may not find anything that they don't already know. It is, however, thoroughly researched and accurate and I have always wanted to produce an authoritative reference book on the status of our bird populations for a wide market. The health of our birds is an increasingly reliable indicator as to the current state of the environment.

Many thousands of ordinary city dwellers, who also love the British countryside, have not failed to notice that the house sparrow and starling are fast disappearing from their urban haunts. In some cases we just do not know the reason why certain species have declined and more research is urgently needed.

There is no science governing which birds are covered; they represent most of my favourite and some of our better known British birds. I have looked at their fortunes over the past 25 years or so and my colour-coded categories are fluid and subject to ongoing change. One harsh winter may cause a dramatic crash in the numbers of a delicate species such as the wren or kingfisher whereas a drought in the whitethroat's African winter quarters can cause its population to halve from one year to the next.

Many of the birds in this book may not be considered 'songbirds' as such by the reader. All birds use some form of communication, however, whether it be a fluty warble or a monotonous one syllable call-note.

There is, of course, much to be optimistic about: for example many raptors and waterfowl have thrived over recent years. Yet it is a sad fact of life that it happens to be our farmland, woodland and garden birds – our true songbirds – that have suffered most at the hands of modern-day man with his advanced technology and sophisticated farming practices.

Note: unlike the bird illustrations, the eggs are shown at actual size. The bird illustrations are taken from *British Birds* by Rev. F.O. Morris (First Edition 1859). The original watercolours were painted by Alexander Francis Lydon (1836-1917) and others. The engravings were produced by Benjamin Fawcett who developed a technique of printing in colour from wood blocks and touching up the prints with hand colouring. The one bird 'unknown' to Morris was the collared dove that had yet to spread into western Europe. This illustration is the work of Rob Hume.

MICHAEL WATERHOUSE

 # *Introduction — by Rob Hume*

For centuries, people have found enjoyment, inspiration and relaxation in the sound of singing birds; and there is no reason to believe that such an emotional response was not evoked thousands of years before.

Apart from its aesthetic appeal, the physical attributes of birdsong are extraordinary; these also serve to highlight the abilities of the average human being. It is impossible for anyone with all five senses working moderately well to imagine what it must be like to be deprived of any one of them. The idea of blindness to a sighted person is too awful to contemplate, but deafness surely cuts people off from their fellows and surroundings still more completely.

Sound has a benefit over light in that it travels around a corner, through a wall, or from the depths of a leafy wood. It is, however, more difficult to describe. None of this is to say, however, that birdsong, or any other sound, has the same effect on all of us; far from it. The connoisseur might be in raptures over a nightingale, while many people listen to a robin at night and are quite happy in the belief that its simpler, smaller voice is that of the nightingale so beloved of the poets. Just as one person may delight in a piece of Mozart or Beethoven and another sees nothing in it (or might merely appreciate a good tune), so the song of a mistle thrush in spring may be miraculous to one person and ignored by another alongside. It is all to do with years of experience, encouragement, learning, identifying and responding to such sounds in our many individual ways.

Our hearing is, as mammals go, not bad but not so very special. Yet we are capable of remarkable feats. Sit anywhere in the house and listen. Waves of sound through the air, hitting a small, flexible drum in the ear, convey a huge amount of information. A scraping noise from another room can be identified immediately as a potato peeler at work on the vegetables. A metallic clink is obviously a fork dropping into the sink; a faint rustle tells a tale on a secret chocolate eater. Even remembered sounds can be thoroughly imbued with meanings and memories: the whirr of a childhood toy, the soft clunk of a particular cupboard door, the drone of a distant piston-engine aeroplane; thousands of such things.

Sounds are heard, some almost felt, and identified with precision as a matter of course – no one really has to try, as they are experienced, stored away in our mental database and continually reinforced or refreshed for the whole of our lives. Birdsong is but one category of sound; but one with the power to enthuse, delight and frustrate.

What do birds hear?
Birds, however, may hear rather differently from us, although it is difficult to be sure. They generally have excellent hearing, even though the ear opening is a tiny one com-

pared with our ear, decorated as it is with its large and complex outer flap. A bird's ear is usually covered over by a layer of tight feathers. In relatively few birds, and none in northern Europe save the farmyard turkey, is the ear opening obvious visually. The way birds hear must have important implications for the way they call and sing. Does the super-fast warble and trill of a wren sound altogether different to another wren? Do these tiny creatures, that live such short, fast lives, really hear the song as if it is 'slowed down', able to penetrate the jumble of sounds and separate out long sequences of tiny inflections that endow the song with so much more meaning? We hear such complex structures only when the song is recorded and played back at a slower speed. But that introduces distortion, especially of the pitch of the sound, which is surely not the way that a bird hears it.

Bird calls and songs have evolved to perform many functions. Drive along a road and much of the surround-sound effect of the moving car comes from the rumble of tyres on asphalt. Modern soundproofing and silencing keeps the engine noise to a minimum, but still the car produces a substantial background hum, a subdued roar. Sharp ears, nevertheless, pick up the fine, thin, high-pitched rhythm of a singing goldcrest with surprising ease.

The faint sound penetrates; it must have been made to do exactly that, to penetrate the dark, dense, overpowering environment of a big conifer forest, the kind of place that this lightest of Europe's birds chooses to inhabit. Similarly, the needle-sharp calls and song of the grey wagtail, and the metallic, grating monosyllable of a flying dipper, are easy to hear above the roar of tumbling water where a torrent rushes through a defile in a deep gorge. These birds' sounds are made to split through the noise of their everyday environment, to communicate information to others of their species.

Such high, sharp notes are always penetrative, but sadly, for many of us, they eventually become inaudible. High pitch deafness is very common in people as they get older, particularly if earlier years were spent in noisy environments. Our ears simply become deadened to the highest pitch. Hearing the prolonged, fast, ticking trill of a singing grasshopper warbler is almost the only way to locate this secretive bird, but many people are resigned to the fact that they may not find one in this way ever again. The bird's ear works pretty much the same as a human ear. Both are sensitive to pitch more than 'strength' or amplitude, the opposite of the case in an insect's hearing. So birds are not sensitive to a much greater range of pitch than we are; but they do seem able to separate out many more notes in a brief moment of time than we can. So it seems that a wren, for example, really can distinguish more in the song of another wren than us, even though the sound obviously lasts just the same few seconds of time; and the wren can control the output of far more minute variations of sound than we are able to in the briefest burst of song.

How do birds produce songs and calls?

Apart from the penetration of sharp calls, the way that the song of even the smallest bird carries over a long distance is striking. How does the tiny body of a willow warbler produce a song that can be heard clearly at such a distance that ordinary human speech, even a shouted conversation, may be hard to hear at all? The song of a mistle thrush, the largest of our typical songbirds, carries for a huge distance, its wild, shouted quality easily identifiable by any experienced listener. And the bittern, that rare and remarkable bird of dense reedbeds, where even another bittern could not see it from more than a few strides distant, produces a deep, hollow booming 'whoomp' that carries a couple of miles. Our effort to reproduce the sound by blowing across the mouth of an empty bottle barely gets across the road.

How do birds produce such sounds? The syrinx is the main vocal organ, the larynx being small and lacking vocal chords. The syrinx is a resonating chamber at the base of the windpipe, with vibrating membranes controlled by special muscles that tighten or relax them. Some birds with no such musculature produce little or no sound, while a single pair of muscles is enough for the pigeons and doves to coo with. Two pairs of muscles create the squeals and rough, hacking noises of falcons but only in the songbirds are there five to nine sets of muscles.

Waders, such as the curlew and redshank, seem to produce a 'song' that is effectively a succession of call notes, whereas the true songbirds exercise more control, producing greater variation and modulation of the notes. Some produce two or more notes together, or at least overlapping, but they lack the resonating chambers of the human mouth, nose and throat that allow a true, open vowel sound. Even the best speaking parrot hardly manages a proper vowel; but an Indian mynah can do it.

What is birdsong?

Birdsong is wonderful, matched only by our ability to hear it and discern the many and varied differences that make it so fascinating and so pleasing. It is not quite everywhere, but near enough so in our small islands. If you adopt a fairly broad definition of song, as Michael Waterhouse does quite rightly in this book, it can be heard from the tops of the highest Scottish mountains to the most open, low-lying marshes and plains; from deep woodland to the exposed ledges of spectacular seabird cliffs on the hardest of our coasts. Perhaps the growl of a guillemot, the cackle of a fulmar or the ringing cries of a gliding kittiwake are not exactly birdsong, but they perform some of the same functions as more conventional song, such as the strident repetition of a song thrush. On the moors, the ecstatic bubbling of a curlew is more obviously a song; if more people knew it and thought about it, surely it would be voted highly into any top ten of songs in Europe, jostling for points with the blackbird and the blackcap.

Some songbirds have a remarkable complexity within their repertoire. Marsh warblers can include mimicry of scores of other birds found within their breeding areas in Europe and their wintering areas in Africa. Woodlarks are known to produce as many as 100 melodic lines in a few minutes of song, with scores of notes per second, although we hear only a rather slow sequence of cadences and diminuendos.

And what of the rasp of the corncrake? A song, surely, if not a musical one. Some years ago, when corncrakes were still widespread in western Ireland, I heard them (but never saw one, then) in a number of places, none more memorable than the central valley of a small, western island called Inishturk. From a distance the cry of a corncrake is a light, simple, double note, like a fine comb scratched across a small wooden box, even a thumbnail on the sandpaper of an old-fashioned matchbox. Closer, it has a deeper, rasping or ratchet quality; your comb must be stiffer, coarser. On Inishturk, at midnight, echoing from surrounding hills, the corncrakes were tearing the air with sharp, hard, crisply defined rattles, like staccato bursts of an old, wooden football rattle. It was no great composition, but what a performance, an indelible experience.

Defining a territory

What functions of bird vocalisations categorise them as 'song'? Popularly, two are given. One is to proclaim a territory; to tell other birds of the same species; *'This is my patch, I claim it, clear off somewhere else.'* Usually this is a male laying claim to a breeding territory in spring. But it can be a male defending a feeding territory in winter, or even a female doing the same. Male and female robins each sing in winter and defend territories of their own.

A singing male has a number of regular song perches around the edge of his territory, as can be seen with a blackbird or a chaffinch. These are species that nest in territories, defended against intrusion by other pairs. The defending pair has sole access to the food within the defended area.

Other species may defend much smaller areas, or breed colonially. Whereas a territorial chaffinch, for example, requires an abundance of caterpillars to feed to its young, and caterpillars are widely but evenly spread through its habitat, species that do not defend a nesting territory eat food that is abundant in a few places but not evenly spread. Territories do not work in such circumstances, but the birds can all find enough food in one place, and there is no need for territorial song.

Finding a mate

Their song, however, has a second main reason: to attract a mate (and, later, perhaps to maintain contact with her and to help reinforce the bond between them). The same (or very similar) song serves both purposes in a territorial bird; other males are warned off, but unattached females are attracted by it and they can assess the quality of the male by the strength and complexity of his song. It is not quite this simple, however, as, once the male is paired, his mate will not want other females coming in to distract him. His song is reduced, often to a brief burst in the morning and evening.

The song of a bird in spring and summer usually indicates a breeding pair, and this is where the song comes into the main story of this book. It is a tool for the bird counter,

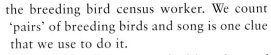

the breeding bird census worker. We count 'pairs' of breeding birds and song is one clue that we use to do it.

Song alone is not proof of breeding, of course. It may be from a solitary male hoping against hope to find a mate. Male wood warblers exploring new areas are particularly prone to sing all summer long and this persistence is a good indication that there is *not* a breeding pair there at all, but just a lonely male doing his best to meet up with a hen.

Monitoring numbers, song is a basic tool in a birdwatcher's armoury, in identifying, locating and counting breeding birds. This is why birdsong is so strongly involved in our attempts to quantify, monitor and understand fluctuations in bird numbers and distribution. It is why the disappearance of birdsong is so worrying, cutting straight to the central issue. If we no longer hear singing skylarks in spring, it is because the skylarks have gone; disappeared, moved on, or whatever. *Why* comes later; the silent skies where once skylarks poured out their ecstatic song carry the first important message that gives rise to real concern. In some cases, the reasons for such declines or disappearances are obvious; or at least, they *seem* obvious. Closer investigation may reveal unexpected complications and unlooked-for relationships. In any case, detailed study is necessary to pinpoint the reasons for declines, if we are to understand exactly what is needed to help declining birds to recover. Nothing beats real facts and genuine understanding.

The work of the conservation organisations, such as the RSPB, which is the one I know best because I happen to work for it, is quite well known publicly, but I am always amazed at the scale and scope of the effort, which really is not widely appreciated. There may be 80 or 100 RSPB research projects continuing at any one time. There is also an abundance of research projects organised by universities, the BTO, English Nature, the Wildfowl & Wetlands Trust, county bird clubs and bird observatories and many other bodies that add to our collective knowledge.

In agricultural areas, the RSPB, for example, is working on many fronts. It has its own farm, to find, prove and promote ways to farm effectively, efficiently but in a bird-friendly fashion. It is deeply involved in shaping such ideas as the new agrienvironment schemes, which help to pay farmers to manage their land in a way that helps birds as well as themselves. In the aftermath of the foot and mouth disease episode, some Devon farmers, who had previously signed up to a special cirl bunting scheme, said that it 'saved their bacon', and there is no doubt at all that it has saved the cirl bunting's bacon in Britain. Without farmers deliberately helping this rare bird, and of course being paid to do so, the cirl bunting would be on the verge of extinction in the UK. Instead, by the end of 2003, it had recovered from a low of 118 pairs in 1982 to almost 700 pairs.

The RSPB has long campaigned for reform of the Common Agriculture Policy across the EU. It had significant input into the Government's Policy Commission on the Future of Food and Farming, welcoming an encouraging indication that Government began to recognise that food production is not the only function of the countryside. The RSPB has recommended that farmers with grey partridges, turtle doves, tree sparrows or corn buntings on their land or near their farm should receive priority for countryside stewardship agreements, and farmers who can supply the entire life-cycle needs of certain birds should score more highly than others.

Many farmers are taking part in experimental feeding of wild birds in winter, using waste grains to support winter flocks of seed-eaters such as finches and buntings. Hundreds of others invite birdwatchers onto their land to map the birds and tell them exactly what they have on their farms and where. Advice on ways to look after these birds is available if they want it.

There are research projects on house and tree sparrows, reed buntings, song thrushes and bullfinches; on choughs (even on cowpats, which encourage insect food for choughs, and the effects of worming chemicals given to cattle which may effectively 'sterilise' their dung). Other projects investigate predators and lapwings and the feeding behaviour of swallows. Research continues into the diets of farmland birds, the effects of intensification of lowland grassland management on bird populations, the indirect effects of pesticides on birds and the benefits to wildlife of newly fashionable non-inversion tillage practices. Researchers are looking at the quality of different types of stubble field and the use of different types of grass margin by grasshoppers and crickets, especially important as food for buntings in summer, when they are feeding their chicks.

Bird conservation, in all its forms, is complicated; and, however much we may wish it was not, the application of solutions to conservation problems is very largely political. But research is central to conservation; good science is essential. It identifies the reasons for declines and helps formulate solutions. Knowledge based on such research helps to plan and put into effect conservation action.

Explaining declines – the corncrake story

Corncrakes, which I listened to with such admiration on Inishturk in 1969, have sadly long gone from most of Britain and even, as I was shocked to find from a map of current distribution in Ireland, from these remote Irish islands in the blue Atlantic. They have disappeared or declined throughout most of north-west Europe; only in eastern Europe are numbers still high and even there they have begun to fall. The spectre of EU agricultural policies being applied in new member states threatens accelerating declines. Why, exactly? The tale is a simple one and the problems easily identified, although the intricate detail took years of research to confirm. Corncrakes used to be found all over Britain and much of mainland Europe; not so long ago there were still people about who remembered them in their childhood in southern England. They are secretive creatures, probably a good meal for a hawk or falcon, but not very quick or manoeuvrable on the wing. They need thick cover the moment they arrive from Africa in early spring – tall yellow irises and nettle beds are ideal – long before their favoured hay crops are sufficiently tall.

In the summer, though, they need hay (although in north-east Europe, natural grasslands play a bigger role, as they must once have done in Britain thousands of years ago). Hay is no longer as widespread as it was. In Britain, especially in the north and west, it is a risky crop at the best of times. It needs weeks to grow and a good period of warm weather to ripen. When the many species of grasses and wild flowers are cut and laid flat and fragrant on the field, it has to enjoy unbroken warm, dry weather, or it gets wet, begins to rot and is fit for nothing. But with the development of different strains of grass the old, flowery hay meadows changed. As hay was replaced by tall, single-species crops of grass cut early for silage, the old situation was changed beyond recognition. Now the corncrake had no time to find a mate, make a nest, lay and incubate its eggs and rear its chicks before the grass was cut.

Mechanical cutters swept up scores of flightless chicks and simply mashed them out of existence. Adult corncrakes, horrifically, crouched before the mower, to lose their legs to the cutting blades. In much of Europe, they still do; researchers in Poland, for example, find this to be a big problem. Corncrakes, already in retreat decades ago, now survive only where farmers and crofters are encouraged – paid – to grow old-fashioned hay and cut it late. And to cut it from the inside out, rather than from the outside of a field inwards, forcing corncrakes into an ever-diminishing refuge in the centre until they face their destiny in the form of the cutter. Growing hay makes little sense to the modern farmer; he usually does it only if he is paid to. Subsidies and special agreements maintain an old-fashioned system that happens to be infinitely better for wildlife and the landscape than the new-fashioned silage. But the corncrake would be gone without such efforts; it remains an 'emergency' situation, but for how long? If the money dries up, the corncrake will go too, even now, when it seems to have been 'saved.'

There are other factors at play, too, of course. Corncrakes of the Western Isles are rarely safe from cats, which roam semi-wild and abundantly through the meadows around the little villages and crofts. Quail-catchers kill corncrakes that are on migration to Africa. But it is the loss of habitat – the important little details of the habitat – that has done for them.

There are many other birds that have declined dramatically across Britain and Ireland, taking their songs with them, for less obvious reasons. Food and habitat, however, seem to be the main factors at work. Climate change may be having an effect and promises more change in future; as indeed there must have been many changes in the past.

Farmland birds

Some changes remain frustratingly difficult to explain, such as the widespread and frighteningly fast decline of the tree sparrow, which, on investigation, seems to have undergone pretty dramatic changes in numbers and distribution in the past (but without so many birdwatchers to record them). Others have gradually given up their secrets to careful researchers: the familiar, humble song thrush and the skylark, the far less familiar cirl bunting and the secretive, elusive stone-curlew. Are there any common factors?

Most of the declining birds are found on farmland. Some species occupy both farmland and woodland, and are typically holding their own or declining slowly in the woods while populations have crashed out on the fields. Other species occupy woodland and gardens and are typically increasing or at least doing moderately well, although early in the 21st century there are signs that all is not well in the woods, either.

In 2000, there were some hopeful signs. The grey partridge, skylark, song thrush, linnet and bullfinch all showed indications of a recovery, although it was too early to be sure whether this was a real turning point. On the other hand, both tree sparrow and corn bunting have become too rare to register on the standard annual breeding birds census. Year-to-year changes are notoriously difficult to interpret, however, and the 2002 Breeding Bird Survey index gives a better overview of recent trends. During 1994–2002, song thrush and tree sparrow have shown significant population increases (up 14% and 12%) while others continue to decline, especially the skylark (a 20% fall) and corn bunting (a substantial 35% fall).

Changing agriculture

What may trigger such substantial, long-term changes? The use of pesticides can do so. Indirect effects of pesticides still take their toll. This is especially so on farmland, of course, but could be a big factor in gardens, too. If we really want pristine gardens with disease-free plants and aphid-free roses, we can spray and scatter all kinds of poisons over them. What will the birds have left to eat? On farmland, most crops are now remarkably weed-free, to the huge detriment of our wild flowers (and the landscapes and joyful experiences that go with them, as well as the insects such as the grasshoppers and butterflies that were once so abundant that no-one took much notice until they were gone). No weeds means no seeds and, in many instances, fewer insects; which, in turn, means nothing for birds to eat. This applies both in winter, when any remaining stubble fields are 'too clean' for seed-eating birds to find a living, and in summer, as there are no insects for them to feed to their young. Most seed-eating birds feed insects to their chicks; the cirl bunting, for example, needs grasshoppers. How many old grassy pastures do you know where grasshoppers still chirrup the summer days away?

Grey partridges – long-term research

While intensive research continues into the problems of many species, it is research on the grey partridge over a much longer period – since 1930 – that first highlighted farmland problems. The Game Conservancy, concerned at the reduction in partridges across UK farmland, found that several factors were involved but chief among them was the lack of insects in summer fields. Like many seed-eaters, partridges nevertheless need an abundance of small insects in spring and summer, because their growing chicks need a high-protein diet. Without insects, too few chicks were surviving. The lack of insects, of course, came about through changing farm practices, especially the use of new, potent chemicals.

Paradoxically, perhaps, the game shooting estates, having begun to put this situation right, created habitat for many birds, beyond the partridges that they wished to shoot.

Thrushes

Song thrushes, among Britain's finest songsters and genuinely deserving a place in this book, have declined quite dramatically in places. Many years ago, it was the blackbird that was the scarcer of the two. Now, blackbirds are generally more abundant while song thrushes have disappeared from some places and have become scarce in many. RSPB researchers have looked into the reasons for this, studying thrushes in Essex and Sussex. The Essex birds breed in agricultural areas with few hedges remaining and little woodland. In Sussex, the thrushes have more woodland and gardens, with less extensive cereal fields. In early spring, there is not a great deal to choose between the two habitats, but as the season drifts on into summer, so the Essex birds face tougher times with the soil drying out and no real option but to plug on in their farmland territories. The Sussex birds can move into woodland to feed, where the canopy and deep layer of leaves and herbs help to maintain a moist soil, from which earthworms can be more easily extracted. These woods probably have more snails, too, which are a favourite food of thrushes. The number of eggs in each clutch laid by song thrushes in both areas is not much different. The survival of thrushes during the hard times of winter is not much different, either. But the Sussex thrushes are thriving while the Essex ones have declined. The reason seems to be that Sussex song thrushes can rear several broods each summer, while Essex thrushes cannot. They manage one brood early on, then give up. Food is hard to find as the year wears on and females cannot get the nutrition to have further broods.

As agricultural practices have changed, so many other species have found life difficult. The song thrush suffers when the land is dried out by drainage schemes and so do many other birds. A wet summer may be good for thrushes, but is bad for larks. Britain, generally, has been dried out by decades of drainage. We may be suffering now as water from the fields and the uplands pours off the land at a catastrophic rate, flooding towns and villages downstream where drainage systems simply cannot cope. A gradual drying out of rural areas, combined with straightening of rivers and streams (and a loss of waterside vegetation, which has been grubbed out to let mechanical diggers get in to dredge the ditches and streams) has caused a steady decline in such birds as snipe, curlew, lapwing, even black-headed gulls and moorhens.

Maximum attack – the lark descending

From World War II, especially, British farmers were rightly encouraged to maximise production; a good job they did. Eventually, production was more than adequate to feed us, but intensification continued, encouraged later by the European Common Agricultural Policy. Subsidies paid to farmers helped to build up food mountains and milk lakes; not so much, now, but production is still largely targeted at maximum yields. A particularly big change came with the switch from spring sowing of cereals to autumn sowing. Now this practice is taken for granted and many younger birdwatchers can remember nothing else but the empty, lifeless, vivid green fields all winter through; but those, like me, who were birdwatching in the 1960s, recall winter fields of stubble, grown through with seeding weeds, with spilt grain adding extra food for flocks of birds. We used to see hundreds of house sparrows, dozens of tree sparrows and, in places, several hundred greenfinches, hundreds of linnets, scores of yellowhammers, a few reed buntings and maybe goldfinches and redpolls, often dozens or even hundreds of chaffinches and groups of skylarks, corn buntings and others, as a matter of course. I remember flocks of 100 turtle doves on wires above stubble fields in August.

Once the harvest was over, the fields of cut wheat and barley were often simply left as stubble over some or all of the winter and were excellent for birds, both in sheer numbers and in variety. With autumn sowing, the fields are quickly ploughed and re-seeded, so that, throughout the winter, there are now just clean, neat, smooth, weed-free fields with nothing for a bird to eat. This seems to have been a large part of the reason for the general decline of seed-eating birds. It has led, also, to a shocking loss of ordinary, everyday countryside flowers, many of which are now amazingly hard to find where once we pulled up handfuls on any short walk to feed to our pet rabbits.

Seeds in the soil have been measured over a remarkably long period. In the mid-20th century there were around 2,000 seeds per square metre in an average UK field, many of them large cereal grains spilled dur-

ing harvest. These were ideal for birds, keeping large numbers alive through long winters. In one study, the average has fallen to 200 seeds per square metre and most of those are tiny weed seeds. A hungry sky-lark now can use up more energy search-ing for food than it can take in by eating it. This has implications way beyond the skylarks that actually nest in these fields. Skylarks breeding on the moors of Wales, northern England and Scotland are declining, too; these 'wilderness larks' cannot survive the winters on fields any more than the farmland larks of the lowlands.

Skylarks breeding on arable land are affected in other ways, too. Skylarks used to breed in spring-sown corn, which was still relatively short and sparse when they laid their eggs, and reared a brood or two of chicks. Now, by early spring, the wheat crop is already dense and tall. Even if there is plenty of food, skylarks find it hard to get at; they just cannot walk easily through such a crop. There is nowhere for them to nest, except on the flattened tractor tracks – the 'tramlines' – through the crop. These make easy places for predators to find nests and eat the eggs and chicks and are in any case likely to be used again by tractors, which simply squash the nests.

Lapwing misfortunes

Other birds such as the lapwing find the intensification and specialisation of farming in arable areas a problem. Lapwings like to nest on short grass pasture or ploughed ground, or in an area where both short crops and bare earth can be found within easy reach. Young chicks need open spaces in which to feed; they are no better than the skylarks at plodding through dense cereal crops.

In mid Wales in the 1970s, when I was finding and counting upland birds for the RSPB, lapwings were common on the edges of the moors and on the wet, open commons where they bred on short damp grass and heath between clumps of gorse. At the time, huge areas of heather moor, common land and bracken-covered slopes – even very steep slopes at the top of the hill where it begins to level out into open moor – were being ploughed, levelled and seeded with rye grass. This created eyecatching squares of bright, smooth green, always incongruous in the otherwise beautifully varied, soft and irregular landscape. The lapwings piled in and nested all over them. At the best of times they were pitifully obvious from a great distance, easy for any passing crow with a taste for lapwing eggs. Then, too, the sheep were let loose or the farmer came along with his tractor and roller, and clutch after clutch of eggs was crushed or trampled by sheep. After a few springs of this, the lapwings, which had, all this time, scarcely reared a chick between them, just began to die of old age, with no young to replace them at all. The arithmetic fell apart; lapwings disappeared wholesale and they are now not common, not even scarce, in most of Wales. They have gone, completely. The irrepressible tumbling, throbbing wings and wailing songs of these fabulous waders has been lost from much of farmed Britain.

On the moors above, huge numbers of sheep have been encouraged as farmers have been paid subsidies according to the number of sheep they have, rather than the area of land they farm. Overstocking, to the detriment of everybody it seems (not many farmers did very well out of it, somehow), has caused dramatic changes in our uplands. More to the point, in some areas, reduced shepherding has exacerbated the situation. At one time the sheep would have been cleverly nudged around the hill and taken down in winter, so that no one part of the hill was heavily overgrazed and damaged. Now, with shepherds too costly to employ (and anyway, who wants to spend all day, every day, tending a flock of sheep?), sheep are left on the hill and encouraged to come to small areas where extra food is provided day after day. Big areas of hill have been ravaged by nibbling and trampling sheep, ruining them for the curlews and lapwings and snipe that used to nest. Other pieces of hill have been left ungrazed and have become sour and overgrown. The old mosaics of habitat have gone and, with them, the black grouse that can no longer survive on poorly managed moors and moorland-woodland edge. It is not just songbirds that have been affected by farming policy changes and the impact on the landscape of rural economics.

Constant change
There is danger in all of this, of course. It is easy to look back and think of Britain in the early 20th century and imagine that this is how it should be: a sort of rural idyll that should be aimed for once again, with thatched cottages surrounded by hollyhocks and roses and country folk singing in the fields. Was this a 'golden age' for birdsong? It was not such an idyllic place, of course. It was a tough place to make a living and farm labourers were overworked and badly paid. Long hours and backbreaking outdoor work in all weathers did little for the working man or his wife and children. And no one can seriously suggest that farming should go back to horse-drawn carts and ploughs, scythes, sickles and steam engines driving threshing machines. Obviously that cannot happen and conservationists who urge change do not propose that it should. Yet anyone watching the old black and white films produced around wartime in Britain, showing the green and pleasant land that was so worth fighting for, will inevitably wonder if that was not a peak period for the rural countryside, its landscape and its birds.

It was a time when agriculture was much more mixed and the village fitted more easily into the countryside scene. Modern industrial estates, retail 'parks', housing and all the paraphernalia associated with bypasses, motorways and their service stations and slip roads grate on the eye and seem sure to be damaging to wild bird populations. They are all taking up ever increasing amounts of space, once full of skylarks and bullfinches. And the monotonous monocultures, especially in eastern England (but spreading, still, elsewhere) have little of the charm of 'Old England.'

Conservation organisations such as the RSPB have a tightly controlled remit. They campaign for wild bird and habitat conservation and raise money for this purpose, so are unable to comment very fully on developments that many of us might regret but which have little or no effect on UK-wide bird populations. That is not, though, in my view, a reason to accept a dreary uniformity of development, a kind of 'dumbing down' of the countryside. There may be regimented country parks where we are all told where to go and what to look at and a replacement of ancient woods with squares of grid-line plantations, however well-intentioned. Far worse are the all-too-familiar wholesale developments around towns and cities of industrial parks, out-of-town shopping developments, motorways, bypasses and their associated infrastructure. These may have had little impact on total populations of birds, yet, but add their considerable weight to a gradual, insidious degeneration of the countryside, and they explain the loss of some birdsong on a local basis, at least.

Changing habitat
Take a look at any old photograph or film and another change is usually evident. Before the 1960s, England, especially, was adorned by millions of towering, billowing elms, among the most magnificent of all our trees. They are all but gone, now, following non-stop infection and re-infection with Dutch Elm disease. Has this affected bird

populations? It is hard to say. At first, some birds, such as lesser spotted woodpeckers, would have benefited. The more recent cycles of growing suckers, which reach 20 or 30ft high and then die back, should surely help these small woodpeckers, too. Yet the lesser spotted woodpecker, like so many other birds, is now in decline; perhaps suffering from competition with great spotted woodpeckers as they have reduced competition for nest sites from starlings.

Go back before the beginning of the 20th century, of course, and things were very different for long periods; in fact, the 'ideal' countryside, as many of us imagine it, was probably short-lived. Writers such as W H Hudson, Edward Grey and Richard Jefferies are firmly based in the countryside of England at a time when it was rich and varied and largely unspoiled. John Clare, however, in his long and detailed poems, bemoaned the loss of his beloved open spaces, as hedgerows and enclosures were being superimposed on the vistas of midland England. Much later, people experiencing the clearance of hedgerows in Huntingdonshire, which became largely open 'cereal prairie', recalled the days when they could scarcely see more than a quarter of a mile in any direction because of the abundance of tall, dense hedges.

It is a fair comment that the contemporary state of countryside birds cannot be expected to match some sort of 'ideal' that might have been the situation 50 or 100 years ago. The bird-life at the time of the enclosures, for example, must have been in a state of great change, as the numbers and variety of countryside species adapted to this massive alteration of rural habitats, and many periods of change since then have all brought some sort of response by bird populations.

There is no obvious 'correct' British bird-life that should be preserved at all costs, any more than a 'correct' UK landscape. It is, and always has been, in a state of flux. But that is not to say that we cannot spot when something is going badly wrong in the countryside, when so many birds are dwindling.

Pesticides and predators

Where do predators fit into the scheme of things? They have, to be sure, been around for as long as their prey, and, so far, have not starved. Some songbird species have done quite well in recent decades; they include the familiar blue tit and great tit, prime prey of the sparrowhawk; a good clue, surely, that the sparrowhawk is not, as some would have it, the cause of the decline of farmland birds such as the skylark (which it rarely catches). But the effects of predation are worth looking at, and probably play a part in the changing fortunes of some species considered in this book.

Controlling nest predators, such as crows, can produce local improvements in breeding success of small birds, and the breeding success of birds such as grey partridges can be depressed by predation, but it is abundantly clear that predation is not the root cause of declines in songbirds or gamebirds in Europe. Several studies show that numbers of songbirds are not related to the presence or absence of crows, magpies and sparrowhawks; at least, they do not decline when these predators increase. If there is a link, it is the other way around; where small bird numbers are high, so these predators are likely to be thriving, too. It is possible, though, that when a songbird has been reduced to a perilous level, predation may keep it at a low ebb even when action is taken to help it recover; it has to be looked at.

The sparrowhawk is a good illustration of a dramatic period in the 1950s and 1960s when many predatory birds declined for no obvious reason. Suddenly songbirds did, too, and small birds were found lying dead in the fields. What was happening? Oddly enough (but with a lesson that still needs remembering today) it was calls for the removal of predators such as the peregrine that helped bring about the work that led to the unravelling of this puzzle. Peregrines are doing so much damage to our birds, said pigeon-fanciers, that they must be culled! How many peregrines were there, then? No one really knew, so a census was organised; and, far from revealing a population booming out of control, it showed one in freefall, declining out of control towards extinction. Worse, the peregrine was suffering like this worldwide, not just in the United Kingdom.

Studies identified the problem, which we now all know about, as the persistence of organochlorine pesticides such as DDT. These bumped off the pests, all right, but remained active within them, so that anything that ate the pests also became affected. Anything that ate anything that ate the pests was poisoned, too. So we had seed dressings killing insects, seed and insects killing small birds and pigeons, small birds killing sparrowhawks and peregrines; and as the poisons concentrated in the bodies of animals at each level, so the predators ate the most. They were killed or effectively sterilised. Their breeding behaviour changed, they were unable to produce sufficient calcium and their egg shells thinned, so the eggs broke before they could hatch. It was a horrific situation, one that was perhaps saved just in time; but it took the birdwatchers to do it. The loss of birdsong, and the disappearance of the hawks and falcons, was the stimulus, then, to remove these deadly substances from everyday use.

It was early in 1964 that I first saw a sparrowhawk. My older, experienced birdwatching friend who was with me at the time said '*I bet you haven't seen one of those this year!*' I did not admit then that I had not seen one before, ever. But in 1964 in Staffordshire you did not see them; sparrowhawks, which should be among the most abundant of our predatory birds, were then practically gone from south-eastern and midland England. This provided a useful 'control' in our studies of small bird numbers. Once pesticides such as DDT and deildrin were banned, sparrowhawk numbers recovered and they become obvious again. Now, with sparrowhawks raiding bird tables in gardens ('takeaways' and 'drive through' for such skilled predators), people began to say that declines in songbirds must be related to the increase in the hawks. They forgot that hawks used to be as common before the pesticide era, let alone that hawks and small birds have co-existed for millions of years.

But things have changed since then, people have messed about with the landscape so much that any 'balance of nature' has long since been toppled. A fair point. But some people had been studying and counting small birds – carefully marking down singing males on maps year after year – and it was possible in some places to look at the numbers of small birds pre-pesticides, during the no-sparrowhawk era and again, post-pesticides, with the sparrowhawk back again. Several of the prey species that sparrowhawks eat increased steadily; in no case was there any evidence that small birds were uncommon before, more numerous while sparrowhawks were absent, and then declined again when they returned. The sparrowhawk, it seems, is exonerated. After all, if the sparrowhawk causes a decline in small birds, it simply does itself out of a living; it would have nothing left to eat.

Doing the sums

Small birds in a healthy environment produce a large surplus of young. Anyone who thinks that the figures sound too good to be true should perhaps consider fish. Each female fish produces tens or hundreds of thousands of eggs. Yet, for the fish population to remain stable, only two eggs – one for the female, one for the male – need to survive, of all these hundreds of thousands. How can nature be so precise? With birds, each pair needs only to produce two young that survive to breeding age to replace itself and keep the numbers up. That assumes that the two survivors live to the same age and also rear two surviving young.

The population can be knocked off balance in a number of ways. If the adults lay too few eggs, the sums do not work. If too few eggs hatch, they go wrong too. If too few hatched chicks survive, then once again the arithmetic is out. Some birds live a very long time; the fulmar, for example, may live for 25 or even 50 years, maybe more, but it does not breed until it is seven years old and then has only one egg each year. It takes a long time to produce one viable youngster. Others are quite different; the blue tit, for instance, lives a few years, breeds before it is a year old and lays as many as 15 eggs. It times them perfectly so that they hatch just when there are millions of caterpillars about on the foliage of trees such as oaks, but it cannot have a second brood because there are none available later in the year. Climate change may be affecting the caterpillars and causing them to hatch out earlier than they used to; so the blue tits, which are proving less readily adaptable, are missing out and cannot feed their chicks as well as they used to. And blue tits that nest in gardens cannot rear so many chicks as those in woods because gardens just do not provide such an abundance of little green creepy-crawlies.

Blackbirds, on the other hand, do not put all their eggs into one basket. They may lay almost as many as a blue tit in a year, but in two or three goes; several clutches of four instead of a dozen in one go. The result is the same but the strategy is different. Tawny owls behave more like blue tits, but lay a much smaller clutch and live longer. They rear the same number of chicks each year, relying on knowledge and experience within a stable territory to get them through. Barn owls, on the other hand, respond more actively to the abundance of food. Instead of three or four chicks each year like the tawny, the barn owl pair rears none when there is insufficient food, two or three in poor years, but maybe six or seven in bumper years when mice and voles are abundant, to make up for the bad years. Short-eared owls do the same but are even more no-madic, moving around to wherever there is plenty of food (voles in grassland) and settling there.

These owls, like some birds of prey, lay their eggs at a rate of one a day over several days but begin to incubate them from the first or second. Blue tits wait until they have laid a full clutch before incubating, so all hatch at the same time. The owls that incubate from the first egg have chicks popping out each day for a week or more, so the first one is already well grown by the time the last one hatches. If food is abundant, the last, tiny chick may get a share and survive. If not, it stands no chance against its older brothers and sisters; indeed, several may die and only the biggest survive, perhaps even killing and eating their own smaller siblings. It is tough being an owl.

All of these different ways of doing the same thing lead towards the two mature offspring that must replace the parents when they die. With small birds, getting back to the beginning of this argument, there may be ten or twelve surplus chicks each year; maybe more if you do the sums over a number of years. They cannot survive; otherwise we would be up to our ears in blue tits, robins and blackbirds. They die in various ways; some starve, some are soaked by cold rain, or cannot reach their food through layers of glazed frost. Others are diseased. Some are caught by cats, others hit by cars, others caught by hawks. Some do not make it past the egg stage, being eaten by magpies or rats, or failing to hatch because any one of these things may have happened to the parent birds. This is normal; indeed, it is essential. Only when things go badly out of balance do the numbers go wrong and populations go up or down over a much longer period.

What is happening close to home?

Other declines are taking place in town and village, garden and park. Why has the house sparrow disappeared from many areas, and diminished in numbers quite dramatically in others, while holding its own in some? Is it that the loss of birds to cars, and cats, has finally caught up with sparrow populations? Surely not, after years of such depredations; but if something else has tipped the balance, do road deaths and cat predation begin to come into play? Sparrows have been put under pressure by increasing loss of winter food (with the loss of weedy fields) and habitat. Or is it the loss of nest sites in roofs and under eaves, in old outhouses and tumbledown sheds, that has played a bigger part? Not so many sheds are left untidy and semi-derelict as used to be the case. Hundreds of thousands of houses have plastic cladding where once there was wood, and ventilation holes in buildings have been filled in and lost to house-hunting birds. Are these factors enough to explain the losses?

Or are sparrows dependent, in some way, on social stimulation, in turn reliant on thriving numbers, so that, if the local population falls below a critical limit, their ability to breed is somehow impaired? It seems possible that this has played a part, but it would only be a small part, after other factors have caused an initial decline.

The good news – plenty of it
It would be wrong to leave this introduction on such a note, with nothing but a catalogue of falling numbers and contracting ranges of British breeding birds. There are many positive changes, too, and recoveries from past declines that could hardly have been expected. The sparrowhawk came back from its pesticide-induced collapse, once the pesticides were identified and withdrawn. The recovery of the peregrine was perhaps more difficult to predict, but nevertheless this magnificent falcon has come back from the dead to numbers hardly experienced before in most areas, although some of its old haunts remain empty. Marsh harriers, down to just three or four pairs not many years ago, are now quite widespread and doing well (other reedbed specialists, requiring more extensive reed marshes, such as the bittern and bearded tit, are finding life more difficult, although bitterns are recovering well given greater opportunity by all kinds of reedbed restoration efforts).

An unexpected spread and rise in numbers has brought another exciting and elegant bird of prey to completely new areas in southern Britain. The hobby, perhaps partly in response to the spread of flooded gravel pits (which encourage large insects, such as dragonflies, which hobbies relish) has become almost commonplace in some areas where it used to be entirely absent 30 years ago. A set-aside field at the end of the drive to The Lodge, near Sandy in Bedfordshire, where I work, attracts 10 or even 20 hobbies on some summer evenings when the chafers are on the wing. From my office window I can see one, two or three dashing across the openings between the pine trees outside on any fine day in September and even October. This seems altogether extraordinary, especially when I remember that, to find a hobby when I was a student, I used to go on camping weekends in the New Forest.

The wonderful woodlark, whose lilting phrases may be heard by night over southern heaths (as I heard my first from a tent in the New Forest on one of those expeditions), has also increased to what a few decades ago would have been unimaginable numbers. The cirl bunting, once common enough to be called the '*village bunting*' by Hudson, withdrew from most of southern England to a final refuge in Devon. Now, due to a special agricultural stewardship scheme and the enthusiastic work of some farmers, it has increased again, although it has not yet shown much inclination to spread. Farmers have helped in the recovery of the stone-curlew, too, in Wessex and the East Anglian Brecklands. Recently a fear of interference by officials in the way they can manage their land has led a few large landowners to ban stone-curlew researchers from their farms and withdraw co-operation from the conservation effort – a worrying and unfortunate development that shows how fragile some of these good-news stories can be.

What the future holds is hard to predict. There are many potential black marks, as we see so many species added to the list of birds that give cause for concern. The dramatic spread of the little egret, however, shows what might happen, perhaps encouraged by a gradual warming of our climate. I once went to a small Pembrokeshire estuary to see my first little egret; I remember it rising suddenly from a hidden creek in the marsh, startlingly and wonderfully white, unlike anything I had seen before. In the next few years I saw one or two more and each time they were superb birds and properly documented in the annual report on rare birds in Britain and Ireland; this was still a species to be treasured. Now it is possible to see hundreds in a day on the south coast and little egrets have bred in several secret places (and one or two published ones, such as Brownsea Island in Poole Harbour and, with a staggering production of 50 young from 30 pairs in 2003, Northward Hill in Kent).

And this is not the only major invasion of a new species into the UK; in the 1950s, the collared dove, after a mysterious spread from south-eastern Europe over several decades, reached East Anglia. Its arrival was kept a secret, then; now, collared doves coo rhythmically and unimaginatively from TV aerials, chimney pots and lamp posts all over the United Kingdom, following a sensational spread and consolidation. No one really knows why.

There will, no doubt, be other mysteries that remain unsolved, whether good or bad news for those of us who take note of our birds as we go about our daily business. It is part of the fascination of birds – and, perhaps, a bit of mystery is no bad thing. But not if it means the wholesale loss of British birdsong from great swathes of our countryside and gardens. That is a different matter altogether and we all must do what we can to ensure that the fields and hedges, woods and parks of the future are not bereft of their melodious blackbirds, ecstatic thrushes and silver-tongued larks, which act so sensitively as barometers of the health of the environment that we depend on as surely as they.

Arctic tern

An early June visit to Inner Farne in Northumberland is one of the most exciting orni-thological experiences imaginable and is a must for those interested in natural history. It is the only Arctic tern colony in Britain that the general public can access. Walking up from the quay, past the little chapel, is similar to participating in an exotic Easter egg hunt. The pathways are lined with the nests of tame yet fiercely aggressive Arctic terns. The intruder is greeted by a crescendo of scolding birds, screaming with anger at the invasion of their privacy. An umbrella is needed for protection as the tern, uttering it harsh staccato cries, raps the visitor on the head with its dagger-like bill.

The Arctic tern is one of the most graceful and elegant of British birds. It has deco-rative tail streamers, delicate tiny crimson feet and a blood red bill. At close sight it is greyer than the common tern and has shorter legs. Like all terns, the Arctic has enor-mous charm and performs the delightful habit in courtship of presenting a sand eel to its mate. The Arctic tern is a bird of northern coastal distribution and unlike the com-mon tern rarely ventures inland. Its annual migration covers a greater distance than any other bird. Twice a year it sets out on a staggering journey that takes it from one end of the globe to another. The round trip is over 20,000 miles as it winters in the Antarctic Ocean.

The stronghold of the Arctic tern in Britain lies in north and west Scotland with the bulk of the population being in the Orkneys and the Shetlands where over 800 colo-nies have been used in the past 30 years. There are two major colonies south of the border, one in Anglesey and another in Northumberland located on Coquet Island and Inner Farne. In the 19th century the Arctic tern nested on the Scillies and 30 years ago 200 pairs bred at the entrance of Morecambe Bay. Once the persecution of the 19th

century terminated with protection, the Arctic tern, un-like other terns, failed to recover in England probably due to climate amelioration. It is interesting that it is not found on the East Anglian coastline. This northerly spe-cies must find the English climate too warm and dry and with global warming it may well retreat further north.

In the 1990s Arctic tern numbers declined by over 50% on the Orkneys and Shetlands. They had been breeding unsuccessfully for some years due to a lack of sand eels, their staple diet. The birds returned each year in smaller numbers only to desert during incubation or in the first few days of the chicks' lives. Sand eels are used in the production of fish-meal and fertilisers. Danish trawlers in particular made big inroads into local stocks in these northern waters. In March 1991 the Scottish Office of the Ministry of Agriculture and Fisheries closed the Shetlands sand eel fishery.

More research is needed into the ecology of the sand eel. Arctic terns are doing well on the Northumberland coast where there is no sand eel fishery. In addition the local marine ecology benefits from nutrients injected into the sea from sewage and agricultural run-off. An absence of fish predators such as cod, due to over-fishing, means that sand eels are multiplying. When fishing, a tern only penetrates a few inches into the water. A lack of fish predators results in fewer sand eels being found at surface level where they flee to escape their pursuers.

There is little doubt that a shortage of sand eels in northern waters has resulted in an overall decline in Arctic tern numbers. This has been exacerbated by an increase in predation on the terns' nesting grounds from mink and Arctic skuas.

Decrease

Avocet

The return of breeding avocets to Britain represents one of the great success stories for global bird conservation. The credit for firm re-establishment must go to the RSPB who provided suitable breeding conditions and protection for the birds at two reserves in Suffolk. The fact that the RSPB adopted the avocet as its logo means that this rare, snow white bird complete with neat black markings and an upswept bill is known to thousands of people across the country. The avocet frequents shallow, brackish coastal lagoons with sparsely vegetated islands for nesting. It sweeps the shallows with its unique bill for tiny aquatic invertebrates and unlike most waders swims a good deal, making use of its partially webbed feet. The avocet is a noisy, gregarious bird and its loud liquid *'klooit'* call can be heard at some distance.

During the 18th century the avocet bred regularly on the east coast of England from the Humber down to Kent; by the 1840s it had vanished. Improvements in sea defences and fen drainage resulted in a loss of brackish pools vital for the avocet's survival. Avocets and their eggs had long been harvested for food by marsh dwellers but as the bird became rare collectors of eggs and specimens moved in. Over a century passed before the avocet recolonised the east coast during World War II. Sea walls fell into disrepair and large areas of the coastline were closed for security purposes. At the same time avocet numbers were increasing in the Low Countries and Denmark. Birds that were dislodged from their Dutch breeding grounds by the flooding of the polders during the war moved to the east coast of England.

By 1970 there were around 150 pairs of avocets breeding at Minsmere and Havergate, both Suffolk based RSPB reserves. Thereafter a big range expansion took place and by 1990 the avocet was breeding at over 20 sites, mostly on reserves where protection from human disturbance and predators was afforded by conservation bodies. Today over 600 pairs breed, from Yorkshire down to Sussex, and birds have even moved inland to the Ouse Washes. Over-wintering takes place mainly in the southern estuaries of Devon and Cornwall.

Protection and sophisticated habitat management are essential if the avocet is to continue to prosper in Britain. It needs the security that tightly run reserves can offer. Black-headed gulls compete for nest sites on the lagoons and predators like foxes and crows need to be controlled. Kestrels have recently started taking chicks from some sites. Above all the avocet is dependent on man-made lagoons. The critical factor for the survival of young avocets is the salinity level. At Havergate the availability of aquatic invertebrates varies from year to year and is reduced by high or fluctuating salinity levels due to drought.

Substantial Increase

Barn owl

The barn owl hunts at dusk. One of the joys of a summer's evening at Newtown in the Isle of Wight is the company of this beautiful white owl. Just before dark it flits across the elm paddocks in front of our house with a silent, buoyant, moth-like flight. It twists and turns with rapidly flapping wing beats and then glides forward as it searches the rough grassland adjacent to the salt marsh for its prey. At night when caught in the car headlights the barn owl appears a ghostly white. When viewed close-to its back is transformed into a stunning golden buff with a peppering of grey.

Newtown provides the perfect habitat for the barn owl. There is little intensive agriculture, just rough grazing around the marshes and a plentiful supply of voles and shrews on which to feed a large brood of young. The barn owl hunts by sound as well as sight and because of its soft plumage makes no noise when it dives on prey. It does not call like a tawny owl but marks out its territory with a blood-curdling shriek. The barn owl does not compete for territory with the tawny. The long wings of the barn owl are more suited to open habitat such as grassland and marshland. It nests in isolated tree holes and buildings and does not need the camouflage that the tawny requires in its woodland haunts. It is lucky that these two owls do not cohabit, as the larger tawny has been known to kill barn owls.

The barn owl benefited from land enclosure and the construction of farm buildings in the 18th and 19th centuries. Around 1900 numbers began to fall with the gamekeepers' lust for killing anything with a hooked beak and the Victorians' passion for stuffed birds. A survey completed in 1930 found 12,000 pairs in England and Wales but in 1985 a census carried out by the Hawk and Owl Trust confirmed a dramatic decline to 4,400 pairs in England and Wales. This frightening fall in numbers took place before that of other raptors, which suffered from the introduction of organochlorine chemicals in the 1950s.

The main reason for the barn owl's decline has been a loss of habitat associated with modern farming. Between 1940 and 1980, forty percent of rough grazing was lost in lowland England. Ninety five percent of our hay meadows have been lost since the war and the switch to silage has greatly reduced the vole population. When tractors replaced horses, haylofts disappeared and modern barns are not suitable for nesting. Nesting sites disappeared with the advent of Dutch Elm disease and the pulling down of old farm buildings. Combine harvesters replaced rickyard threshing and together with improved methods of crop storage caused the number of rodents to decline. The barn owl is now most numerous in areas of mixed farming or areas of marshland and damp grassland.

On top of the ravages of modern farming came the introduction of toxic chemicals in pesticides; owls, like the sparrowhawk, being at the top of the food chain suffered greatly. Britain is at the northern end of the barn owl's range and as a result it suffered from a series of harsh winters from 1940-1980 as it particularly dislikes long periods of frost, snow and rain.

Although the present population of 5,000 pairs is under one half of what it was 50 years ago the decline seems to have halted and numbers have stabilised. The barn owl is a difficult bird to survey as it is largely nocturnal, less vocal than others and its numbers fluctuate in line with the short-tailed vole cycle. The future now looks much brighter with breeding success and chick survival rates having improved over the last 25 years; organochlorine problems have now largely disappeared. The use of rodenticides to control warfarin resistant rodents around farm buildings is still a danger but with global warming and the provision of artificial nest boxes the barn owl can look to the future with some confidence.

Stable

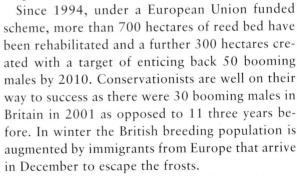

Bittern

I have only once met with a bittern and that was on the Cob Lake at Malltraeth in Anglesey, immortalised in *Shorelands Summer Diary* by artist Charles Tunnicliffe. A brown bird with rounded wings that I initially took for a large owl flapped lazily across the brackish pool. The bittern is a secretive bird that seldom ventures into the open and rarely takes to the air. It is a master of camouflage. When the bittern suspects danger it freezes with its head and neck stretched vertically. Then its golden-buff plumage blends perfectly with the patterns created by its reedy home.

The territorial song of the bittern is a far carrying boom that can be heard as far as three miles away. The boom resembles a fog horn and individual males can be identified by their calls. Two hundred years ago the bittern was not uncommon but with the draining of marshes and persecution they were pushed back to the fens and lost to Britain as a breeding bird by 1870. Eggs were stolen by collectors and many birds were shot to satisfy the insatiable demands of the Victorian taxidermist. Bittern was also a much sought after item of country fare.

A reduction in persecution resulted from the *Wild Birds Protection Acts* of the 1880s and together with the stimulus of climate amelioration, breeding was once again proven in 1911 in the Norfolk Broads. The population then peaked in the mid-1950s with 80 booming males and by this time it was breeding in seven counties. In the 1970s no bitterns were breeding outside East Anglia and Lancashire and these were practically all found on the RSPB reserves at Minsmere and Leighton Moss.

Since 1994, under a European Union funded scheme, more than 700 hectares of reed bed have been rehabilitated and a further 300 hectares created with a target of enticing back 50 booming males by 2010. Conservationists are well on their way to success as there were 30 booming males in Britain in 2001 as opposed to 11 three years before. In winter the British breeding population is augmented by immigrants from Europe that arrive in December to escape the frosts.

Why was there a renewed decline in bittern numbers in the 1950s? Herons, which have a similar food range, were contaminated by organochlorine pesticides in the 1960s. A number of factors probably came into play including water pollution from agricultural run-off and sewage effluent, harsh winters, disturbance from recreational boating and even the presence of coypus! The large majority of bitterns breed on well managed reserves. Reduced reed harvesting results in reed die-back and scrub encroachment. A failure to maintain reed bed ditches that were once used to transport harvested reeds leads to clogging by vegetation, which again destroys valuable habitat for the bittern.

Dangerous Decrease

Blackbird

The cock blackbird ranks as one of our best known garden birds but never seems to occupy pole position in our affections. He may not have the charisma or friendly charm of the robin but he is a handsome bird and together with the blackcap and nightingale represents one of Britain's three most accomplished songsters. Shakespeare certainly saw the glamour of the cock blackbird when he wrote: *'The ousel-cock so black of hue with average tawny bill.'* The female blackbird on the other hand is a dowdy brown bird that invariably fails to attract attention.

The blackbird begins its rich fluty song with a series of powerful warbled notes and finishes up with a number of faster scratchy ones. WH Hudson wrote of the blackbird: *'its charm consists in the peculiar soft, rich, melodious quality of the sound and the placid leisurely way it is delivered.'* Richard Jefferson agreed yet felt the song ended in a disappointing fashion: *'the blackbird sings in a quiet leisurely way, as a great master should; unfortunately the great master too often ends his performance unworthily with an unmusical note, or he collapses ignominiously at the close.'* The only real drawback to the blackbird's song is its short duration. Starting in early March, he only performs for four months of the year, peaking during the great dawn chorus in May. Sir Edward Grey wrote: *'Listen attentively and consider how the song of the blackbird gives tone and spirit to the whole. A dozen or more different species of birds are taking part, but it is the notes of the blackbird that the chorus could least spare.'*

The alarm call of the blackbird can be heard in garden roosts throughout the year, especially if a cat or fox is stalking the undergrowth. A chorus of metallic 'spinking' cries will continue long after the intruder has departed.

The blackbird has demonstrated a great ability to profit from man's modification of his environment and has earned its place as one of the most successful British birds of this era. Historically the blackbird lived in the woodland edge and numbers must have decreased as the woodland was cleared. The Enclosures of the 18th century led to an expansion on farmland via a network of associated hedgerows. The late 19th century, in turn, witnessed a remarkable explosion into urban areas. The planting of ornamental shrubs in gardens provided nest sites and today the density of blackbirds in British oak woods is one tenth that of gardens.

The past 25 years have seen a worrying decline in the blackbird population for which there is no obvious reason. Common Bird Census (CBC) surveys show a 30% fall in numbers. The blackbird certainly benefited from warmer climatic conditions in the first part of the 20th century; however there is little reason to conclude that it suffered from the colder winters in the late seventies and early eighties. The blackbird is less susceptible to hard winters than the song thrush and it quickly recovered from the extreme winter conditions of 1962-3. A 'twist in the tale' could come from present-day global warming. Blackbirds are being encouraged to nest earlier and earlier, which leaves them more susceptible to spells of cold wet weather in early spring.

Agricultural intensification has contributed to their decline on farmland, with a resulting lack of spring tillage for feeding and fewer hedgerows for nesting. Blackbird densities are lower in counties dominated by winter cereals. In these areas fields are ploughed and sown directly after the harvest. This results in a dearth of winter stubbles that provide a rich source of food for many different species during the harshest season of the year.

Two other species, the magpie and sparrowhawk, have demonstrated a remarkable adaptability to man's urban development and thereby may have contributed to the blackbird's decline. The feeding of birds has become a widespread and popular activity and as a result predators have been drawn into the garden. Domestic cats have always been ruthlessly destructive in urban gardens. They have now been joined by the cock sparrowhawk, which targets garden bird tables, and together with numerous magpies that systematically hunt the shrubs and hedgerows during the nesting season, the garden has become a dangerous home for the blackbird.

Decrease

Blackcap

The arrival of the blackcap in Derbyshire around the third week in April is the event in my ornithological calendar that really marks the commencement of springtime. The chiffchaffs have been with us for nearly a month although this year cold east winds have delayed the arrival of the willow warblers. It is 8th April on a sunny yet frosty morning and I am walking the dogs in London's Brompton cemetery. Suddenly a few fluty notes waft out from the canopy above; it is surely a robin. Then a burst of rich, melodious song sends a thrill down my spine. The blackcap, which many people think is the equal of the nightingale, has arrived. It is surely appropriate that it is singing on the edge of Chelsea before moving on to some woodland glade deep in the country-side.

The first sighting of a blackcap is clearly etched in my mind. Two sleek grey birds were fidgeting in a *ribes* shrub on the edge of my small garden in Blenheim Park; the contrast between the cock bird's black head cap with the reddish brown cap of the female was unforgettable.

Now that the nightingale has become so rare we must be grateful for the blackcap's success for its song is quite beautiful. In the *Charm of Birds* Sir Edward Grey wrote:

'For perfection or moving quality of voice I should place the blackcap with the black-bird and the nightingale in the first class of British songbirds. His song is loud, exceedingly sweet but also spirited; it is not very long, but is frequently repeated: there is not great variety, but the thing done is absolutely perfect. There is not a note that fails to please or is not a success. The tone does not stir us so inwardly as that of the blackbird, but it is sheer delight to listen to. Of the blackcap, indeed, it has been said that, like the gipsy before the castle gate, "he sang so very completely"'.

The blackcap has been the most successful of our warblers with the Common Bird Survey showing increases of over 50% from 1994–2000. It breeds as far north as the Great Glen and has even been recorded nesting in Shetland and the Orkneys. In England, as a result of its recent success, the blackcap has spread out of its favoured woodland habitat and moved onto farmland. British blackcaps winter in the Mediterranean and thereby, unlike other warblers, escape the effects of drought in the Sahel (to the south of the Sahara); on a longer migration the blackcap would be exposed to such dangers. Having a shorter distance to travel the blackcap arrives back earlier in its nesting area giving it more flexibility to raise a successful family. The blackcap has adapted its migratory behaviour and many now winter in Britain. These are thought to be eastern

European breeders. Their ability to utilise winter foods such as berries of holly, privet and ivy has resulted in improved survival over the harshest period of the year. The blackcap has also benefited from the provision of artificial food supplied on garden bird tables.

Substantial Increase

Black grouse

There are few more exciting ornithological experiences than a visit to a black grouse lek. This is a traditional piece of ground where their complex courtship ceremonies take place. Black grouse are polygamous and the lekking ground is where the males display and establish a pecking order. The cocks joust as knights of old, hopping up and down with their beautiful white tails spread out like a fan. The watching females select the fittest males from the centre of the lek. Once they have mated they nest alone. The best time to visit the lek is at first light towards the end of April. My first experience of this ritual was at Allenheads near Hexham. There was a light fall of snow on the hill and before I caught sight of the birds I could hear their eerie bubbling calls wafting across the valley.

Sale particulars for our small farm in Derbyshire, drawn up just after World War I, state: *'an excellent wild pheasant and blackgame shoot'*. I doubt if any blackgame have been seen in our valley for well over 60 years. There was a small lek a few miles from our home on the edge of the Staffordshire Moorlands but the colony became extinct in 1999 and that was in a county where 252 birds were shot in one day during the 1880s (on Cannock Chase).

Ninety-five per cent of all British black grouse have been lost over the past century. By the early years of the 19th century black grouse had been shot to extinction in many English counties, the last bird being shot in Kent in 1851. In 1905 black grouse had disappeared from nearly all our southern heathlands and more recently they have died out on Dartmoor, Exmoor and the Quantocks.

Habitat loss as a result of agricultural intensification has been the main cause for the demise of the black grouse. The black grouse likes a mosaic of heather, grassland, damp rushy hillsides and sparse birch and pine woodland near the moorland edge. Birch buds and young conifer shoots are a favourite food. Sheep grazing and high stocking densities destroy the heather and birch scrub. Over-grazing removes vegetation that supports invertebrates consumed by chicks in the first fortnight of hatching, in addition to destroying the bilberries and the nutritionally rich flowers of cotton grass. Sheep grazing often causes serious problems as they tend to graze the moorland margins, a critical zone for black grouse. Agricultural subsidies have encouraged a switch from rough grazing to improved pasture through drainage, reseeding and the use of fertilisers.

Following the sharp population declines of the early 20th century there were some localised temporary increases in Scotland and Wales as a result of afforestation in the 1950s. Black grouse particularly like the developed shrub layer of heather and bilberry in young plantations; however, once the canopy closes over, the ground cover is lost and the habitat is no longer suitable.

Conservation schemes and voluntary bans on shooting are badly needed if the black grouse is going to survive in its limited strongholds of Scotland and the north Pennines. New forestry plantations not only encourage predators but they are often protected by lethal deer fences. The birds fly into them with disastrous effects and wherever possible they need to be taken down. It is no coincidence that the black grouse does best where gamekeepering is most intensive. Stoats and weasels are the most dangerous predators closely followed by the fox and crow. The greyhen is not the best of mothers and cold wet weather during fledging invariably results in the loss of chicks.

Dangerous Decrease

Black-headed gull

The black-headed gull returns to its breeding grounds on the Newtown estuary like clockwork on 1st March. I associate those screaming cries with warm spring days and I am immediately reminded how much I have missed the frenzied choir. The name is misleading as one or two recent arrivals are just beginning to regain their chocolate brown heads that they lose in winter.

In the south of England the black-headed gull breeds on salt marshes and small coastal islands. In the north it moves onto the hills and moors where it nests in colonies on boggy lakes and marshes. The black-headed gull has the widest inland breeding distribution of any seabird. On the coast it tends to be found in the company of terns; it is absent from rocky shores, the characteristic nesting place of other gulls.

The black-headed gull is an adaptable, successful bird that can be found almost anywhere. During the autumn it moves inland, following the plough on farmland, fighting for food at rubbish tips or just scavenging in St James's Park. In the short winter afternoons it can be seen flying out in a formation of thousands to roost on a suburban reservoir.

The black-headed gull started to expand inland towards the end of the 19th century. Driven by hard weather it moved up the Thames estuary finding food in the docklands and along the embankments. It has now become a town bird and is a classic scrounger in the London parks. One hundred years ago this small gull suffered from random egg collecting for food particularly at the more accessible southern colonies. A steady population decline brought it close to extinction although it survived better in the north. One of the main reasons for local losses was the draining and enclosure of breeding marshes for grazing.

The Seabirds Protection Act of 1869 assisted the black-headed gull's survival and in 1938 it was estimated there were 35,000 pairs breeding in England and Wales. As a result of general conservation, restricted egg collecting, a reduction in shooting and the creation of new sites like gravel pits this number increased to 100,000 pairs in 1973, peaking at over 200,000 pairs during the 1985-7 Seasonal Colony Register. In winter there may be as many as three million birds resident in Britain, two-thirds from the Continent.

A further decline in black-headed gull numbers over the last 25 years is well illustrated by events at the Needs Ore colony at the mouth of the Beaulieu River in Hampshire. For years this represented one of the most successful colonies in Britain not- withstanding an annual egg harvest.

In 2003 the gulls failed to return. Maybe global warming has started to take its toll and their patience has suddenly snapped after a combination of bad weather, high tides and strong winds caused no chicks to fledge. The last straw was probably a pair of peregrines that settled on the salt marsh during the mating season. Black-headed gull colonies are very susceptible to predation. The National Trust built a scrape at Newtown and one summer when the water level dropped a fox moved onto the island and destroyed the entire colony. I have also watched carrion crows come in and steal chicks on a regular shuttle basis.

In the Mink-Seabird Project Study area (west coast of Scotland) sites where mink were controlled against those with no mink control revealed a breeding performance of 1.22 and 0.51 chicks fledged the nest respectively, suggesting mink reduced productivity by 58%.

Decrease

41

Black-tailed godwit

At Newtown in the Isle of Wight, black-tailed godwits assume the role of avocets at Minsmere. These beautiful waders are the aristocrats of our estuary and they winter at Newtown in internationally important numbers. When they return from their nesting grounds in August some birds still sport their stunning chestnut breeding plumage. In flight they are instantly recognisable by their distinctive white rump, black and white wing bar and long legs that project well beyond the tail.

As they probe the mud at low tide with their long bills a few birds will be wearing brightly coloured rings on their stilt-like legs. These identification tags prove that the Newtown godwits have migrated from Iceland. There are two sub-species of black-tailed godwit in Europe and each has a different success story to tell.

The Newtown birds form the race *islandica*. They nest in Iceland and winter on English estuaries. This race also breeds in the Faeroes, the Shetlands and the Orkneys in very small numbers. The sub-species *limosa* breeds from England across continental Europe to Russia and winters in Africa. This species is struggling as a breeding bird in Europe whereas the English wintering godwits (*islandica*) are increasing at an encouraging rate.

The western European breeding population is concentrated on the Low Countries and west Germany and is threatened by general agricultural intensification. In Britain the black-tailed godwit became extinct as a breeding species by 1850, with large scale

drainage of their traditional fens and wet meadow habitat, egg collecting and shooting taking their toll. They returned in 1952 with a recolonisation of the Ouse Washes in Cambridgeshire. The UK population reached a peak of 87 pairs in 1976 with 90% being held in the Ouse Washes. Numbers declined dramatically in the Ouse Washes due to spring flooding, reaching a low of four pairs in 1990. The flooding is thought to have been caused by a combination of higher rainfall and faster run off due to changes in land use.

Conservation efforts are taking place at a satellite colony in the nearby Nene Washes where the water table on the well-grazed wet grassland is maintained at a high level, but where surface flooding is prevented after mid-April. High densities of grazing animals have also to be avoided if trampling losses are to be overcome. Godwits started nesting here in the 1980s, reaching 24 pairs in 1990.

The black-tailed godwit is a loosely colonial nester. This provides effective communal defence against predators such as crows. When the population drops, this species is unlikely to survive in isolated pairs as nest predation by mink, stoats and weasels poses a serious threat to breeding success.

The UK wintering population has rocketed to 15,000 birds with internationally important sites in the Dee, Ribble, Stour, and Mersey estuaries. Black-tailed godwits feed apart from other species in tight flocks that can number several hundred. Their diet consists of invertebrates, particularly lugworms and ragworms.

In their breeding territories godwits feed on earthworms. If we are to enjoy their evocative *'wacka-wacka-wacka'* mating calls in Europe over future years, Common Agricultural Policy grants will have to switch further away from production and fall more heavily into the area of environmental protection.

Stable

Blue tit

This active, acrobatic and intelligent little bird is the most common visitor to the bird table. Even though it was originally a bird of deciduous woodland it has long lived in close association with man. One is just as likely to find its nest in a wall crevice as in the garden nest box. As a child I was fascinated by the tiny nest, snugly built with moss and hair, containing a dozen red-brown spotted eggs. The blue tit has a cheeky charm. It has learnt to steal cream from milk bottles by tearing the foil off the top and even more annoyingly will peck the putty from windows presumably in search of insects. Its song is a trilling, *'tsee-tsee-tsee'*.

The blue tit is both adaptable and mobile which no doubt accounts for the steady and gradual increase in numbers over the past 25 years. It is a bird of oak woodlands that in winter will either move into gardens or forage through the woods in mixed species flocks. The huge increase in garden feeding has greatly benefited the blue tit as has the provision of nest boxes that provide welcome protection from predators. In years when beech mast and other natural foods are plentiful blue tits are less dependent on garden feeding. The agile blue tit can feed on the tips of the thinnest twigs whereas the heavier great tit is more dependent on ground feeding. Interestingly in the two severest winters this century, blue tits were badly affected in 1946-47 when there was no beech mast crop but much less so in 1962-63 when beech mast was plentiful.

Nesting begins in mid-April and hatching is timed to coincide with the caterpillar flush. The blue tit only has the one large brood and on average, of the ten youngsters that leave the nest in summer nine will die by the following spring. Only one bird needs to survive for the population to remain steady. Blue tits are particularly susceptible to winter starvation and predation at the bird table by sparrowhawks. Breeding densities in suburban gardens may approach those in woodland but reproductive success is relatively low. Caterpillar numbers are lower in an urban environment and artificial food has a relatively poor nutritional value.

Recent observations at RSPB reserves and in gardens have demonstrated that the blue tit population could be heading for troubled times. Global warming has caused the caterpillar flush to come a fortnight earlier and as a result many chicks are dying of starvation. Whereas in the past ten chicks fledged per nest, today it might only be two. It appears that birds respond to length of daylight first and air temperature second.

From time to time an irruption from the Continent takes place causing the local British blue tit population to soar. This situation arises from a series of good summers and mild winters followed by the onset of severe weather and a consequent food shortage.

Increase

Brent goose

On a still, winter's morning the background noise in the Newtown estuary is deafening. The resident choir consists of 'bubbling' curlew, 'piping' redshank, 'mewing' lapwing, 'whistling' wigeon, and, perhaps most vocal of all, 'growling' brent geese.

Two distinct races of brent geese winter in Britain. The pale-bellied variety breeds in Greenland and Spitzbergen and visits Ireland and Lindisfarne respectively. The Newtown birds represent the dark-bellied race. They breed in Arctic Russia and Siberia and winter in north-west Europe, over 50% along the southern and eastern coasts of England.

The brent goose is the same length as a mallard; it is Britain's smallest goose. It is a true seabird, roosting at sea in the night-time and sharing the coastal mudflats with shelduck during the day. The brent goose has only recently adapted its feeding habits to graze on arable farmland and pasture behind sea walls.

The favoured diet of the brent goose is *zostera*, or eel grass, one of the few flowering plants that grow submerged in saltwater. In the 1930s, disease devastated the eel grass on both sides of the North Sea and brent geese numbers fell by 75%. The world population of dark-bellied brent fell to around 15,000 and remained at this level until the mid-1950s. A dramatic increase in numbers took place in the 1970s and by the 1990s the world population had exceeded 250,000.

Wintering birds have benefited from a recovery in the eel grass and a ban on shooting. Around 25 years ago the brent goose diversified its habitat and moved onto agricultural land. It began to take young shoots of grain once the eel grass and salt marsh plants were exhausted in late winter. Another recent reason for its success has been a long series of successful nesting seasons due to favourable climatic conditions on its Arctic nesting grounds.

The current healthy population levels are likely to be maintained as long as its foreshore and estuarine habitats remain free from development or excessive recreational usage. It will also help if alternative feeding areas are established via set-aside schemes, as with the barnacle goose.

Substantial Increase

Bullfinch

One of the added bonuses of the morning paper run to the village shop at our home in the Derbyshire Dales is the likelihood of meeting a pair of bullfinches. The little road that runs the mile or so downhill is flanked by thick straggling hedges which are interspersed with young ash trees. This is the perfect habitat for the beautiful bullfinch. When viewed close to, the jet black head and the pink underparts justify the cock bullfinch's claim to be one of Britain's prettiest birds.

It is very secretive and from my car all I glimpse is a flash of white rump as the bullfinch dives for cover. It normally only reveals its presence by way of a distinctive far-carrying piping call. Hudson writes: *'his call and alarm note is a low, piping, musical sound, very pleasant to hear. The male sings in the spring, and so it is said does the female; but his strain is short and so feeble that it can be heard only a distance of a few yards.'* I have rarely heard the bullfinch's soft song. It takes the form of a series of creaky piped notes descending in pitch.

One hundred years ago Hudson described the bullfinch as rare in most districts. It was persecuted by gardeners for its propensity to feed on the buds of fruit trees, and was trapped as a cage bird on account of its beauty. *The Wild Birds Protection Act* of the 1890s halted the decline of the bullfinch. Numbers increased throughout the early 20th century, with an acceleration in the 1950s when it spread into more open areas such as farmland, parks and suburban gardens.

The sparrowhawk is a notorious woodland predator that hunts low and fast down hedgerows, surprise being its main weapon. It is interesting to note that the expansion of bullfinch numbers in the late 1950s coincided neatly with a decline in the sparrowhawk population brought about by chemical poisoning. Conversely, bullfinch numbers have declined by 55% over the past 25 years while sparrowhawk numbers have increased. The sparrowhawk has undoubtedly played a part in the demise of the hedgerow-loving bullfinch, yet general agricultural intensification over the last three decades has been the real culprit. Not only have thousands of miles of hedgerows been lost altogether, but many straggling hedges have been relaid with the assistance of government grants.

The bullfinch is primarily a seed-eating bird with a particular liking for the seeds of the nettle, dock and bramble, in addition to tree seeds such as those of the ash and elm. It is only in the late winter and early spring when these natural foods are exhausted that the bullfinch turns into a garden pest and attacks fruit and flower buds. Cleaner farming and extensive spraying of weedy areas have taken their toll, not just on the bullfinch but also other seed eaters such as the tree sparrow and corn bunting. Dutch Elm disease has also cut off an important source of tree seeds.

Dangerous Decrease

Buzzard

When we arrived at our home in Derbyshire nearly 20 years ago, the sighting of a buzzard was a cause for major celebration and one that might occur every other year. Today it is commonplace to see this chunky raptor soaring in spirals above our valley and mewing loudly.

For the last decade buzzards have been spreading eastwards from their stronghold in the south-west of England and Wales, where they are so common in places they do not merit a second glance. I was staying with friends in Gloucestershire recently and I awoke to a pair of buzzards sitting under an oak tree outside my bedroom window. I threw open the French windows and within minutes they were specks in the sky, rolling and turning together in the early morning sun over a dense bank of golden deciduous woodland.

Buzzards frequent diverse landscape characterised by wooded valleys with small farms. These units typically contain hedgerows, copses and plenty of pasture. Lightly grazed scrubby slopes that hold rabbits and small rodents are much favoured. Extensive afforestation, particularly in upland regions, reduces the amount of open country available for hunting.

At the beginning of the 19th century buzzards bred in most counties across Britain. Numbers started to decline around the middle of the century through persecution, with the contraction reaching a peak in Edwardian times. Buzzards were exterminated in lowland England by gamekeepers, but during the two World Wars, when keepering was dramatically reduced, their fortunes revived. The number of professional gamekeepers fell from 20,000 in 1911 to 5,000 in the 1970s. The earlier level of persecution was unforgivable as buzzards are essentially carrion eaters with a particular weakness for rabbits. They are, however, versatile predators, and will turn to snakes, squirrels and birds, the latter meaning it will always grab the attention of gamekeepers.

In 1954 the outbreak of myxomatosis decimated the rabbit population which caused a big decline in buzzard numbers. Recovery in the 1960s was slow due to the use of organochlorine chemicals. Sheep carrion became impregnated with dieldrin and aldrin used in dipping. This in turn affected the buzzard's breeding productivity through egg-shell breakage.

These toxic chemicals were banned in 1966 and the rabbit slowly developed its immune systems to myxomatosis. The future for the buzzard is bright. With limited persecution this graceful raptor is rapidly spreading eastwards across England and numbers are back to around 15,000 breeding pairs.

Substantial Increase

Capercaillie

One could be forgiven for mistaking this giant woodland grouse for a wild turkey. A displaying cock capercaillie on its forest lek with its erect head and fanned tail is a truly intimidating sight; so territorial is the 'caper' that it has been known to attack both hikers and tourists' cars. The song of the cock bird is one of the weirdest sounds in the ornithological world. It commences with a rattle and ends with a series of popping notes that imitate a cork exiting a bottle.

Conservationists are currently fighting to save this charismatic bird from extinction in Britain for a second time. The last 'native' bird was supposedly shot in Aberdeenshire in 1785. A Scottish Act of Parliament of 1621 that prohibited the buying or selling of 'caper' suggests that it was becoming scarce even at that time. The capercaillie frequents old Caledonian pine forest with undergrowth of heather and bilberry. Its disappearance resulted from the destruction of the natural pine forest together with persecution by hunters. It was successfully reintroduced to Perthshire from Sweden in 1838 and proceeded to spread throughout eastern and central Scotland.

The capercaillie's maximum distribution was reached just before World War I at which time many trees were felled and this temporarily halted its expansion. The creation of the Forestry Commission in 1919 initially proved a further benefit to the capercaillie. Since then, the population has crashed and may have reached as low as 1,000 birds. Following a survey during the winter of 2003-4, it is now known numbers are increasing thanks to targetted conservation. There are thought to be approximately 2,000 capercaillie in Britain today.

The main reason for its decline lies with the depletion of its favoured pinewood habitat. The open canopy provided by Scots pine allows light to reach the ground permitting the growth of a shrubby vegetation that includes bilberry and crowberry. The 'caper' eats such shoots, seeds, berries and buds and only supplements its diet with pine needles in winter. Over-grazing by sheep and deer reduces the shrub and herb layer and prevents the forest from regenerating. Deer are becoming an increasing threat to our woodland birds. The erection of deer fences up to three metres high causes deaths to flying capercaillie and blackgame; grants are now available for their removal.

Over-shooting on many northern estates hastened its decline although a ban is now in place. In the 1950s the capercaillie was regarded as a pest by foresters and nests were destroyed. Since 1982 the rights for 'caper' shooting have not been let on Forestry Commission land. Increased predation by foxes and pine martens has not helped its cause and the importance of climate change should not be underestimated. Increased June rainfall in north-west Scotland over recent years has resulted in poorer chick production by female capercaillies.

Dangerous Decrease

Carrion crow

The carrion crow is a highly successful, cunning rogue. It is a notorious egg thief and predator of nestling birds. At my home in Derbyshire I placed a fox-proof fence around some ponds with the ever hopeful objective of providing a sanctuary for the wild duck. In early spring, before the protective lush vegetation has grown up, the surrounding fields are strewn with broken mallard's eggs. From high up on its watchtower the sinister crow has patiently watched, waited and burgled.

The carrion crow is a relatively solitary bird, whereas the rook is gregarious. It is best differentiated from the rook by the black bill and throat and the neater plumage without the 'leg trousers.' The voice of the crow is very similar to the rook but is characterised by a harsher 'caw' repeated several times in succession.

Crow numbers have increased by over 60% during the last 25 years. With the decline in gamekeeping between the wars numbers began to increase. Farmers have ceased to persecute the crow to the extent they once did. Modern stock rearing practices mean that lambing is now usually conducted inside farm buildings and as a result the crow is seen as less of a pest.

It is a canny bird that breeds in isolated pairs. It leaves the nest at the first sign of danger. The crow is therefore difficult to shoot at the nest but the recent introduction of the Larsen trap can help control numbers. It preys on gamebirds and songbirds alike, so predator control is yet another example of how well-run sporting estates can benefit our songbirds.

The crow's opportunistic nature has allowed it to move into urban habitats such as

parks and cemeteries. It has adapted well to modern agriculture and has benefited from the substantial increase in available carrion in the form of road kills.

The carrion crow is substituted by the Hooded Crow in the northern uplands, with which it interbreeds in a hybrid zone. This corridor in Scotland continues to push northwards as a result of climatic amelioration.

Substantial Increase

Chaffinch

On a sunny day in early February, perhaps after a spell of cold wet weather, comes one of the milestones of the birdsong year. Sir Edward Grey used to note the 5th February as a possible date for hearing the chaffinch. The song is a series of short trills with a final flourish, and is repeated at regular intervals. Hudson described it: *'a loud song and a joyous sound – "gay as a chaffinch" is a proverbial saying of the French; but there is also a note of defiance in the song, as in the crow of the cock.'* Warde Fowler compares the manner of the song to *'a bowler running with quick steps up to the wicket and then with the overhand turn of the arm delivering the ball'*. He tells us that when the chaffinch first begins to sing it cannot for some days *'deliver the ball.'* It fails to complete its terminal flourish.

The chaffinch was the first bird that came to Robert Browning's mind when contemplating the joy of an English spring:

> *Oh, to be in England*
> *Now that April's there;*
> *And whoever wakes in England*
> *Sees, some morning, unaware,*
> *That the lowest boughs and the brushwood sheaf*
> *Round the elm-tree bole are in tiny leaf,*
> *While the chaffinch sings on the orchard bough*
> *In England—now!*

Browning's delight in the chaffinch does not emanate from its musical abilities. It is not so much a brilliant performer as a vigorous one. The chaffinch remains one of Britain's two most prolific birds and as such in springtime its song becomes part of our everyday lives. As part of its repertoire it has a very distinctive double call note, a sharp *'clink'*, that is repeated from a territory or when the bird is alarmed.

I always associate the chaffinch with success. Not only is it an enthusiastic songster but it also wins first prize for nest building, constructing one of the tidiest and snuggest nests of

all British birds. Above all it is one of the very few British farmland birds that has bucked the trend and is increasing in numbers. During the first half of the 19th century the chaffinch's range increased northwards through Scotland and into the Hebrides, no doubt aided by coniferous afforestation.

The great strength of the chaffinch has been its ability to use a number of different habitats as a source for a varied diet. For most of the year it is a seed eater, feeding on both woodland and crop seeds picked from the ground. In winter large flocks feed on beech mast and throughout the year the chaffinch can be relied on to search for rich pickings under the garden bird table. In the breeding season the chaffinch turns into an insect feeder collecting caterpillars and flies for its young. It is this varied diet that has enabled the chaffinch to weather the storm of agricultural intensification more successfully than other farmland birds.

Not surprisingly CBC numbers have increased by 25% over the past 25 years. There was a serious slip in the late 1950s when it was suspected that chaffinches were suffering from the use of toxic chemicals in seed dressings. These have thankfully now been banned and after the hard winters in the early 1960s, chaffinch numbers have risen steadily.

Increase

Chiffchaff

The most eagerly awaited event in the bird calendar is this bird's arrival. The chiffchaff is the true herald of spring; its presence lifts our spirits and reminds us that summer weather is just around the corner. It is not the first swallow or the first cuckoo, both of which arrive in April, that excites us, but rather the dual note, '*chiff-chaff*' song that can be heard as early as the second week in March. Grey wrote a moving description of its arrival on our shores: '*he is forerunner of the rush of songbirds that is on its way to us and will arrive in April, and therefore enrich our woods, meadows and gardens with still further variety and quality of song. That is why the first hearing of the chiffchaff moves us so each spring. He is a symbol, a promise, an assurance of what is to come.*'

There is a brief resumption of the song in late September, a relatively quiet time of the year for birdsong with winter approaching. The chiffchaff is about to commence its long journey back to Africa and the song reminds us of the balmy days of spring. Grey wrote: '*then comes the moult, and the bird falls silent till September when energy is restored and expresses itself in a subdued repetition of the song – a sort of quiet farewell before the chiffchaff leaves us on its long journey southwards.*'

Unlike its close cousin the willow warbler, some chiffchaffs over-winter in Britain. The best way of telling these two warblers apart is by their song but there is also a subtle difference in habitat preference. The chiffchaff avoids treeless areas as it needs mature trees for song posts. It feeds within the foliage whereas the willow warbler forages low down in the shrub layer. The willow warbler is much the more abundant of the two species.

A sharp decline in chiffchaff numbers took place in the early 1970s when the population halved. Since 1985 numbers have risen strongly, so much so that the chiffchaff count is 50% up over the past 25 years. Looking at the broader picture their numbers fluctuate and there is no discernible long term trend.

Weather conditions in its wintering grounds are almost certainly the most decisive factor in these population changes. The chiffchaff's most southerly winter quarters lie within drought-affected areas south of the Sahara. The drastic decline in chiffchaff numbers from 1970–74 tracks the patterns of the Sahel rainfall deficit. The chiffchaff tends to over-winter to the north of most warblers, especially in the Mediterranean, hence it returns earlier to Britain. In adverse drought conditions its overall numbers are not badly affected, as fewer chiffchaffs than whitethroats, for instance, make the Saharan crossing.

Increase

Chough

My first meeting with this energetic bird was one summer in the mid-1990s. I was entertained by the lively aerobatics of both species within the space of a few days in sharply contrasting surroundings. The chough is a close relation of the jackdaw with a long thin curved beak. The British chough has a crimson beak whereas the alpine chough that is found on the Continent has a yellow beak. They are birds of the high mountains and sheer coastal cliffs. Both birds are spectacular performers in flight; their acrobatic displays include steep dives with closed wings and somersaults in mid-air. One day I was watching the Alpine chough riding the up-draughts at Ronda's famous gorge in Andalucia, the next enjoying the cartwheeling antics of its British counterpart along Jura's raised beaches.

Britain lies at the northern extremity of the chough's range and there is an interesting correlation between its decline and the cold winters of the 19th century. It is a bird of coastal cliffs that feeds on larvae and soil invertebrates such as crane flies, ants, spiders and beetles. By the end of the 19th century the chough had disappeared from most places in Britain and it stopped breeding in Cornwall around 1950. A survey completed in 1963 demonstrated 130 pairs mostly breeding in Wales. Twenty years later the figure had risen to 260 pairs of which 80 bred in Scotland, the large majority at their Islay stronghold. Today's figure is probably nearer 350 pairs of which one half breed in Wales and many of these have moved inland. In 1991 a local survey on the Isle of Man concluded approximately 70 breeding pairs were present. A pair returned to breed in Cornwall in 2002 for the first time in over 50 years. The chough is now slowly increasing in Britain from an extremely low base.

The chough needs a habitat characterised by low intensity livestock farming with unfertilised turf for foraging. Favoured feeding grounds are rough unimproved grassland grazed by sheep and particularly cattle, machair and coastal turf. Any changes to the cliff top ecology that might diminish the close cropped sward can be detrimental to the chough. Removal of livestock results in bracken and scrub development. It is easy to understand why the rocky cliffs on the west coasts of Islay and Jura are favoured by the chough. The deer come down to the shore to feed on the seaweed and graze the coastal turf and there are many suitable nesting sites on cliff ledges, in caves and in ruined buildings. Animal dung is an important source of invertebrates for the chough. The dung of deer and wild goats on Jura's western coastal turf provides a rich source of insect life for these birds. It is also unlikely that any livestock in this remote area would be wormed with drugs such as Ivermectin which destroy insects known to feed and lay eggs in animal dung.

Increase

 # *Cirl bunting*

I have enjoyed cirl bunting song twice, once near Agen in France and again in Andalucia, but never in Britain. This is not altogether surprising as the cirl bunting is essentially a Mediterranean species and at the northern edge of its range in southern England. There were probably less than 150 pairs in Britain in 1989, nearly all concentrated in the small coastal strip of south Devon, one of the warmest spots in Britain. The cirl bunting has much in common with the yellowhammer. The attractive male has black and yellow head markings and an olive rump. Its monotonous trill, often performed from the top of a high hedgerow, resembles the first part of the yellowhammer's song. The cirl bunting frequents southward-facing slopes on chalk escarpments. It prospers in a mixed farming environment with a patchwork of small fields and can often be found along the borderline of downland and farmland.

The cirl bunting was first recorded as a separate species in Britain around 1800. There is a theory that the cirl arrived in Britain towards the end of the 18th century with the advent of warmer weather. It is interesting to note that the eminent ornithologist Gilbert White completely omitted the bird from his *Natural History of Selborne*. WH Hudson writing a century later in *Hampshire Days* refers to the cirl as the '*village bunting*' whose favourite singing place was in the churchyard. Both Hudson and Edward Grey found the cirl as common as the yellowhammer, which frequented more open ground.

A marked decline in cirl bunting numbers was noticed in the early 1950s. The cooler, wetter summers and harsh winters such as that of 1962-63 introduced a less favourable environment for the cirl but it was the change in agricultural practices at this time that fuelled its decline. The cirl bunting relies heavily on open stubbles for sources of winter food. After the war, with a move away from mixed farming to intensive cereal production, arable crops were planted in the autumn and no winter stubbles remained. During the agricultural recession between the wars, stubbles were left as rough grazing for sheep and the ground produced vast amounts of weed seeds. Cirl chicks are fed exclusively on insects, particularly grasshoppers, and the adult birds collect their food in grassland rich in invertebrates. With the widespread introduction of insecticides in the 1960s such habitat became scarce.

The RSPB has proved that with selective conservation and the co-operation of a small group of farmers there is hope for the future. Farmers provided unsprayed winter stubbles in small fields enclosed by thick hedges through Stewardship Schemes in the cirl bunting's core area of south Devon. The population responded immediately and was estimated at 380 pairs in 1997. Assisted by warmer summers and milder winters the cirl might now be able to expand out of this refuge area.

Increase

Coal tit

For a tiny bird the coal tit has a big personality. It is the smallest of all visitors to most bird tables. It is handsome, acrobatic, and above all shows real spirit when feeding alongside bullies such as the great tit. The coal tit is best recognised by its jet black crown and the white flash on its nape. It is very vociferous and constantly announces its presence with a series of call notes which can be heard at long range, the most common of which is a high pitched *'peecho-peecho-peecho'*.

The coal tit flourished in the 19th century and expanded its range in the face of afforestation. It is similar to the goldcrest in that it has a particular liking for evergreen trees and therefore prospered with the planting of coniferous woods and exotic evergreens in gardens. This expansion continued into the 20th century with the establishment of the Forestry Commission and on to the present day, so much so that the CBC 25-year index is up over 60%.

The coal tit is a sedentary species. On account of its small size it has an inability to carry fat reserves and therefore suffers in hard winters. Ironically it appears to cope with adverse weather conditions better than other members of the tit family. The coal tit takes advantage of its great agility and feeds on the underside of snow-laden branches in coniferous woods. Its thin bill is ideal for foraging amongst the pine needles. The coal tit faces little competition in its coniferous surroundings, the only disadvantage being a lack of nest holes, which often forces it to nest at ground level amongst tree roots.

Another advantage lies with the coal tit's ability to store food in a similar fashion to the nuthatch. The availability of beech mast in the autumn is important to the coal tit. In poor beech mast years there is more movement into gardens where it enjoys the riches of the peanut feeder.

Collared dove

I often wonder whether the disappearance of the house sparrow from around our houses and farm buildings has anything to do with the success of the collared dove. This slim little dove is one of Europe's most remarkable birds. It only arrived in Britain in the early 1950s having taken just 20 years to spread up from the Balkans.

Collared dove numbers have increased by over 200% in the last 25 years and its monotonous, mournful cooing has replaced the cheeky chirping of sparrows around thousands of houses. The collared dove seems to have taken over the house sparrow's historic role – that of the classic sponger. Wherever man resides, the collared dove is always just around the corner; stealing the chicken's grain, sharing a meal with the farm animals or scrounging under the bird table.

The reason for its explosive expansion remains a mystery but its high reproductive output must be an important factor. The collared dove has a particular liking for parks and gardens, where it can find evergreen trees and shrubs for both roosting and nesting. Eggs can be found in the nest most months of the year. It produces up to five clutches a year and will often start a new clutch while still feeding the previous fledged brood.

Unlike its close relative, the turtle dove, the collared dove keeps clear of open countryside and is not dependent on weed seeds for its diet, thereby not exposing itself to the deprivations of intensive agriculture as do other seed eaters. Numbers have recently begun to level off and we are probably even witnessing some local decline as farmyards become tidier with better protection for livestock and poultry food stores. At the end of the day I cannot help but feel that the more dominant collared dove has edged the house sparrow out of its traditional farmyard setting.

Substantial Increase

Common sandpiper

It is mid-May, the month Wordsworth referred to as *'the golden time'*, and I am on Speyside in the Highlands of Scotland. Fresh green vegetation has appeared everywhere. The broom is looking bonny on the riverbank. The young beech leaves are a delicate lime green and shade a carpet of bluebells below. The sycamore and silver birch have burst into leaf and the mountain ash is adorned in white flower. The alder is slowly unfurling yet the ash is still stubbornly lifeless. I am wading down an angry river with only a pair of restless sandpipers for company.

Common sandpipers, which in days gone by were known as *'summer snipe'*, arrive with the primroses. They have recently completed the long journey from sub-Saharan Africa to their northern nesting grounds. As the pair flit up and down the river on stiff bowed wings, I am reminded of Edward Grey writing in *The Charm of Birds*: *'sandpipers give the impression of happy affection, as the pair flit about together, piping pleasantly as if each enjoyed the other's company.'* They are nervous birds, which perpetually bob their heads and jerk their tails when perched on a riverside rock.

Common sandpipers are found on upland streams, rivers and clear hill lakes with stony margins. They are often found in the company of the dipper although the latter tends to frequent higher altitudes where the gradients are steeper. The sandpiper's nest is never far from water, usually tucked away in the riverbank or amongst shingle which contains light vegetation.

On migration, particularly moving north to breed, they can be found at a wide range of sites. They have visited my ponds in Derbyshire and I once met with a bobbing bird on Vanbrugh's Grand Bridge at Blenheim. It seems they are beginning to follow the example of their cousin, the green sandpiper, and over-winter in Britain. For the last two seasons I have enjoyed a solitary bird wintering in the Newtown estuary in the Isle of Wight.

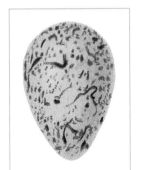

Common sandpipers began to withdraw from their lowland breeding areas to the uplands around 150 years ago. They ceased breeding in Cornwall in the first half of the last century and nesting on Dartmoor has not been recorded since 1962. The decline may well have been caused by pollution, especially if near industrial areas and mines as in Wales. In more rural areas the activities of ramblers and anglers have resulted in a vulnerability to recreational disturbance.

Although the population is now reasonably stable there is some evidence of a shallow decline in their northern heartland over the last 50 years. The decrease has not been fully explained. However, they could be suffering from the acidification of our rivers, which decimates the insect fauna. This has stemmed in part from the huge increase in upland coniferous plantations since the last war.

Decrease

Common tern

The members of the elegant tern family are generically described as 'sea swallows.' In the Newtown estuary, the arrival of the common tern in April from its wintering grounds off the coast of west Africa is as much the herald of spring as is the swallow in the farmyard up on the downs. The shrill *'kik-kik-kik'* calls of the common tern can be heard long before it is seen hunting up the muddy channels at low tide, propelled by its playful butterfly flight.

The common tern is the most widespread tern in Britain although the 12,500 breeding pairs are actually outnumbered by the Arctic and Sandwich terns. The common tern can today be found on many inland sites where it has colonised gravel pits along riverine floodplains. Other members of the tern family tend to stick entirely to coastal sites, but the Arctic tern rarely nests south of a diagonal line drawn from Northumberland to Anglesey.

Common and Arctic terns are frustratingly difficult to tell apart when airborne. The Arctic tern is an altogether daintier bird with longer tail streamers and a shorter head and bill. The common tern's bill has a black tip whereas the Arctic's is blood-red overall. When stationary on a shingle bank, perhaps the best distinguishing feature is the longer legs of the 'heavier' common tern.

The early part of the 19th century saw a decline in common tern numbers due to egg gathering and from shooting associated with the Victorian millinery trade. *The Seabirds Protection Act* of 1869 marked the turning point in their fortunes and numbers peaked in the 1930s.

Many colonies declined over the following 50 years and the common tern now seldom nests in Wales or south-west England. Predation by larger gulls is a prime reason for this tern's decline. A colony on the Isle of May in the Firth of Forth once held over 5,000 pairs but they deserted in 1956 as a result of competition from herring gulls. I have holidayed for many years on the Isle of Jura in the Inner Hebrides. When I first visited, there was always a tern colony on the small islands beside the Loch Tarbert boathouse. Today one is fortunate to see a single pair screaming out above Glenabattrick Bay. The celebrated raised beaches on Jura play host to an ever increasing number of sinister black-backed gulls.

The common tern has fared better than other members of the tern family and over the past 25 years their numbers have increased by around 10%. Unlike the little tern they are not so susceptible to human interference, witnessed by the fact that in 1987 over 300 pairs bred at Leith docks in Edinburgh. The most important factor in their success lies with their ability to colonise new sites, particularly inland, on the islands and banks of gravel pits. Common terns have even started to nest in the London area where the first pair bred at Cheshunt in the Lea Valley in 1963. By 1990 there were over 200 pairs nesting.

Conservation projects have also helped stabilise numbers. Purpose-built rafts and islands have been colonised at many inland and coastal sites. With the introduction of rafts at Blaydon Water numbers increased from 17 pairs in 1977 to 129 pairs in 1990.

Increase

 *Coot*

I have held a deep affection for the coot since my childhood when I used to wander along the fringes of Blenheim Lake in Oxfordshire. A large man-made lake represents the perfect habitat for this weird looking waterbird. The coot needs expansive open stretches of shallow vegetated water on which it can feed and breed. It is a bottom feeder that requires emergent plants for nest anchorage and concealment. It is also often to be seen grazing by the lakeside.

I have vivid memories of the coot from those carefree days. The nest was often in reeds close to the bank. It was easy to catch a glimpse of those delicious buff-coloured, black-spotted eggs. When the eggs hatched, the nest became an important refuge for the chicks, as underneath this floating platform lurked danger. Blenheim Lake is notorious for its large pike and this sinister predator takes a terrible toll on the chicks as they skim over the water. One minute they would be serenely following the parent bird, the next, with an eruption of water, they would be gone.

The coot is a noisy and aggressive bird with a loud high-pitched cry that resembles its name. Although gregarious in winter it becomes very territorial during the breeding season, particularly on smaller expanses of water. It scampers across the water with head down and wings outstretched to see off any intruder. The coot appears immensely buoyant, as it sits well out of the water. It is in fact a most effective diver, going down

to depths of four to five feet to pluck vegetation from the lake bed. Air is pressed out of the plumage and the bird gives a little leap forward that produces the impetus for submersion.

The coot is a bird of lowland Britain, where it frequents slow-moving nutrient-rich waters. It is therefore absent from much of the Highlands of Scotland. Large numbers migrate from the Continent to join our resident birds in the winter. Birds come from as far away as Russia, which might seem surprising as the coot looks strangely laboured in flight.

The coot has benefited greatly from a close relationship with man. Since the 1950s the acceleration of road building has led to an enormous demand for building materials and the creation of large gravel pits. In similar fashion to the tufted duck, the coot has greatly benefited from the creation of this new habitat, and in the last 25 years numbers have risen by over 20%. In excess of 90% of all coot nest on lakes, gravel pits and reservoirs. Linear waterways, canals and rivers represent minor habitat. The coot has become increasingly tolerant of humans. It now breeds happily on ornamental waters such as St James's Park in London, where it seems to thrive on bread fed by the tourists.

Increase

Cormorant

In the early 1980s I had a charming little weekend house beside the lake in Blenheim Park. I would be lucky if I experienced a couple of cormorant sightings a year on my many wanderings around the lake. One day in November 1996, I returned to find over 40 cormorants above the cascade. A similar story could be recounted today at countless inland sites across England.

The cormorant has moved inland from its traditional coastal habitat in increasing numbers over the past 25 years. This expansion has resulted from a combination of factors. Maritime fish stocks have certainly decreased yet new man-made habitat in the form of gravel pits and reservoirs, coupled with an increase in fish farms and 'put and take' lakes, has irresistibly enticed the cormorant into the countryside. The Breeding Bird Survey demonstrates a 23% increase in the population between 1994 and 2000, with a substantial rise in numbers breeding inland in England and Northern Ireland.

This behavioural change resulted in a serious conflict between conservation and fishing interests. There was probably a slight fall in the cormorant population until the 1960s. Full protection was introduced into Ireland in 1967 and into Britain in 1981 by way of the *Wildlife and Countryside Act*. In the 19th century the cormorant suffered from egg

collectors, was harried by fishermen on the more accessible inland colonies and was shot on inland waters in winter. The cormorant today can be shot under licence and research is currently under way to ascertain whether it is harmful to managed fisheries. It is still illegally and quite possibly unfairly persecuted as by preference it takes eels on freshwater lakes. In some places the cormorant may actually be beneficial by helping to control predatory coarse fish.

Inland colonies keep expanding in south-east England. At one site in Essex nine pairs first bred in 1981 and by 1990 there were 356 pairs breeding. It is thought these birds may have come from the tree-nesting population in Holland.

The cormorant is one of the characters of the coastline. It is almost reptilian in appearance and often perches on a rock with wings spread to dry its feathers. The cormorant is the only web-footed bird that does not put out a waterproofing oil on its feathers and as such must dry itself after each feeding session. It is bigger than a shag with a distinctive white throat. It breeds on the rocky shores of north and western Britain and Ireland. On the coast the cormorant prefers to feed in shallow bays and estuaries where it preys on flatfish such as flounders.

Increase

 # Corn bunting

The corn bunting is Britain's largest bunting and possibly our least glamorous bird. It has a drab, scruffy appearance and likes to perform its rather irritating song from an unattractive strand of barbed wire or telephone line. Edward Grey described the corn bunting as the *'carthorse amongst buntings'* and he wrote in *The Charm of Birds*: *'he has the habit too of sometimes taking a short flight with legs hanging down, as if it were too much trouble to tuck them up neatly in flight like other birds: this adds an impression of slovenly disposition to clumsiness of body.'*

The song, which is emitted from a prominent perch, is a series of accelerated jingling notes which are often compared to the sound of a bunch of keys being shaken. Grey wrote: *'I can even imagine that corn buntings like barbed wire. On wire then, by preference, the corn bunting will perch and grind out the noise that is his song. This suggests to me the sound of two hard pebbles triturated against the other.'*

Its love life is complicated and exhausting. The corn bunting is polygamous and both male and female mate with several partners. The males return to their breeding sites in winter, to be joined in April by the females who stay in winter flocks until springtime. The females carry out all the nest building duties while the males court other hens!

As suggested by its name the corn bunting is closely linked to agriculture. It will come as no surprise therefore, that along with the English partridge and tree sparrow, no other birds have been so cruelly devastated by modern farming. The corn bunting's decline has been accelerated by the fact that it is a sedentary species that never moves far from its nesting site. It is possible to travel hundreds of miles and never hear a corn bunting's song and then suddenly move into a pocket of birds. It is consequently susceptible to local specialisation or intensification of farming and is threatened with extinction in some areas.

The corn bunting's name is, of course, derived from an association with cereal crops, particularly barley. It thrives on the chaff and wastage left on stubble fields after harvest. Historically, harvesting barley tended to be inefficient, with a higher proportion of wast-

age than in current times. Wheat comes relatively cleanly off the stalk. Thirty years ago, farmers were happy to accept a 2-3% wastage at harvest. With modern-day mechanisation and improvements in harvesting techniques farmers expect a 0.25% wastage. The agricultural depression of the 1870s led to a substantial decline in the total area of cereals under cultivation in Britain, which continued until 1940. There was a parallel decline in corn bunting numbers until they stabilised during World War II. During the 1970s and 1980s, numbers began falling dramatically again to the extent that the British Trust for Ornithology's (BTO) Common Bird Census shows an 86% decline over the last 25 years.

The switch to autumn sown corn has exaggerated the problem as the corn bunting likes to feed on winter stubbles in large flocks with other finches. If it is lucky enough to find winter stubbles in its neighbourhood it is highly unlikely that these fields will provide the winter seeds vital for survival. Modern-day herbicides have all but exterminated common weed seeds such as charlock; only a few weeds such as fathen and knotgrass remain. It should not be forgotten, too, that fewer weeds mean fewer insects in the summer. Insects represent a vital food source for chicks at nesting time.

British agriculture is now largely polarised with grassland in the west and north and cereal growing in the eastern counties. The corn bunting is virtually extinct in the livestock areas. This is primarily due to a switch from haymaking to silage making. The corn bunting used to rely on hayfields where grass seeds were plentiful. Hayfields were mown later in the year than modern-day silage fields. The application of inorganic fertilisers on silage fields results in weeds and wild flowers being suppressed by the rigorous grass sward.

There are a few localised areas in which to enjoy the corn bunting. These specialised habitats clearly demonstrate the corn bunting's demise at the hand of modern farming elsewhere. The machair grassland in South Uist rings with its jangling song. The crofters' farming practices take us back to pre-war Britain. Mechanisation is primitive and hay is still cut late in the summer. It is hardly surprising that the Hebrides also represent a last bastion of the corncrake.

At Sandwich Bay in Kent a 'mixed farming' habitat still persists. A few arable fields lie adjacent to the reclaimed water meadows and, of course, they sit beside the famous golf courses. The links provide a large expanse of 'dirty' rough grassland untouched by pesticides. Finally, I often drive through the Grampian plain in north-eastern Scotland. The weather locally is harsh, with late frosts, and as a result farmers do not sow their crops until spring, which results in an abundance of winter stubbles and a welcome food source for the flocks of seed-eating finches.

Dangerous Decrease

Corncrake

In May the flower-rich Hebridean machair rings with the cries of nesting waders. One song stands out in its originality; it is the rasping call of the corncrake. The corncrake is a difficult bird to monitor. It is a shy creature and at its most vocal between midnight and 3am. The song, which can be heard at some distance, is reminiscent of a piece of wood being drawn against the teeth of a comb.

The corncrake's song was once a familiar sound in the English countryside. A decline set in around 1880 with the introduction of machine-mown hay. The old-fashioned method of harvesting with a scythe meant that the hay crop was cut later and nests and chicks escaped destruction. The corncrake had effectively disappeared from England and Wales by 1960. Shortly afterwards the development of silage hastened its decline in Scotland. The corncrake had become the classic Harvard case study as to how modern farming techniques can destroy bird populations. A survey completed in 1978-79 confirmed there were 750 calling birds in Britain with only 12 south of the border. When a similar report was published a decade later the figure fell to 550 and no birds were registered in England.

The corncrake migrates north from south-east Africa through Morocco each spring and makes the return trip via Egypt. The increasing desertification of the Sahel, with a resulting loss of cover, must make the journey more hazardous. When the corncrake arrives in Britain it needs tall, rank vegetation in which to conceal itself. Damp meadows associated with the low intensity farming of the crofting regime provide the perfect habitat. These might contain iris, *Phragmites* reeds or nettles, all providing the perfect nesting cover.

Agricultural improvements have resulted in a loss of herb vegetation at field margins and reduced the density of plant species in grasslands together with the invertebrate fauna. Loss of hayfields to permanent sheep pasture and the earlier harvesting of meadows in June rather than mid-July have been the main culprits. Fewer young birds will be killed if the meadows are mowed from the centre outwards thereby allowing the chicks an escape route. Corncrake recovery schemes with Government funding have now been put in place and the farmers agree emergency changes to the management of their hay crops. This has been particularly successful in the Inner Hebrides, such as on Tiree, and corncrake declines appear to have been halted in the nick of time.

Predation by mink and domestic cats around crofts takes its toll. On the machair in the Outer Hebrides hedgehogs have been destroying the eggs of many different species of nesting bird.

Dangerous Decrease

Cuckoo

There is no more awaited sound in the country calendar than the voice of the cuckoo. It arrives in England from its African winter quarters around the third week in April. As William Wordsworth reminds us the cuckoo is more often heard than seen:

> *O blithe new-comer! I have heard,*
> *I hear thee and rejoice.*
> *O cuckoo! Shall I call thee bird,*
> *Or but a wandering voice?*

When the cuckoo is seen in flight it is often mistaken for a sparrowhawk. The cuckoo has a longer tail, pointed wings and grey plumage.

Sadly the cuckoo is heard less and less in present day Britain. Although it is widely distributed across the countryside it usually occurs in low densities. The carrying distance of the male cuckoo's song creates an impression of abundance. The female cuckoo's song is less widely known and can best be described as 'a bubbling liquid trill.' Widespread declines in cuckoo numbers were first noticed in the 1940s and 1950s with the onset of colder springs and wetter summers. There are thought to be around 20,000 breeding pairs in Britain today with the CBC recording a decline in excess of 30% over the past 25 years. The Breeding Bird Survey reports a worrying 15% decline in the last five years.

The female cuckoo usually lays in the nest of one specific species all her life, which suggests genetic inheritance from her own experience. Eighty percent of 'breeding events' take place in the nests of meadow pipits, dunnocks and reed warblers. A very few species such as the blackcap and spotted flycatcher have become cuckoo resistant and desert if the cuckoo lays in their nests. The cuckoo has even developed egg mimicry, laying eggs closely resembling that of the host species. It is one of the wonders of nature. The blind chick has the ability to eliminate competition within hours of hatching. It heaves the host eggs and chicks out of the nest with the use of a hollow in its back. The female may produce between 12 and 25 eggs in host nests each year.

Cuckoo mimicking dunnock

There could well be a link between the decline of the host species and that of the cuckoo. The meadow pipit has declined in the cuckoo's upland habitat and the dunnock in its woodland habitat. This hypothesis does not hold entirely true as reed warblers are increasing in areas like East Anglia, which have witnessed a sharp decline in cuckoo numbers. The cuckoo is a long distance commuter and perhaps the fall in numbers is the result of conditions in its winter quarters. The timing of droughts could disrupt the cuckoo's migration schedule. Although it is not known exactly where British cuckoos winter in Africa it is thought to be south of the Equator.

The cuckoo is one of our few birds adapted to handle the hairy caterpillar as a staple food source. A decline in this vital food source is more likely to be responsible for the cuckoo's demise. There are many varieties of hairy caterpillar and the garden tiger moth is currently in severe decline. Its reddish 'woolly bear' caterpillar has disappeared completely in some areas. The once common garden tiger moth has declined by 44% across Britain in the last 30 years. The tiger moth spends the winter as small larvae and these seem to be able to cope less well with the warmer, wetter winters that Britain has been experiencing of late. The larvae are prone to fungal infections that thrive in such conditions. The number of moths recorded at Rothamsted Research, the oldest agricultural research station in the world, has declined by 60% since the 1930s.

Decrease

Curlew

At our home in Derbyshire a wrought iron curlew perches proudly above the old coach house with its long curved bill pointing into the prevailing wind. The blacksmith who created this magnificent weather vane was exhibiting at the Chelsea flower show and I could not resist placing an order. The curlew is my favourite bird. I am lucky enough to enjoy its company for most of the year. Around 30,000 curlews nest in Britain, predominantly in the damp uplands, with three times that number wintering on our estuaries.

The curlew arrives in Derbyshire just in time for Cheltenham week and proceeds to delight us with its bubbling song and undulating display flights for the next two months. In the autumn and winter I enjoy its melancholy call note on the Solent in the picturesque estuaries of Beaulieu and Newtown.

In *The Charm of Birds*, Edward Grey hit exactly the right note when he wrote of the curlew:

'of all the birdsongs or sounds known to me there is none that I would prefer to the spring notes of the curlew. As a rule the wonderful notes are uttered on the wing, and are the accompaniment of a graceful flight that has motions of evident pleasure. The notes do not sound passionate: they suggest peace, rest, healing, joy, an assurance of happiness past, present and to come. To listen to curlews on a bright, clear April day, with the fullest of spring still in anticipation is one of the best experiences that a lover of birds can have. On a still day one can almost feel the air vibrating with the blessed sound.'

The winter call note of the curlew, a melodic *'corlee'*, can be heard at all times of the year, but just occasionally on a mild day in mid-winter a few notes of the beautiful spring song can be heard. Grey captures the atmosphere brilliantly in one of the most evocative passages of English literature I know. He wrote in *'The Charm'*: *'but even at this season [winter] on a mild day one may be surprised to hear a single bird give a few of the joy notes, just enough to revive memory of the past spring and to stir anticipation of the next one.'*

Sadly the curlew is yet another example of our most accomplished songsters, along with the blackbird, song thrush and nightingale, to have declined in the last 25 years. The Breeding Bird Survey gives a figure of 35% although this predominantly applies to farmland and curlews could be doing a little better on our heather uplands. Historically the breeding range of the curlew was confined to the latter habitat, yet towards the end of the 19th century there was a vigorous expansion into new lowland sites, such as cultivated river valleys and heathland. This happy situation had halted by 1950. Thereafter a decline set in precipitated by agricultural improvements such as land drainage, over-grazing, and the reseeding of moorlands, in addition to afforestation of our heather uplands, all of which combined to destroy nesting habitat.

The decline of the curlew can be well illustrated by farming practices at our home in the Derbyshire Dales. The limestone uplands are characterised by large tracts of permanent pasture where the late hay crop has been replaced by two earlier cuts of silage. From May through to July the countryside echoes with the humming of silage machines. What chance does a nesting curlew have? The nest, eggs and chicks are destroyed by the blades of the grass cutter. Those few nests that survive are plundered by predators such as the fox and carrion crow. There is no local fox hunt and the great estates have long since been split up and there are few gamekeepers on the ground. Ground nesting birds have little chance to survive this onslaught. The lapwing has all but disappeared from our dales and it will surely not be long before we lose both the curlew and the skylark.

Decrease

Dabchick

It was the afternoon of the Queen's Jubilee. The sun had obligingly returned and I walked down to a small pond in our local valley in Derbyshire. I sat on the bank and enjoyed the antics of colourful dragonflies while listening to the scratchy song of whitethroats and the lazy ditty of a reed bunting. From behind the tiny island came the spooky whinnying trill of a dabchick.

There was no sign of the bird. The dabchick, or little grebe, is a secretive bird that likes to conceal itself in emergent vegetation and unlike the great crested grebe does not sport a conspicuous plumage. I walked around the margin of the pond, and amongst some lilies on the far side, about a yard from the bank, was a platform of dead vegetation. I lifted the weedy lid off the nest, which cleverly camouflaged the three stained white eggs.

The dabchick frequents large lakes and gravel pits like the great crested grebe. It also chooses to occupy tiny areas of water, such as my local farm pond, which contain shallow muddy bottoms and an abundance of vegetation, both emergent and submerged. It thrives on suburban ponds and lakes and can even be found on such celebrated waters as St James's Park and Buckingham Palace Gardens in the heart of London.

Nests on small ponds and lakes tend to be more successful than those on rivers and streams due to the greater incidence of flooding on running waters. The nest is, in effect, a floating platform that is anchored to surrounding vegetation; thus drought or flood conditions invariably spell disaster.

Global warming is working in the dabchick's favour. Over the past 25 years their numbers have increased by around 15% despite serious reverses during the cold winters of the 1980s. These small grebes are very susceptible to periods of prolonged frost and the notorious winter of 1962-63 nearly caused their extermination in northern Britain.

Aside from intermittent setbacks caused by unfavourable climatic conditions, the last 150 years have seen the dabchick expand its range throughout the north of England and Scotland. The increased availability of nesting sites with the introduction of canals, reservoirs and, at a later date, gravel pits, has been responsible for the little grebe's success. Modern-day recreational activities do to some extent act as a check to both grebes' success. The wash of a passing boat can all too easily flood a floating nest platform.

Perhaps the most serious challenge to its future welfare comes from the recent explosion in the mink population. These ruthless killers wreak havoc on the wildlife that shares a similar waterside habitat, such as the water vole and moorhen. One ray of hope is the fact that the mink is relatively easy to trap. It cannot resist walking into a cage trap baited with old smelly fish or even dog food. Trapping requires a considerable infusion of human time and cash resources.

Increase

Dartford warbler

The Dartford warbler was first recognised as a British bird in 1773 when a pair was shot on Bexley Heath near Dartford in Kent. It was not until 1806 that a nest was discovered. The Dartford warbler is out of place in Britain. It is really a bird of scented Mediterranean hillsides yet in England it has clung on in small numbers amongst the gorse and heather of our rapidly diminishing southern heathlands.

The New Forest is now the stronghold for this species. I once came within a few feet of this handsome little bird when concealed behind a small gorse bush while wildfowling on the sea wall at Exbury. It had a cocked tail, a slate head and wine-coloured underparts. Its jerky movements gave the impression of a restless energy and, indignant at my presence, it scolded me with a soft buzzing *'churr'*. The Dartford warbler's song is very similar to that of the whitethroat as is its display flight. It ascends vertically while singing and then dives back down into the undergrowth.

The Dartford warbler frequents heathland dominated by gorse and heather: it is a bird of scarce and threatened habitat. It is insectivorous and subject to huge losses following cold winters. As a result of a series of mild winters in the 1990s numbers have multiplied to nearly 2,000 pairs. After the harsh winter of 1962-63 it was estimated that only a dozen or so pairs remained in England. Like many birds that are susceptible to the ravages of nature the Dartford warbler is capable of a quick recovery as in good summers it will rear two or three broods.

The Dartford warbler occupies a large territory and has a propensity to skulk in gorse. It is difficult to find but nevertheless suffered at the hands of egg collectors in the 19th century. Gorse is the most productive feeding place as it is richer in invertebrates than heather. It also provides good shelter from snow in winter. Other warblers migrate south in winter but the Dartford warbler stays on to face the harsh weather, suffering as a result. Most birds are not surprisingly concentrated in the southern counties of Surrey, Hampshire and Dorset. There is plentiful habitat in East Anglia but the birds would be vulnerable to the cold east winds.

Although much of their favoured habitat is now protected by SSSIs with conservation and management strategies in place, our southern heathlands have disappeared at an alarming rate over the past 100 years. An area of 30,000 hectares of Dorset heathland late last century had been reduced to under 6,000 by 1980, the losses mainly due to forestry, agriculture and urbanisation. Uncontrolled fires, often started by tourists, present another problem that leads to the spread of birch and bracken.

Substantial Increase

Dipper

In the few seconds it takes for my salmon line to traverse the angry waters of the River Spey, I often wonder whether the white bobbing ball downstream is just another module of frothy jetsam or the brilliant white plumage of a dipper. Its snow white chest can be seen at a distance either as it splashes around in the shallows or as it curtseys on a rock out in the middle of the tumbling stream.

The dipper is unique among songbirds in that it swims on or under the water. In fact it is a much more polished performer below water than above. As it dashes upstream uttering its sharp *'zit-zit'* call note with a fast, direct, no-nonsense flight that reminds me of a starling, it suddenly alights on the water with an untidy belly-flop before vanishing below the surface in search of food. Here the dipper's strong legs come into their own. It walks upstream along the riverbed searching for caddis larvae, tadpoles and minnows while the angle of its body deflects the water upwards giving increased stability to its progress. As it forges against the strong current the wings are used for additional propulsion.

The warbling song of the dipper seems in perfect harmony with the rushing water. Sir Edward Grey wrote in *The Charm of Birds*:

'his song seems to be part of the rippling water, from which he is never away. "I hear thee where the waters run" may well be said of the dipper. His song is very sweet and lively; it has no marked beginning or close, but goes on indefinitely. It is as if "beauty born of murmuring sound" had passed into the bird who was giving it back as song to the stream from whence it had come.'

The dipper is found where fast-flowing streams run over gravelly, rocky beds and where there is an abundance of invertebrates, particularly caddis larvae and mayfly nymphs. Dippers are scarce when the waters are acidic as this reduces the small fish and insect populations. Since the War the Forestry Commission (now Forestry Enterprise) has planted large areas of our uplands with conifers and carried out associated drainage. Many river catchment areas are heavily planted with conifers that have the ability to trap acidifying air pollutants on their foliage. The acidic rainwater finds its way quickly into the river system.

The dipper is a good indicator of acidity and other water pollution in our river systems. River pollution caused by agricultural run-off and prolonged periods of extreme weather will also affect dipper numbers. It is a sedentary bird that stays in its breeding habitat during the winter months. The Waterways Bird

Survey reports a drop of 14% over the last 25 years but numbers tend to fluctuate with no long-term trend. In the 19th century the dipper declined in the flourishing manufacturing areas of the Pennines and the tin mining districts of West Cornwall.

Decrease

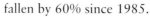

Dunlin

Two thousand of these small waders over-winter with us at Newtown on the Isle of Wight. They provide a constant source of pleasure as they perform their agile aerobatics above the estuary. When the peregrine hunts across the marsh, dunlin explode into the sunlit sky, wheeling and turning, snow white one moment, jet black the next, like a shoal of panicky fish escaping the attention of the dreaded pike in the shallows.

The dunlin represents the most common visitor to our estuaries, with a total of 500,000 birds wintering along the shores of Britain. The breeding population is less than 10,000 pairs concentrated in two main habitats, wet upland moorland and coastal zones such as the machair in the Outer Hebrides. Nesting dunlin congregate in the peatlands of Lewis, Caithness and Sutherland, and the western coastal zone of North and South Uist.

There has been a noticeable downturn in the dunlin's fortunes in Britain over the last 25 years both as a breeding bird and as a winter visitor. The Flow Country in Scotland holds around 40% of Britain's breeding population of dunlin and huge tracts of this unique habitat have been lost to blanket conifer planting. Afforestation in this area has reduced the dunlin breeding population by approximately 20%. Research has shown that breeding dunlin stay well clear of newly afforested areas, almost certainly because plantations act as refuges for predators.

The machair coastal strip of the Uists holds around 25% of the total dunlin breeding population in Britain; here, sinister predators threaten their survival. The mink is a ruthless killer and large numbers have escaped from fur farms on Lewis and spread throughout the islands. Hedgehogs were released on South Uist and now prey on the eggs of numerous wading birds on the machair. Hedgehogs are not native to the Western Isles and were introduced on South Uist in 1974, since when their numbers have grown to more than 5,000. On the two Uists and Benbecula breeding snipe, dunlin and ringed plover have fallen by 60% since 1985.

Breeding birds in Wales, Cornwall, Devon, the Pennines and south-west Scotland are in steep decline; agricultural intensification and disturbance from ramblers have added to the problems nesting dunlin face from afforestation.

Wintering birds are also facing problems in their estuarine habitat. Land claim and barrages result in a reduction of food availability in an estuary and are likely to result in fewer waders being supported by a particular site. The loss of wintering birds correlates closely with the spread of spartina, a plant which has spread rapidly in the upper shore zone of many estuaries. The loss of high-level mudflats removes a crucial winter feeding ground. The decline of wintering numbers is no doubt also linked to the recent run of mild winters in north-western Europe. Birds tend to remain on the Continent and only move to Britain if the weather becomes harsher.

A few dunlin remain on our estuaries all year where they look particularly handsome in their summer plumage, sporting a distinctive black belly and rich chestnut brown back. The bill is slightly curved and the call an evocative reedy '*treep*.' When dunlin frequent tidal mudflats they feed on ragworms; however on their moorland breeding grounds the diet changes to insects.

Decrease

Dunnock

At first sight the dunnock, or hedge sparrow, appears an ordinary bird. Its very name implies dullness. It is plain-coloured in appearance, meek, furtive and unobtrusive in manner. To the casual observer there is little exceptional about its song. Dig a little deeper and I guarantee it will become a favourite.

This delicate little bird should always be called by its alternative name, the dunnock. There is nothing remotely 'sparrow' about the dunnock. The house sparrow is a robust, noisy bully with a heavy seed-eating beak. The dunnock on the other hand has the characteristics of a warbler. Its beak is thin, as with all insect-feeders, and its song like most warblers is musical. The dunnock might not be one of our most accomplished songsters but most writers seem to agree that the song has spirit and uplift and it is a determined performer. The thin high-pitched tinkling song, with a similar structure to that of the wren, can be heard both at dawn on a glorious summer's day or during a blustery spell of wet weather in January. Like the mistle thrush it sings for us when others have their heads down and gives us a taste of the spring season to come.

Sir Edward Grey wrote: '*the song is quite adequate in loudness, and is pleasant, but there is little shape or feature by which to remember it.*' WH Hudson found the song uplifting if not particularly polished, when he wrote: '*the song may be said to be pleasant because it is a natural sound and is heard in the open air when the sun shines, when leaves and blossoms are out, and it expresses the gladness which is common to all sentient things. But it has none of the rare qualities which are requisite to make a pleasant sound anything more than a merely pleasant sound.*' I disagree with Hudson's assessment that the dunnock is one of our least attractive birds. The dunnock's heavily streaked reddish brown back and wings, ash coloured crown and bluish-grey neck give it a most attractive countenance. It also lays that wonderful blue egg, '*as blue as a cloudless June sky*', enthused about by broadcaster Percy Edwards.

The dunnock is a sedentary bird that frequents woodland scrub and low bushy cover. It favours areas of thick low vegetation such as brambles, ivy and wild rose, and feeds on tiny insects on the ground under trees and shrubs in addition to adjacent open spaces. It would

have prospered under the ancient system of coppice management where clearings were created in the dense forest. It is infrequent in closed canopy woodland. The dunnock's rapid spread was accelerated by the coming of Enclosure hedgerows. It prefers low trimmed hedges and unlike the robin does not need a tall song post. The dunnock has, like the blackbird, adapted well to an urban environment and by the end of the 19th century had moved into gardens, parks and churchyards.

The unexplained decline of the dunnock began after a spell of cold weather in 1975 and over the last 25 years the CBC has registered an all-habitat decline of around 45%. Interestingly enough there was a rapid recovery after the hard winter of 1962-63. The reason for the substantial decline in numbers is simply not known, although locally the grubbing out of hedgerows and the advent of Dutch Elm disease cannot have helped. The related loss of tree canopy encouraged the growth of ground vegetation previously restricted by shading, which in turn reduced the amount of bare ground on which dunnocks like to feed. This situation, coupled with general agricultural intensification, which leads to greater competition for sharply reduced food sources, cannot entirely explain the dunnock's decline, as numbers have also fallen in urban areas. Little research to date has been undertaken on the dunnock; however there must be a strong possibility that a widespread use of garden pesticides is behind its decline in suburban Britain. Unlike the flourishing tit family that feeds on insects in trees, the dunnock forages at ground level. This would make it much more susceptible to modern gardening practices such as spraying, which devastates insect life.

Decrease

Fieldfare

When I first hear the gruff, chuckling calls of the fieldfare high in the autumn sky I am reminded that winter is around the corner. The winter thrushes, fieldfares and redwings arrive from the north in October. I was once out stalking on a wild autumnal day at Glen Affric in the Highlands, when hundreds of fieldfares dropped exhausted out of the mist, having just crossed the North Sea. The fieldfare is a member of a select group of winter visitors to Britain that, until recently, did not stay on to breed.

The fieldfare migrates to Britain from its breeding grounds in northern Europe. In its winter quarters it feeds in huge flocks on hawthorn berries or spreads out on farmland and short grass in search of leatherjackets. The total population of around one million birds is constantly on the move, pushing south if the weather deteriorates.

The first British breeding record was in Orkney in 1967. It then spread south to Shetland and onto the mainland, with recordings in the Pennines and a pair as far south as Kent by 1991. British breeding fieldfares are probably linked to Scandinavian stock. The fieldfare uses a wide range of breeding habitat, so a number of breeding pairs no doubt go unrecorded. Even so it is thought no more than twenty-five pairs nest in Britain.

The central European population has experienced a century of range expansion, having formerly bred as far west as Poland and east Germany. It has now reached France and the Netherlands, having colonised Switzerland in 1923. A consolidation in Britain could yet take place from these Central European birds rather than from the Scandinavian population. Colonisation is likely to result from late migrants lingering in suitable habitat. It is essential that human disturbance is avoided if such colonies are to become established.

The fieldfare is a handsome bird with a blue-grey head and rump. It has a distinctive song, a mixture of whistles, squeaks and chuckles, not unlike the starling. The nest is

similar to the blackbird's, with a layer of grass overlying a mud cup, and is located in diverse habitat such as forestry, moorland valleys or even in tussocks on the ground. Like its close cousin, the mistle thrush, the fieldfare is an aggressive bird that boldly defends its nest from predators.

Stable

Fulmar

At first sight one might be forgiven for thinking of the fulmar as 'just another seagull', but there is much more to this ocean-going bird than meets the eye. The fulmar is in fact a petrel and is related to the albatross. It is distinguished from other seabirds by its complex tubular beak structure. Along with the collared dove it is the great success story of the British bird world. A little over 100 years ago there was one small colony of 20,000 birds on St Kilda. Today they have colonised our entire coastline and even nest in inland quarries and occupied buildings. Most interestingly, for hundreds of years this romantic bird was the mainstay of one of the most specialised yet antediluvian economies in the western world.

Each year in the second week in August young fulmars were taken from their nests on the island of St Kilda. Each fulmar contains half a pint of rust-red oil that is spat out and used as a defence mechanism against intruders. This foul smelling fluid was sold to the mainland for medicinal purposes and lighting fuel. Fat extracted was sold as grease and fulmar feathers were bought by the Government for stuffing army mattresses. The carcasses of the young birds were then salted and stored for the winter months. In

1830 some 12,000 birds were caught by the islanders. By 1900 demand for fulmar products fell away and the St Kildan economy collapsed.

A second fulmar colony was founded on Foula in the Shetlands in 1878; Ireland was colonised in 1911, England (Yorkshire) in 1922 and Wales in 1931. It is thought the original colonists spread out from Iceland where a more adaptable new genotype favouring expansion had developed. The population on St Kilda exhibits different characteristics in that the local birds feed on plankton and avoid nesting in ruined buildings. There is little doubt that the broader diet of the Icelandic population has contributed to its success as the birds exploited the discards from the whaling and trawling industries. Today there are around 600,000 breeding pairs in Britain of which one-tenth nests on St Kilda. It is estimated that the population is growing at 3–4% a year. Interestingly there was a marked fall in their numbers on the Shetlands in 1988 with the reduced availability of sand eels.

The fulmar lives a long life with the oldest British ringing recovery on the Orkneys proving it to be over 40 years old. It does not breed for at least five years after fledging and is very noisy at the nest producing a hoarse, rapid, cackling call. After breeding it disperses widely into the Atlantic Ocean. It is thought that a general warming of the east Atlantic has produced a more favourable ecosystem for the fulmar.

Substantial Increase

 *Gadwall*

The drake gadwall ranks amongst my favourite wildfowl. In my early thirties, when working in the City, I rediscovered a childhood interest in birds. This stage in my life was closely associated with two enchanting places: Blenheim Park, where I was lucky enough to have a small weekend cottage, and the Itchen valley which was close to my parents-in-law's house at Bramdean.

At both locations I developed a deep affection for this handsome duck. From a distance the drake appears an understated grey but at close quarters delicate shades of grey, black and white are revealed along with chestnut flashes on the upper wing. Gadwall frequent well-vegetated, quiet, inland lakes and slow-moving streams, as they feed on emergent and submerged water plants rather than land-based plant material. Blenheim Lake and the River Itchen proved the perfect habitat for these inland ducks. In flight both sexes are easy to identify with their distinctive white wing patches and snow white belly and underwing.

The gadwall is one of Britain's great wildfowl success stories. They did not nest in Britain until a pair was caught at the Dersingham duck decoy in 1850 and then released into the wild in Norfolk as pinioned birds. By 1875 a substantial population had arisen from this source, the duck having spread into the Breckland waters and mixed with over-wintering Continental birds.

For the next 50 years or so their spread was slow. In 1909 a small colony was established at Loch Leven, which built up to around 40 nests a year. It is not known whether these were feral birds; although it is thought they might have been natural colonists from Iceland. Gadwall colonised the Broads in the 1950s, no doubt benefiting from a combination of the nutrient enrichment of the waters from sewerage, agricultural run-off and pollution. Since then the gadwall has spread into southern, central and north-western England and up to the Hebrides.

Wintering and breeding numbers have increased dramatically in the last 25 years. The wintering population, which mainly comes from Russia, has more than doubled to 15,000 over the last decade and breeding pairs are probably nearing 1,000. A substantial proportion of the birds ringed in Britain during the summer have been recovered in France or Spain.

The reason for their success lies with an ability to exploit man-made habitat. They have benefited greatly from the significant increase in the number of nutrient-rich freshwater sites, such as gravel pits and reservoirs that support lush submerged vegetation. Although it is a dabbling duck, by stealing pond-weed from feeding coot, gadwall are able to feed in these deep artificial waters. With so much unused habitat across the country the prospects for the gadwall would seem excellent.

Substantial Increase

Garden warbler

One day towards the end of April the 'warbling choir' that prevails in the hawthorn bank at my home in Derbyshire is reinforced by a new arrival. The song is not as rich and loud as that of a blackcap and it contains grating notes reminiscent of a whitethroat. It is a well sustained, sweet, even warble and quieter, mellower, and more rapid than that of a blackcap. The liquid sound reminds me of a 'babbling' brook.

The garden warbler arrives in Britain a fortnight later than the blackcap. It is inappropriately named as it rarely occurs in gardens. It is a discreet bird that likes the dense undergrowth of my hawthorn. The garden warbler is the most nondescript of our migrant warblers; it is a heavy looking specimen with pale brown plumage. It makes up for its blandness with a beautiful song. Sir Edward Grey particularly liked the length of the song although the blackcap received top marks. In *The Charm of Birds* he wrote: *'the garden warbler goes on and on for a longer time and yet never seems to liberate its voice upon the air so completely as the blackcap does. In other words, a garden warbler's song seems always on the point of an achievement, to which only the black-cap attains.'*

Garden warbler numbers fluctuate from year to year and there is no obvious long-term trend. The population on farmland is less stable than that in their favoured woodland habitat. Overall numbers have increased substantially over the past 25 years but that is because they started from a relatively low base. There was a trough in the mid-seventies when the Sahel rainfall deficit was at its worst. Recovery was quicker than that of the whitethroat as the garden warbler winters further south and outside the drought zone. One can only imagine the garden warbler had problems crossing the Sahara when the drought was severe.

The widespread damage caused by the gales in October 1987 may well have resulted in local increases. The garden warbler frequents open woodland that is interspersed with scrub. Newly created clearances will quickly become overgrown with brambles and thick undergrowth. Blackcaps use a very similar habitat but have a preference for the deciduous trees whereas the garden warbler utilises the scrub zone; as a result two birds with much in common manage to co-habit quite successfully.

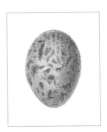

Increase

Goldcrest

It took me 50 years to find a goldcrest's nest. I was walking on the lawn at my brother's house on the edge of the Berkshire downs. My attention was momentarily caught by the busy antics of two tiny birds high up in an old yew tree. What looked like a ball of moss and lichen was suspended under one of the topmost boughs. Emanating from this snug hammock came the cries of a hungry family. The goldcrest's nest is a miracle of construction. The mossy cup is glued together with spiders' webs and is bound to twigs on the underside of an evergreen bough.

The goldcrest is one of nature's wonders. It is remarkable enough that they survive harsh winter conditions. Even more extraordinary is the fact that many thousands migrate across the North Sea from Scandinavia to over-winter in Britain. In the old days it was thought that these little birds, hardly bigger than bumble bees, hitched a ride on the back of short-eared owls.

The goldcrest is a vociferous bird and if it was not for its far-carrying high-pitched calls, 'zi-zi', it would easily be overlooked. The tinkling song has a pulsating quality and a thin terminal flourish which makes it difficult to distinguish from the treecreeper. Edward Grey described its song in *The Charm of Birds*: '*Its voice, as we should expect, is very high-pitched; the little call notes are like needle-points of sound. The song has little volume, but on a still day can be heard from some distance. It suggests to me a tiny stream trickling and rippling over a small pebbly channel, and at the end going over a miniature cascade.*'

Of course, hundreds of thousands of these gutsy birds fail to survive a hard winter. After the terrible winters of the early sixties, which decimated the goldcrest population, their numbers rose tenfold to hit a peak in 1975. Since then the CBC 25-year average has shown a fall of over 50%. Although numbers fluctuate depending on the severity of the winter, the goldcrest does not seem to have responded to a series of mild winters to the degree one would expect. Like the nuthatch they suffer greatly from hoar frost and ice coating on trees. A lack of these conditions over the past decade has given rise to a small population increase.

The goldcrest and coal tit are the dominant species in conifer plantations, and as such increased their range northwards with 19th century afforestation. The goldcrest does not move into deciduous woods until the population reaches saturation point in its favoured coniferous habitat. It is yet another of nature's miracles that these minute birds hatch up to 10 eggs, and start to lay a second clutch when the first brood is only half grown. This is nature's way of coping with near extermination, which is what took place during the winter of 1962-1963.

Decrease

Golden eagle

The sheer size and majesty of the golden eagle is breathtaking; its wingspan reaches over seven feet as it quarters the Highland skies. It is Britain's most charismatic bird; the 'lion king' of the feathered world. I came within yards of a soaring eagle as I moved over a ridge while out stalking on Jura in the Inner Hebrides. It was a young bird with conspicuous white patches on its wings and the base of its tail.

The golden eagle is not a prolific breeder and will not mate until five years old. It lays only two eggs and invariably the biggest chick ends up eating its smaller sibling. It has never been common and historically was severely persecuted with the spread of upland sheep farming in the first half of the 19th century. The golden eagle reached its low point in 1870 when only 80 eyries were used regularly in Scotland. The latter half of the 19th century saw a decline in sheep farming and conversion of much land to deer forest; with this change in land use persecution was relaxed.

The eagle ceased to breed in England in the 1780s and had left Wales by 1750. In 1969 a pair bred once again in the Lake District and has remained until the present time. Numbers increased slowly with a reduction in gamekeepers between the wars but there was a setback in the 1950s when breeding productivity was affected by toxic chemicals from sheep dips. Sheep carrion forms a major part of the eagle's diet. In days gone by this led to unfair persecution by shepherds. A survey in 1982 produced 424 pairs nesting in Scotland and numbers have remained static ever since. Illegal egg collecting continues to be a problem and the eagle is still persecuted on the eastern moors where it is not welcome on account of its weakness for red grouse. Other threats stem from a loss of habitat caused by overgrazing and blanket conifer planting particularly in the far north and west of Scotland.

The golden eagle's diet consists of a combination of carrion and live prey. Research has demonstrated that eagle density is related to the amount of carrion available in late winter. Western Scotland and the Inner Isles have long been a stronghold owing to plentiful sheep and deer carrion; on a deer forest the eagle will also feed on the gralloch. An old ghillie on Jura told me that when sheep were taken off a particular area of the island the eagles deserted their local eyrie. Breeding success is highest in the east Highlands and the Inner Hebrides where there are greater amounts of live prey such as grouse, ptarmigan and hares.

The eagle's range can be as wide as 20,000 acres. Territories are very constant and it is estimated there is room in Scotland for around 600 pairs.

Stable

 *Golden plover*

The golden plover is an aptly named bird. When the low winter's sun catches a flock roosting on a mudflat their upper parts appear a delicious golden brown. These agile little plovers lead a golden life. They inhabit some of the most beautiful wilderness in Britain. In summer their mournful fluty whistle can be heard high up on their heathery nesting grounds. In winter they execute dashing aerobatics as they wheel playfully over our southern estuaries in tight flocks.

Sadly, the future for these delightful birds looks bleak. During the 19th century golden plover bred across most of upland Britain. Only 30,000 pairs breed in Britain today and serious losses have taken place on Dartmoor, Wales and the southern Pennines. On their upland nesting grounds they have been hit by afforestation, disturbance by hikers and walkers in addition to over-grazing and the general deterioration of their moorland habitat. In Caithness and Sutherland, afforestation in the 1980s displaced 20% of the breeding population, which represented 2% of the entire British population. Ironically the highest breeding densities are on well-managed grouse moors, where the heather is short in carefully burnt strips and in good condition. Intensification of agriculture in the uplands, encouraged by EEC subsidies on sheep, led to overgrazing and ultimately the loss of heather to grassland. This practice together with the reseeding of rough grassland has led to a dramatic decline in nesting golden plovers. Only on a well-managed grouse moor does one find sheep numbers strictly limited and vermin tightly

controlled. Afforestation not only leads to the destruction of habitat but also encourages vermin such as crows and foxes. Often in summer, the 'goldie' will share its territory with a pair of dunlin, giving added protection from predators. Both off-duty partners from each species associate closely on the ground and in flight, hence the dunlin's nickname, 'the plover's page.'

In the autumn golden plovers move south and east to over-winter on our estuaries and lowland agricultural habitat. They particularly like to feed on flat ground adjacent to estuaries with a diet of earthworms and beetles. Around 350,000 'goldies' winter in Britain, although some of our breeding birds will move further south to France and Iberia. Agricultural intensification on their wintering grounds, such as the loss of permanent pasture to plough, is now taking a serious toll that leaves their future a grave concern.

Goldfinch

During winter, 80% of the goldfinch population emigrate to the Continent, many to Belgium and Spain. They arrive back in Derbyshire just before Easter and enrich our garden throughout the spring and summer with their delightful busy antics. Their liquid tinkling song can be heard incessantly as the birds flit from tree to tree with their bouncy undulating flight. They are beautiful and acrobatic finches. I will never forget the sight in winter of a pair of goldfinches feeding on an old thistle in the snow in our bottom meadow. Maybe they were a pair from Scotland or the north of England. They hovered and hung with great agility on the tall weed, their crimson and yellows dazzling against the glare of the snow.

The memory always takes me back to a lovely passage written by Pamela Grey about a goldfinch on its nest:

'One of the prettiest nests ever found was a goldfinch's. It was in a yew tree, and the outside of the nest was made of green lichen: the lichen you find on beech bowles and wooden pilings. The inside was incredibly soft to the touch, which was possible only by a very long stretch, so the bamboo ladder was fetched to get a clear sight of it. Then it was found to be lined completely with dandelion "clock" each little sphere detached from the many that make the round of the puff. Another nest, this time lovely in its environment, was again that of the goldfinch. Holding my face deeply into a pyramidal apple tree in full blossom in order to enjoy the light filtering through the mass of petals that clustered on the boughs so thickly as to shut everything else out, I became aware of the ruby mask of the goldfinch, sitting on her nest not ten inches away. She never stirred; happily I had insinuated myself very gently into "this world of light". Neither did I withdraw hastily. I stayed long enough to see how this rose and gold of sunlit apple-blossom could be deepened by this touch of red.'

Goldfinches underwent a big contraction in their numbers during the 19th century. They thrive on common seeds and are a very easy cage bird to feed; coupled with their attractive song and colouring goldfinches became a popular victim of the commercial bird trapper. In 1860, 132,000 were caught in a year near Worthing, which lies on the main migration route. Increasing enclosure and ploughing of marginal land, characteristic of this time, compounded the problem. Relief finally came in the early 20th century with protection and an agricultural depression, which increased the weedy areas on which they like to feed.

Goldfinch numbers today are relatively stable. There was a sharp fall from 1975-85 probably caused by the widespread use of new, efficient fertilisers in Britain and in their European winter quarters. They use their long thin bills for opening the seed heads of thistles, dandelions, teasels and knapweeds. It must be said that goldfinches have not been hit as badly as other seed-eating finches such as the linnet. Goldfinches feed on tree seeds like birch and alder and are not so dependent on arable seeds. Thistles and dandelions flourish on waste lands and old pasture and are less easy to control with herbicides than other weeds because their windborne seeds disperse so widely. They do use the bird table as an early spring top-up when food resources are scarce, but not so frequently as the greenfinch. Goldfinches are susceptible to cold weather in their Franco-Iberian wintering grounds in addition to shooting by the local rural communities.

There is no more appropriate collective name for this goldfinch than a 'charm.' In one of the most delightful passages in *The Charm of Birds* Grey wrote of the goldfinch:

'the song is rather trivial, a tinkling sound but happy; and as the birds are so constantly on the move, now in one place and now in another, the garden is always being enlivened by them. Indeed goldfinches give a touch of lightsomeness to the heaviest day in July. They suggest to me what the ash does among trees. July is the month in which to appreciate the ash. When the leaves of oak and beech are dark, impenetrable to sunshine, and stiff, almost stubborn, to the breeze, then observe the ash. The leaves are graceful on long stems, and are stirred by a gentle air, and the foliage is so open that the light seems rather to permeate and be welcome than to be excluded. In the early spring green and bright autumn colours of other trees the ash does not compete; even in bareness its stout branches tipped with black buds are without the grace of other trees in winter; but in midsummer it has a gracious presence. No day in midsummer can be unrelievedly heavy if there are goldfinches in the garden and an ash tree in the field beyond.'

Stable

Great crested grebe

The great crested grebe can justifiably lay claim to being one of the most eloquent and charming of British birds. Their springtime mating display is a delightful and exciting experience for anybody who appreciates the mysteries of nature. The two birds face each other with their chestnut ruffs and jet-black tippets erect. Then with their beaks full of vegetation they commence their penguin dance, raising themselves from the water, paddling frantically and shaking their heads from side to side.

It is this very elegance that led to their near extinction in the middle of the 19th century. The skin of the underside, with its thick white feathering, was considered a substitute for animal furs and was made up into ruffs and used for trimming garments. By 1860 there were only about 40 pairs left in Britain, mainly in Cheshire and the Norfolk Broads. Eggs were highly prized by collectors and in many areas the birds were shot to protect fish stocks.

Help came at the eleventh hour with the introduction of the *Bird Protection Acts* in the 1870s. Numbers have increased steadily ever since and a national survey undertaken in 1975 estimated the British population stood at 7,000 adult birds.

Great crested grebes breed on large shallow lakes which provide a good runway of water for their long takeoff and reedy margins for nesting. In the breeding season these extensive tracts of water echo with their harsh purring growls. The main increase in the grebe population came in the 1960s and 1970s with the provision of additional habitat in the form of new reservoirs and the flooding of gravel pits. Since 1975 their numbers have risen by around 15% and have stabilised at around 8,000 birds.

Leisure activities such as waterskiing and small boat recreation on large lakes create disturbance and inhibit successful breeding in many areas. Predation by large pike should not be discounted as a check on their expansion although the adult birds' charming habit of carrying their stripy chicks on their backs when out on open water provides a welcome refuge from underwater ambush.

Increase

Great skua

The sighting of a great skua or 'bonxie', as it is known in the Shetland Islands, is an exciting moment for any bird lover. Not only is it a rare bird on account of its northerly distribution but it also has great physical presence. It is a heavy, thuggish-looking brown bird with a stout hooked bill, short tail and distinctive flashes of white on its wings. The very name, great skua, suggests aggression. It will drive humans away from its nest site with a blow to the head and is powerful enough to tip a gannet into the sea by grabbing its wing in flight. The great skua is a true pirate of the high seas. It belies its heavy stature by twisting and turning acrobatically in flight as it harries other seabirds in order to terrify them into disgorging food.

The great skua breeds in loose colonies on coastal grassy moors. I have enjoyed the antics of this charismatic bird on a trip to St Kilda with the Scottish National Trust. On the journey home we stopped off at the enchanting island of Mingulay and were surprised to see a great skua so far south. This expansion southwards is likely to continue as the 'bonxie' successfully exploits its marine environment. It breeds predominantly in areas colder than northern Scotland such as Iceland, Norway, Spitzbergen and Bear Island. Colonisation from its Shetland heartland initially tended to be northwards into the Arctic.

By 1774 six pairs were breeding on Foula in the Shetlands and three pairs on Unst. In the early 19th century there were 30 pairs nesting on the Shetlands and they were tolerated by the farmers because they drove off white-tailed eagles. The great skua suffered persecution at the hands of collectors until 1900 at which time it was afforded protection. By 1915 it had spread to Orkney and by 1945 it had colonised the Outer Hebrides. The population doubled every year until 1970 and today there are over 8,500 pairs breeding in Britain, nearly 90% on the Shetlands.

During the 20th century the great skua benefited from an expansion in the offshore fishing industry. In a similar fashion to the fulmar it followed trawlers picking up the offal discards. Recent action has been taken to cut back on small discarded white fish by increasing fishing net mesh sizes. The great skua also forages on surface shoals of sand eels. In the late 1980s sand eels began to disappear around the Shetlands and the seabird populations crashed. In March 1991 the Ministry of Agriculture closed the local sand eel fishery and skua numbers increased once again. It should not be forgotten that a current absence of predator fish means that sand eels are not so easily found on the surface of the sea.

Despite the cutback in offal discards and sand eels the great skua has thrived, demonstrating a resourceful nature. It will scavenge on rubbish tips and the carcasses of stranded sea animals and kill lambs in distress. Above all it will take the eggs, young and adults of other seabirds. The colony on St Kilda has grown from 145 pairs in 1994 to 271 pairs in 1997. It is estimated that 40,000 such seabird kills are made by skuas on St Kilda each year and 200,000 on the Shetlands. Small seabirds such as petrels and puffins are most at risk.

Substantial Increase

Great spotted woodpecker

It has been said of the great spotted woodpecker that its traditional 'drumming' call is one of the most evocative sounds of an early spring morning. If so I am very lucky to have an old sycamore outside my bedroom window, which our resident pair uses as a drumming post.

Before the advent of the bird table these pretty birds were more often heard than seen. They announce their presence either through a harsh '*tchich*' call-note or through their 'drumming', which is predominantly reserved for the mating season. My resident pair in Derbyshire commence drumming as early as January. 'Drumming' is both a way of marking out a territory and a method of communication between the pair; both sexes drum. This technique is unique to the woodpecker family and was originally thought to be a vocal form of communication. It was soon recognised that the sound emanated from the beak striking against the bark of a tree trunk, at a remarkable rate of some 16 blows a second.

A serious contraction in great spotted woodpecker numbers took place at the beginning of the 19th century and by 1860 they were extinct in Scotland and scarce in the north of England. Many reasons have been offered for their decline including predation by red squirrels and competition for nest holes from starlings. The most likely reason is that the contraction coincided with a period of active woodland management in Britain, and their natural habitat was steadily eroded. There was much felling of woodland at the time together with the introduction of highly managed coppice systems.

Towards the turn of the century their fortunes improved and the woodpeckers spread north and recolonised Scotland. There is an interesting passage in *The Charm of Birds* when at around the same date Grey wrote that he spied a great spotted woodpecker on an open moor in Sutherland amongst some beech trees: '*it is so interesting to see a bird of this species so far north in so wild a place; and to find it so tame*'. It should be remembered that 100 years ago this woodpecker was less common than the ground-feeding green woodpecker. The reverse is true today. Their increase around 1900 was no doubt assisted by a period of climate amelioration, which benefited arboreal invertebrates on which woodpeckers fed.

A steady expansion took place until the 1970s when the population growth moved up a gear with the advent of Dutch Elm disease. The great spotted woodpecker thrives on rotting wood which provides both an excellent food source and an abundance of nest holes. A favourite food is the larvae of scolytid beetles that live in the trunks of infected elms for at least two years after the trees have died.

Dutch Elm disease subsided in the 1980s yet great spotted woodpecker numbers have increased by 60% over the last 25 years. The popularity of the garden bird table may well be behind this happy situation. Woodpeckers began moving into parks and suburban gardens in the 1950s and a very high percentage of garden-feeders today report a visiting woodpecker. The householder now has the opportunity to view this highly attractive bird at close quarters. Both sexes have crimson under their tail but only the male sports a crimson patch on his nape. Young birds are characterised by a red crown.

Substantial Increase

Great tit

Although it was originally a bird of deciduous woodland, the suburban garden is tailor-made for the great tit. It takes to nest boxes more readily than the blue tit and is an enthusiastic recipient of artificial food at all seasons of the year. The great tit is the bully of the bird table. It is an aggressive feeder and constantly threatens the smaller blue tit with its stout beak.

The great tit is one of the earliest songsters of the year, commencing its repertoire in January. It produces a variety of repetitive notes with a metallic or ringing quality suggesting the use of a saw or a bell. Sir Edward Grey wrote in *The Charm of Birds*: '*the notes ring out loud, vigorous and clear: to one who knows the ways of a great tit the sharpness of his notes suggests the sharpness of his beak.*'

There was a marked spread of great tits in Scotland early in the 20th century that was attributed to afforestation and a warmer climate. The latter half of the century witnessed a steady increase in the British population fuelled by garden feeding. There were temporary decreases in the cold winters of 1978-79 and 1981-82. The great tit, being bigger than the blue tit, has greater fat reserves and is probably not as vulnerable to cold weather unless conditions include a prolonged cover of snow. Beech mast is as important to the great tit as it is to the blue tit but being more of a ground-feeder the great tit suffers to a greater extent in such harsh conditions. The woodland population remains stable in most years; however great tit numbers on the more marginal farm-land habitat fluctuate widely according to the winter weather. The availability of nest holes is vital to the great tit and the loss of hedgerow trees due to Dutch Elm disease may have affected the farmland population.

In the spring and summer great tits feed on insects taken from trees and bushes. As with the blue tit the young fledglings are brought up on the caterpillars of moths. In the three weeks during which the pair rears the brood they can destroy as many as 8,000 caterpillars. There is currently worrying evidence that global warming has caused the caterpillar flush to decouple from the tit's breeding cycle resulting in much lower productivity at the fledgling stage. This could quickly have an adverse effect on the future tit population.

Increase

Greenfinch

There are two distinct characteristics that make the greenfinch a garden favourite. It is a harbinger of spring. Its distinctive song, a series of twills and wheezes, can be heard from a prominent hedgeside song post as early as the first week of February. On a wet, windy winter's day its repetitive long drawn out call-note fires one with anticipation of warmer times. WH Hudson was captivated by it as he wrote in his *British Birds*: *'the charm of this perpetual summer music of the greenfinch is its airy, subdued character, as of wind-touched leaves that flutter musically.'*

The sheer beauty of the cock bird makes it irresistible and the brilliance of the yellow wings can best be seen when it feeds on the bird table. Of all the members of the finch family, the greenfinch is most partial to a free feast of garden peanuts. Edward Grey captured the exotic nature of the greenfinch when he described it in *The Charm of Birds* as *'green as a parrot may be green and with a touch of yellow.'*

On balance the greenfinch appears to be coping rather well with modern society and overall numbers are relatively stable. A general decline on agricultural land has been counterbalanced by an increase in suburban areas as a result of widespread garden feeding. The vast winter flocks of finches that used to be seen in the countryside are now history.

Agricultural intensification has taken its toll. Favourite weed seeds have become less plentiful as a result of the increased use of herbicides. Greenfinches have a greater preference for cereal grains than other finches. Harvest wastage is no longer available to the degree it once was; more efficient machinery and a move from spring ploughing to autumn ploughing being the guilty parties.

Fortunately the greenfinch has been able to adapt to alternative food sources. Its strong conical bill enables it to forage in a wide range of seed-bearing trees and shrubs now planted in urban gardens. Mortality used to be high amongst greenfinches in spring when seeds are hard to find but, today, peanuts are displayed in many gardens throughout the year. As a result of this adaptability the greenfinch is probably one of the few farmland birds that has increased in numbers over the past decade.

Increase

# *Green sandpiper*

I shall always associate this attractive wader with my small farm in Derbyshire. This might come as a surprise to many people as we could not live further from the coast if we tried. We bought Parwich Lees the first week in August 1986. The day we moved in I took a short walk down the valley and past an ancient dew-pond used for watering the cattle. A bird that looked strangely like a large house martin propelled itself into the sky uttering a high pitched '*klu-eee-weet*' cry. It had dark underwings, a distinctive white rump and a twisting, corkscrewing, snipe-like flight.

The green sandpiper is one of the first migrants to fly southwards each summer. It nests in forest swamps from Scandinavia to Siberia and the majority will winter in Africa. It arrives in Britain in midsummer and visits shallow freshwater sites, no matter how small. I have seen a bird pass through our ground in Derbyshire as early as 8th June and as late as 26th September. When moving south it likes to travel down the central spine of the country whereas on its northern journey it takes the more direct coastal route.

Sir Edward Grey took the first visit by a green sandpiper to his home in Northumberland as the beginning of the autumn migration and the winter birds. He wrote in *The Charm of Birds*:

'*In most years, on some day in early August, a bird flies up from the edge of one of my ponds. It is larger than a common sandpiper and it utters a cry that is more sharp and piercing than that of a redshank; sometimes there are two or even three birds and they may settle again, but generally there is only a single bird and it flies away with a sharp and repeated cry and is heard and seen no more. It is a green sandpiper.*'

The green sandpiper has only been known to nest in Britain twice, once in 1917 in Westmorland and again near Inverness in 1959. On its nesting grounds this species has a switchback display flight, and as with the greenshank, its musical song and mating display are the main indication of breeding. Interestingly the green sandpiper builds in a tree, often using the old nest of a crow or thrush or even a squirrel's drey.

With the advent of mild winters more and more birds over-winter in southern Britain. The green sandpiper has a preference for freshwater springs and chalk streams where the water seldom freezes, and here it probes for aquatic invertebrates such as beetles, flies and crustaceans. The watercress beds in the Itchen valley are my favourite spot for enjoying green sandpipers. A sighting on Christmas Day near Tichborne is etched in my memory. Over 1,000 birds now winter with us in England.

Greenshank

It is early October in the Newtown estuary on the Isle of Wight. A watery sun has risen out towards Spithead and the autumn mist is lifting slowly off the downs. The tide is well out and the crisp morning air vibrates to the piercing cries of countless waders. From amongst this feeding frenzy one particular voice stands apart; it is the unmistakable fluty, trisyllabic call of the greenshank.

Four birds take off simultaneously from a muddy channel in the salt marsh. This in itself is unusual as it tends to be a solitary species. Greenshank are noisy waders and easy to recognise on take-off with their dark wings contrasting with a white rump. They are particularly distinctive in the winter months when they appear almost white as they forage in the shallows on long green legs.

Over 1,000 pairs breed in the Highlands of Scotland but in all likelihood these Newtown birds nested in Scandinavia, where it is an abundant breeding species. The largest numbers of British greenshank are seen in the autumn when these Scandinavian migrants pass through our estuaries en route to their African winter quarters. Most of the Scottish breeding population is thought to winter in south-west Ireland.

In Britain greenshank breed in wild country such as the rough boggy moorland of the Flow Country or the forest bogs of Deeside and the Spey Valley. They are easy to find on their breeding grounds as the male has a delightful switchback display flight where it gains height rapidly and then glides down singing musically as it descends.

The nest itself is difficult to find, which was fortunate in the 19th century as greenshank eggs were much sought after by collectors. During this period greenshank extended their range as Scottish woodland was felled.

The British breeding population today remains relatively stable. Figures produced in 1978 demonstrated a loss of 130 pairs due to afforestation in the Sutherland and Caithness peatlands. This represents a 12% reduction in the national breeding population. Drainage of pools used for feeding, egg-collecting and recreational improvements such as the use of all-terrain vehicles, pose an ongoing threat to the greenshank on its nesting grounds in Scotland.

Losses have been partly offset by local increases in the Outer Hebrides. SSSIs are now being declared on large areas of moorland that represent potential nesting habitat.

Green woodpecker

On a grey, damp, misty November morning in the Derbyshire Dales, a carrion crow grunts from across the valley, a robin proclaims its winter territory with a thin warble, and a boisterous great tit calls as it shuttles to and from the bird table. Suddenly a sharp cry pierces the autumnal gloom; it is the happy laughter of a green woodpecker.

The green woodpecker is Britain's most exotic bird. Its loud ringing call and brightly coloured plumage seem better suited to the equatorial rainforest than upland pasture. It is a shy bird but its mocking 'yaffle' call carries a considerable distance announcing its presence. Parkland and deciduous woodland are the favoured habitat.

Unlike its cousin, the great spotted woodpecker, the green woodpecker is a ground-feeding species with a diet that consists mainly of ants. As such it is susceptible to cold weather, especially when a heavy fall of snow makes feeding difficult. The harsh winter of 1962-63 caused severe losses amongst the green woodpecker population. A period of stability followed until a cold spell in the early 1980s caused a further decline. There has been a rapid increase in numbers since that time and there are now thought to be well over 25,000 breeding pairs in Britain. It is not understood why the green woodpecker has been so successful of late but it may well be linked to global warming.

In the mid-19th century the green woodpecker declined in Scotland and northern Britain, perhaps due to trophy shooting. In the 1940s it recolonised north-west England and the first confirmed breeding record in Scotland was in 1951. The reason behind their spread was said to lie with the widespread planting of coniferous woodland after the war that allowed the wood ant to increase in abundance. This now seems unlikely as the green woodpecker tends to favour deciduous woodland when given a straight choice.

Local declines in the south-west, eastern England and west Wales may well result from a downturn in sheep husbandry in favour of arable farming, in addition to the introduction of the myxomatosis virus. Close cropping by sheep and rabbits gives rise to a short dense turf which with its higher exposure to the sun, supports larger and more varied ant populations than longer grass swards.

Increase

# Grey partridge

Aside from the thrill of pitting one's wits and physical reactions against those 'aerial aces' amongst gamebirds, the red grouse, there were two overriding memories of an August visit to the High Walden Moor above Aysgarth.

There was the sheer beauty of the panoramic views down Wensleydale to a sunlit Castle Bolton. Then there was the charm of glimpsing the unexpected, and sadly nowadays unusual sight, of a covey of English partridges. As we drove up the dale sandwiched between the freshly cut hay meadows, a pair of grey partridges lovingly shepherded their family of four immature 'squeakers' alongside a drystone wall. It was one of those enchanting moments nature gives us which *'penetrates the affections and abides thereafter in the memory'*.

The low ground in the valley bottom and the rushy white grass immediately below the heather moorland is today one of the few areas in Britain where the grey partridge prospers. Farming practices have changed little since the war and the ground is well keepered, hence potential predators such as the stoat, fox and carrion crow are tightly controlled.

Grey partridge numbers have fallen 90% since 1970 and there are now significantly fewer than 100,000 pairs in the entire British Isles. One hundred years ago there was practically a pair to every field; indeed these charismatic gamebirds were once so abundant that had they not declined from their former peak, they would now be the tenth most common bird in Britain. Prior to 1940 it was estimated that two million grey partridges were shot annually in the country.

The grey partridge reached its peak levels from 1880 to 1914 following the agricultural revolution which spawned increased cereal production and field boundary enclosures which necessitated planted hedgerows. Shooting became very popular in Edwardian times and with it came a significant increase in the number of gamekeepers. A reduction in the partridge population took place after World War I with a sharp decline in the number of keepered estates, as tenants began to acquire their own farms. The level of nest predation is an important factor in the population regulation of the grey partridge.

A dramatic decline in partridge numbers took place in the 1950s with the revolution in farming practices and the widespread introduction of chemical sprays. Stubble burning and autumn ploughing became common, which resulted in greatly reduced food sources for adult birds over the winter months. More efficient harvesting has led to less grain spillage and a loss of hedgerows has meant fewer nesting sites and greater predation. Nests became concen-

126

trated making easier pickings for both foxes and badgers.

The introduction of pesticides in the never-ending quest for higher cereal yields has been the real villain behind the demise of the English partridge. Partridge chicks need an abundant supply of insects during the first three weeks of their lives. The preferred insects tend to be crop pests such as aphids, weevils and sawfly larvae, all of which are decimated by the application of insecticides. Insect numbers are also affected by other areas of farmland management, particularly the reduction in the practice of undersowing cereals with clover.

Food for adult birds consists chiefly of plant material such as the leaves and seeds of grasses, cereals, clover and weeds; seed heads of chickweed are particularly favoured. Much of this food source is eradicated by the application of herbicides.

Ironically one of the few areas where partridges do well is on a specialist shooting estate where conservation methods are introduced and the land is well keepered. Conservation headlands around fields with a width of up to six metres left unsprayed enhance the growth of plant species on which insects thrive. The recent introduction of 'set-aside' requires that fields should not be mown or sprayed until early July when the breeding season is effectively over.

The real problem lies with chick survival. The Game Conservancy's research demonstrates that only three chicks per brood survive (20%) which is well below what is necessary to keep the population going. With 'set-aside' and agri-environmental measures providing more food for chicks, should we not be doing better? The answer is that there are still far too few insects for the needs of partridge chicks. The benefits of conservation headlands have been outweighed as crop management in the fields has intensified. We need yet more radical conservation methods to be introduced into our arable farming policies.

Perhaps it is just too late for the grey partridge and their numbers will follow those of the corncrake. How I already miss the loud grating call of this most English of birds from across the valley on a summer's evening at my home in Derbyshire.

Dangerous Decrease

Grey plover

The grey plover is a Jekyll and Hyde character. While wintering in Britain it appears a solitary, miserable bird; hunched-up and dejected it sits on a mudbank longing for the summer. A transformation takes place on its northern breeding grounds in Siberia. It becomes aeronautically active over its territory, executing a delightful butterfly flight as it courts its mate. The drab grey-brown plumage is replaced by a stunning combination of jet-black underparts and sparkling grey and white upperparts. In winter the grey plover can be identified in flight by a distinctive black patch under each wing. It is a larger and stouter bird than the golden plover. Its wistful call consists of three notes, 'tee-oo-ee', containing a low middle syllable.

The grey plover winters in warm climates, therefore its distribution in Britain remains essentially to the south. There has been a huge increase in the winter population since the 1970s with a doubling of numbers each decade reaching a maximum of 40,000 in the late 1990s. A series of highly successful breeding seasons in the Arctic, aided by milder weather, has been a major factor in their success. In the past the grey plover was hunted extensively throughout Europe and the relaxation of this pressure may have aided its recent increase. The Wash and Chichester Harbour represent two of the most important wintering sites. Birds that move through Britain are probably on their way to the West African coast.

Recently wintering numbers have fallen back and the count of 38,000 in 1999-2000 was the lowest since 1992-93. Over the past few years there have been increases in wader

numbers on our east coast sites and decreases in the west. The estuaries of Suffolk, Essex and the Thames are muddier than those on the sandier west coast and thus very rich in food. The disadvantage of the east coast is that weather can be harsh. With the advent of much milder winters it appears that the wader population is moving further east and the grey plover is wintering in greater numbers on the Waddenzee on the Continent.

Global warming could have adverse effects on their northern breeding grounds at some future point. If the treeline moves northwards part of the grey plover's tundra habitat will be destroyed. It nests on lowland tundra, north of the tree limit, and excludes coastal locations.

As with most waders, estuarine land claim for industrial and leisure development, or the creation of barrages, poses the greatest threat to the grey plover's wintering habitat.

Increase

Grey wagtail

The grey wagtail is far from 'grey.' It is one of our prettiest birds and certainly the daintiest. It does have a blue-grey back yet the bright yellow underparts and greeny-yellow rump complement its exotic tail. The long thin tail is constantly flicked as the wagtail flits here and there after waterside insects. As it bobs up and down on a boulder in a roaring stream it gives the impression of perpetual motion. This exuberance also shines through when the grey wagtail is airborne. It has a graceful bouncy flight when it announces its presence with a high pitched metallic cry, *'tschizzik'*, that is more penetrating than that of the pied wagtail.

The grey wagtail is the true water wagtail. It spends the summer on fast-running upland streams, often in the company of the dipper. It particularly favours watercourses lined with deciduous trees as it supplements its diet of aquatic invertebrates with caterpillars and spiders. As such, unlike the dipper, which exploits the larval stages of aquatic insects, the grey wagtail is not affected so badly by the acidification of its watery habitat. Like its cousin, the pied wagtail, the grey wagtail is a partial migrant and moves down to lowland waters in winter with some birds continuing through to France and Spain.

In the winter months the grey wagtail can be found on cress beds and sewage farms and is never far from man-made features such as weirs, sluices and reservoir overflows. It is this relatively new habitat that has encouraged the grey wagtail to expand into eastern and southern England over the past 50 years whereas previously it was only common in the hilly areas of the north and west.

In the 19th century the grey wagtail managed to cope with polluted waters, especially streams and rivers into which sewage flowed, as a result of an abundance of insects. Numbers peaked around 1960 and were devastated by the savage winter of 1962-63. The then picked up again following a series of mild winters in the 1970s only to fall back in the early eighties. The population decreased by 33% following the harsh winter of 1978-79 and by over 40% after the 1981-82 winter.

Insect-feeders are more susceptible to harsh winters and the grey wagtail's winter habitat, the lowland watercourse, always freezes first. The dipper remains in its upland home of rushing streams that are highly unlikely to freeze and as a result fares better during inclement weather. Surveys show a drop in grey wagtail numbers over the past 25 years but this probably results from a high starting level before the cold winters of 1978-79 and 1981-82 set in. The population has now picked up and stabilised and with more mild winters we should see an increase in lowland areas.

130

Guillemot

A boat trip from Seahouses to the Farne Islands in June will prove a memorable occasion for any lover of the natural world. The Pinnacle Rocks on Staple Island will take the breath away. This is one of the largest guillemot colonies in Britain. The stench of guano, the growling of thousands of auks standing shoulder to shoulder like tiny soldiers each aggressively defending a postage stamp of bare rock where they incubate a single pear-shaped egg clutched between their legs – there are few more extraordinary sights in nature.

Guillemots, razorbills and puffins are all members of the auk family. Where there are tens of thousands of guillemots on the Farnes there are only a few hundred razorbills. The guillemot has a dagger-like bill and chocolate brown upper parts whereas the razorbill has a square-ended beak with black plumage. The guillemot returns to its clifftop nesting grounds in February after months on the open sea where its staple diet is the sand eel. It is a strong swimmer and is capable of diving up to depths of 150ft.

Surveys undertaken in 1985 demonstrated that guillemot numbers had doubled since 1970 making it the most numerous of our seabirds. The population continues to expand to the extent that there are now around one million pairs in Britain. The main colonies are in Scotland and many of them are increasingly over 10% per annum. The main reasons for the guillemot's success lies with a plentiful supply of food and an availability of suitable nest sites. The guillemot can dive deeper than other sea birds, for example terns. This enables it to tap into a wider variety of small fish such as sprats and sand eels.

Guillemot distribution in the 19th century was much the same as today although southern colonies such as in Kent and Sussex decreased markedly as a result of human interference. In Victorian times the birds were shot for sport and their eggs taken for food and by collectors. Luckily these colonies formed a relatively small proportion of the population as a whole and relief came with the introduction of the *Wild Birds Protection Act* in the 1880s.

Being divers, auks are still threatened by fishing nets and oil spills. The latter became a serious problem from 1940 onwards although recent legislation such as the prohibition of cleaning out tanks at sea has eased the situation. There have also been surprisingly few accidents during the extraction of North Sea Oil.

The guillemot's delicious looking egg is pear-shaped for a good reason. When knocked in its crowded colony it revolves like a top in a tight circle centred on the small end, rather than rolling off the ledge into the sea.

Substantial Increase

Hawfinch

Only once have I seen this secretive bull-necked finch in Britain. The happy experience coincided with my 50th birthday and took place in Exbury gardens on the edge of the New Forest. Exbury is a glorious rhododendron garden. A mass of exotic colour is shaded by the canopy of the old forest. From the very top of one of these mature trees emanated a totally unfamiliar sound. A loud and distinctive *'clip'* call revealed a shy hawfinch slipping away through the treetops.

The hawfinch is unmistakable. It is Britain's largest finch and sports a massive bill and short tail. It is a wary bird and its pretty chestnut head and reddish-brown upper parts are rarely seen as it flits through the high foliage. The unique feature of the hawfinch is its tall deep bill. The beak can exert a crushing force of 100lbs when it is used to crack open cherry stones. The hawfinch thrives in well wooded areas of broad-leaved trees and feeds on the seeds of hornbeam, yew and wych elm. In the spring it forages on beech buds, in the summer it takes insects and in the winter it invades cherry and damson orchards.

The hawfinch dramatically expanded its range in the second half of the 19th century assisted by the growth of cherry orchards and suburban gardens. As with the bullfinch it was considered a pest by the fruit growers and persecuted until given protection in the 1880s. The population then remained stable for a century when a mysterious decline set in around 1990.

A reduction in the habitat of cherry orchards and broad-leaved woodland may well be behind its demise. The hawfinch population is estimated to have fallen by 40% in the past decade. Over 15 million mature trees disappeared overnight in the notorious October gale of 1987 and as 75% of hawfinch nests are found in deciduous woodland, the storms would have had a significant effect on both feeding and breeding habitat.

The hawfinch often breeds in loose colonies and because its nest is usually located in mature trees, early in the season it is very susceptible to woodland predators such as grey squirrels, crows and jays. These egg thieves are thriving as gamekeepers in modern Britain are a scarce resource. If the hawfinch is suffering from a reduction in favoured habitat, such predation can only compound the problem.

The hawfinch has not as yet visited garden bird tables although it is known to do so in many areas of the Continent. If it takes a venturous leaf out of the greenfinch's book, its prospects may well improve in the future.

Decrease

Hen harrier

The hen harrier is a handsome, charismatic and spectacular raptor. There are few more exciting experiences in the world of nature than to watch its dramatic aerial antics. During the courtship display its buoyant, graceful flight turns into a frenzy of aerobatics. The harrier climbs, turns a somersault at the summit and plunges with folded wings. Equally sensational is the aerial food pass where the cock bird calls its mate off the nest and drops prey to her in mid-air. The female is brown with a distinctive white ring on her long narrow tail whereas the smaller male is a combination of grey and snow-white with black wing tips. At a distance he could be mistaken for a seagull.

Yet there is another side to this beautiful bird that brings it into conflict with man and places it at the forefront of one the countryside's most contentious political debates. Beneath those stunning looks and lazy wingbeat lurks a sleek predator that quarters its moorland habitat for prey with ruthless efficiency.

The hen harrier has been persecuted by gamekeepers for many years and on a limited basis is still harassed on grouse moors. Its natural habitat is rolling heather moorland interspaced with patches of bracken and rushes. It nests on the ground in thick heather or in young conifer plantations. The harrier takes voles, the chicks of nesting birds and fully grown grouse. Nineteenth-century persecution banished it to Orkney and the Western Isles where the relatively small number of sporting estates concentrated on wildfowl as opposed to grouse. After World War II the harrier recolonised the mainland and in the 1960s spread to northern England and Wales. This rise in the population resulted from a reduction in gamekeepers and a substantial increase in the number of new conifer plantations. Young forestry not only provides secure off-moor nesting sites but also a plentiful number of voles.

The British population of hen harriers has remained static over the past 15 years and if anything has shown a small increase. In the 1960s it was thought there were 350 pairs in Britain and by 1989 there were 550 with a noticeable increase in the Isle of Man and Northern Ireland. There has been less persecution on grouse moors but offsetting this, habitat has been lost as post-war plantations have matured making them unsuitable for harriers.

It is unfair to polarise the harrier argument as between grouse-shooting landlords and conservationists. Landlords are very often the best conservationists. Grouse shooting is the most economic form of land use on our heather uplands. The quickest way to destroy this scarce habitat is to graze too many sheep and to plant forestry that also encourages vermin. A well-managed moor means sheep are restricted and the heather is burnt in cycles to encourage new growth. This provides the perfect environment for many breeding birds such as merlin, golden plover, curlew and dunlin. The Langholm report illustrated how harriers thrive when heather moorland is not managed for grouse. Gamekeepers were taken off the moor, sheep overgrazed the hill, and white grass quickly took over from heather. In the short term meadow pipits replace grouse and the hen harrier population increases; longer term the harrier's food supply will dry up and their numbers will decrease again. The overall result is that a unique heather habitat disappears.

Hen harriers and productive grouse moors are like chalk and cheese. A harrier is not just a ruthless killer but it also causes serious disturbance. I have read in certain bird books that a harrier causes grouse 'to go to ground'; far from it, the terrified birds will lift off the hill in a huge pack and leave the moor altogether. Another complication is that the grouse is a cyclical bird and when stocks are low the presence of harriers can be fatal. There are two sides to this debate and some sort of compromise on harrier numbers must be reached. The harrier moves down to low ground, particularly estuaries, in the winter.

Increase

Heron

The heron frequents lowland Britain, no doubt because more fish are available on the lower reaches of rivers, on estuaries or along the coastline. This big bird is a familiar distraction to any motorist as it flaps slowly across the countryside on broad round wings, with legs trailing and uttering its loud, harsh *'frank'* call. Likewise at the seaside, holidaymakers will see a sinister bird with a threatening dagger-like bill standing motionless in a rock pool, patiently awaiting a meal. At my home in Derbyshire we could not live further from the sea if we tried, yet when I stocked my ponds with trout the herons appeared overnight.

The heron has been persecuted by fishermen for generations. There was some early conservation in Britain when falconry was important, but by 1800 hawking had fallen into decline. The heron was a prestigious quarry: and heronries located on large estates were often preserved. The heron was also considered a delicacy at the table, and unfledged young in particular were taken and served at medieval banquets.

The 19th century saw an increase in persecution that led to the dispersal of many large colonies. Egg collecting caused the extinction of the last heronry in Rutland in 1830. By 1890 it was thought there were over 200 heronries in England and Wales with 6,000 nests. In 1954, protection was granted against shooting and today there are around 10,000 nests in Britain.

Hard winters with prolonged frosts are the most common form of mortality. First year birds are thought to be more susceptible to harsh conditions, being inexperienced foragers. It has been said that one reason the heron commences nesting early in February is so that the young birds can have more time to find their feet before the onset of winter. The hard winter of 1962-63 devastated heron numbers by 50%. It took much longer than usual for the heron to recover from this particular winter. It is thought that this was the result of toxic chemicals. DDT and dieldrin accumulated in prey from the bottom of the heron's food chain upwards. Like the sparrowhawk, the heron suffered from being at the top of the pyramid and experienced a decrease in reproductive rates, manifested in eggshell thinning.

In 1928 the celebrated ornithologist, Max Nicholson, organised the original census of heronries in Britain and its success indirectly gave birth to the British Trust for Ornithology in 1933. Heron numbers today have never been higher, although nearly 10% of ringed recoveries result from deaths against overhead wires. A certain amount of illegal killing remains with increased stocking of freshwater fisheries.

Heronries are noisy nurseries and fun to visit. There is even a small colony in Regent's Park. The nests are located in the tops of trees and built with thick sticks. They are often long-established and birds only move on if prompted by fishing interests, or as a result of the felling of commercial woodland. The heron will range many miles from the heronry in search of food, and even visit fields and haystacks in its quest for small rodents.

Substantial Increase

Hobby

The aerial agility of the hobby is remarkable. Its narrow, scythe-shaped wings result in speeds so fast that it can fly down a swift or even catch a bat in flight. This graceful little falcon can cover huge areas with a minimum amount of energy. I have only once seen the hobby at our home in Derbyshire, which must represent the most northern part of its range; one minute it was overhead and in a flash it folded its wings and disappeared down the valley.

The last 25 years have witnessed a rapid expansion of the hobby northwards that may be linked to increases in its dragonfly prey supplies and a decreasing dependency on its traditional heathland habitat. The hobby is insectivorous for most of the year but switches to bird prey when breeding. In the 1950s there were no more than 100 nesting pairs in Britain; although not a danger to gamebirds it was heavily persecuted in the past. In the 1960s it was still thought to be a bird of our southern heathlands but more recent research has shown that it was under-recorded and more birds had been breeding on farmland and in woodland than originally thought. The hobby is a very secretive bird and difficult to observe around the nest. Pesticides had little effect on the population maybe because of the high proportion of aerial prey taken. By the late 1990s 624 pairs were recorded breeding in Britain.

The main threats to the hobby come from nest predation by crows and squirrels, shooting on migration and egg thieves; it has most attractive eggs prized by collectors. The hobby is a trans-Saharan migrant that arrives late in May to take advantage of the warmer weather and increasing insect numbers. In a similar fashion the chicks hatch in mid-July to coincide with an abundance of young swallows. The nest is usually placed in an old crow's nest amongst an isolated clump of tall trees or shelter-belt. Display flights, including food passes, during the mating period can help locate the nest site as can the male's noisy 'kew-kew-kew' calls as he brings in food to his partner.

Substantial Increase

House martin

The house martin occupies a special place in my childhood affections. Each year about half a dozen of these delightful little birds would build their nests at our home in south Oxfordshire. The house martin is the most accomplished builder in the martin/swallow family and I would watch in fascination as the birds constructed a cup of mud pellets under the eaves of the house. While the house martin went about its work moulding the damp mud into place, it sang happily, a soft chirruping twitter. As soon as their nests were completed they had to fight off the attentions of avaricious house sparrows that were intent on taking over their homes.

The house martin has a distinctive white rump and a shiny blue back. It has charming little legs covered in white feathers and 'woodpecker-like' claws that allow it to cling to a vertical face. Historically the house martin nested on cliffs and in caves but today 99% build on man-made structures, which suggests the species is much more widespread than it was 1,000 years ago. Air pollution forced it out of cities at the end of the 19th century and it only returned to nest in Greater London in 1966 as a result of the *Clean Air Act* passed a decade before.

Like the swallow, the house martin has a close association with man. It is a social bird that used to breed in large colonies in farmyards or under bridges. Over recent years several large colonies have decreased markedly and birds have dispersed to housing estates and individual homes making them difficult to census. A celebrated colony used to be located under the arches of Clifton Hampden Bridge over the Thames near Oxford; that reached 513 nests in 1952. Today it is largely deserted, maybe because of increasing vibration from traffic. This clearly demonstrates the mobility of the bird.

Although the Common Bird Census currently reports the house martin population as stable coupled with a recent recovery, the last 25 years demonstrate a decline of over 30%. The house martin's mobility mitigates the negative effects of drought in its African winter quarters, thus the problem probably lies in its breeding grounds. The house martin feeds on aerial insects at a higher level than swallows. As man has sanitised his villages, towns and farms the amount of airborne insect prey has been reduced. Pesticides have taken their toll across the country and, with agricultural intensification, mixed farming has been replaced by regional specialisation and with it a loss of livestock, particularly in the south-east. The presence of animals guarantees a good supply of insect life.

A primary limitation to the house martin's distribution is the availability of nesting materials. It needs a good supply of liquid mud within a few hundred yards of the nest site. If the building materials are located further away the mud is in danger of drying and will not attach to the wall. The filling-in of farm ponds and the loss of muddy puddles on account of drier weather causes the house martin localised problems. Maybe the recent recovery in its numbers has something to do with the dramatic decline of the house sparrow?

Decrease

House sparrow

My generation was brought up to dislike the house sparrow. It had been considered a pest in the countryside for several hundred years. The sparrow descended in enormous flocks onto the ripening corn before harvest. It loved to tear flowering plants apart in the garden. Sparrow Clubs were set up in the early 19th century to eradicate it from every village.

There is definitely something unattractive about the house sparrow's personality. It is noisy – it chirps and doesn't sing – it is thuggish-looking, boisterous and messy. It is a pugnacious bird that at my childhood home in Oxfordshire used to bully the house martins and take over their nests under the eaves.

In my schooldays it was probably the most familiar bird in Britain, living as it does in close proximity to man. It was invariably to be seen hopping around farm buildings. It could be found in suburban gardens, parks, railway stations; it has even been known to nest on ships and down mines. Something started to go wrong in the 1970s and it began to disappear from all its favoured habitats, urban, suburban and rural. I now rather miss it around my farm buildings in Derbyshire and I have finally seen its point. On closer inspection the cock sparrow is actually a handsome bird. It is a creative opportunist that colonised the world; the ultimate 'cheeky chappie' with an in-built mistrust of man that never became too confident in his presence. It is a clever bird that builds an untidy nest – when it can be bothered – nearly always in sight but just out of reach.

By 1940 the house sparrow had reached all the remotest places in Britain. Its numbers must have peaked at the beginning of the 20th century when the horse was replaced as the principal form of transport. In those days there were easy pickings for the sparrow; corn spilt from the nosebag, undigested grain in droppings and straw bedding for foraging. It is thought there are some six million breeding pairs in Britain today; that represents a decline of around 55% over the last 25 years. The house sparrow is a very sedentary bird that spends most of its life within one mile of its birthplace. Over 60% of breeding house sparrows occur in human habitats. Falls have been greatest on arable farmland and it is thought that changes in first year survival are most likely to have driven this decline.

Although the sparrow used to represent a pest on agricultural farmland, now only about a third of the total live in this habitat. The intensification of farming practices since the 1970s has been responsible for its decline. Huge reductions in the availability of invertebrates and seeds have resulted from the use of pesticides. While adult birds feed on seeds, nestlings require protein, which they obtain from invertebrate foods. Harvesting has become more efficient, meaning less spilt grain, and improvements in grain storage result in a lost foraging opportunity. There are fewer small stockyards around the country, which produces yet another lost foraging area. Seeds are sown with dressings that are likely to decrease the palatability of the seed to birds. Finally, and maybe most importantly, the decrease in the spring sowing of crops gives rise to a lack of stubble fields where the sparrow would flock over the winter months. In pastoral areas the shift to silage making, with earlier and more frequent cuts, provides fewer seeds and fertiliser application has a negative impact on invertebrates.

Declines in the sparrow population in towns have had the greatest impact on the total British population and this is where it is more difficult to put a finger on the cause. Atmospheric pollution, for example from lead-free petrol, could be detrimental to insects, such as aphids, which the chicks require for healthy development. This fuel contains volatile organic compounds as lead substitutes. Other reasons for their decline could be predation from cats, tawny owls and sparrowhawks – the latter two having recently taken to an urban environment – and a lack of nest sites resulting from modern building materials such as plastic cladding. Roof spaces have increasingly become sealed off to prevent access by birds and the sparrow is a hole nester.

A loss of food supplies is likely to be the most serious factor affecting the sparrow population in urban areas. This could be caused by a decline in the insect population as mentioned above, which would hit the nestlings, or through a lack of seeds, which would result in winter starvation amongst firstyear birds. Our urban streets are much cleaner than previously and on top of this there has been a loss of 'brownfield' sites due to city development plans. The weeds on such sites are likely to provide a higher quality food source than household scraps.

Dangerous Decrease

Jackdaw

Cheeky, bold, creative, cheerful, boisterous, endearing; these are all adjectives that apply to this small crow. The jackdaw is a real character. It will doggedly fill your chimney up with sticks, feed with the farmyard animals and perch on a sheep's back to acquire nesting material. It even lays delicious eggs. When I was a boy we would hunt for jackdaw's eggs in the old oaks in Blenheim Park. The jackdaw produces an egg with a rich dark yolk similar to a gull or plover.

The jackdaw's call is a high-pitched *'chack'* from which it takes its name. It is a social bird that roosts and feeds communally with other members of the crow family, especially rooks. Although jackdaw numbers have greatly increased this century there was a decline in the 1960s. Interestingly the fall in numbers was not nearly so marked as that of the rook and the recovery was much quicker.

The use of organochlorine chemicals in seed dressings affected the productivity in both species, however the jackdaw's relative immunity reflects its generalist feeding habits. The jackdaw exploits a more diverse and ephemeral package of food resources. It is less of a specialist feeder than the rook. The latter has a long thick bill for probing the soil whereas the jackdaw has a shorter bill that takes food from the surface in addition to shallow subsurface invertebrates such as the larvae of moths, flies and spiders.

As a result of its broad diet the jackdaw was less affected by the move to early autumn ploughing than the rook. The jackdaw's success results from its adaptability. It takes more weed seeds than the rook and in May it will move into woodland and take defoliating caterpillars. It will scrounge at domestic refuse pits, eat sheepcake in farm troughs and feed in rural gardens. At the end of our Derbyshire garden I kept a pheasant feeder full of wheat and it was invariably occupied by aggressive jackdaws.

Large numbers of jackdaws are found in those areas where cattle and sheep are grazed and livestock food is available in periods of cold weather. The jackdaw has disappeared from many upland sites where there is little grassland and few buildings for nesting. It is a hole-nesting bird that may well have benefited during a short period in the seventies from the number of dead trees resulting from Dutch Elm disease.

It was thought that a substantial reduction in jackdaw numbers in East Anglia during the 1960s was a result of the general conversion of pasture to cereal production. It is much more likely that the jackdaw population suffered from the effects of pesticide poisoning. Recent research has demonstrated that the jackdaw thrives in cereal dominated counties, especially barley-growing areas. It all goes to show that the jackdaw has a catholic diet and hence its success.

Increase

Jay

The jay is one of my favourite birds and is surprisingly exotic for a member of the crow family. It is both decorative and noisy. The plumage is distinctive with a white rump, bright blue wing coverts and a pinkish-brown chest. It is a shy and secretive woodland bird with a screaming cry. As with the bullfinch, all that is often glimpsed is a flash of white rump as the jay dives into the dense canopy.

WH Hudson unerringly describes the chilling call in *A Foot in England*:

'A little later a jay screamed at me as only a jay can. There are times when I am intensely in sympathy with the feeling expressed in this ear-splitting sound, inarticulate but human. It is at the same time warning and execration, the startled solitary's out-burst of uncontrolled rage at the abhorred sight of a fellow-being in his woodland haunt.'

The jay has a close association with oak trees. The only time I see a jay at home in Derbyshire is in October when it moves significant distances to collect acorns. For the balance of the year it is a sedentary bird, never moving far from the nest site. It has a mixed diet but acorns are a staple food in most months. In two months during the autumn the jay makes hidden stores and each bird's larder can consist of more than 2,000 acorns. The jay has a remarkable memory and even when thick snow covers the ground they seem to know exactly where to dig for a meal. This colourful bird is responsible for the large-scale dispersal of acorns and hence propagates oak trees.

During the nesting season the jay will take the fledglings and eggs of other woodland birds. One hundred years ago the jay was in full retreat. It was not only persecuted by gamekeepers but its bright blue wing feathers were in demand for the millinery trade and for fishing flies. As mentioned earlier, gamekeeper numbers have since fallen from 20,000 in 1911 to only 5,000 in the 1970s. The jay has also benefited from afforestation programmes since World War II which have created new habitat. Although they prefer deciduous woodland they have spread north, taking advantage of new coniferous plantations in addition to moving into suburban parks and gardens. The greatest concentration of jays in Britain remains Sussex, Hampshire and Kent, an area that forms the most heavily wooded region of the country.

Although the jay remained fairly stable in its woodland haunts until the late 1980s, the CBC survey has pointed to a small decline in numbers over the past 20 years. The jay is a difficult bird to monitor as it can range widely and is secretive in its movements. It does not seem to have been affected by pesticides or harsh winters. It is more likely that jay numbers are curtailed by shooting in woods that are also occupied by reared pheasants. The jay is a wary bird but many are shot when woods are driven for gamebirds. In today's world gamekeepers themselves are unlikely to pose much of a threat to the overall jay population.

The population fall mentioned above may also be linked to a decline in the jay's staple food source. Oak trees have recently contracted a stress-related condition known as 'oak die-back' where the crown of the tree perishes. Interestingly the condition tends to be more prevalent in individual and hedgerow trees. The jay's recent decline has been more marked on farmland habitat than in its traditional woodland habitat.

Decrease

Kestrel

An enjoyable way to relieve the boredom of a long car journey is to count the kestrels. This delightful raptor has learnt to exploit thousands of miles of grassy motorway verges that harbour voles. The kestrel is our most common and familiar bird of prey and is often to be seen hovering by the roadside searching for a meal with its tail fanned out and wings flapping frantically. The two sexes are different in appearance. The female's plumage is heavily barred and streaked whereas the male sports a distinctive blue-grey head and tail. The kestrel is normally a quiet bird that utters its shrill 'kee-kee-kee' cry in courtship.

'Adaptability' is the word that springs to mind when considering the kestrel. It can be found on cliffs, moorland, farmland and even in the heart of cities. In a special survey carried out in 1977 well over 300 nesting pairs were reported in London. Seventy percent of the kestrel's diet consists of voles and mice while the balance is largely made up of insects such as beetles and caterpillars. In an urban environment it has learnt to take sparrows and starlings.

One hundred years ago the kestrel was unfairly persecuted by gamekeepers. Numbers picked up after the war only to suffer a setback with the onset of the organochlorine chemical problems in the late 1950s. This manifested itself particularly badly in the cereal producing areas of eastern England. The kestrel population then made one of the quickest recoveries in the 1960s, possibly helped by its ability to exploit undisturbed roadside verge habitats. At much the same time the kestrel began its expansion into our towns and cities.

A further decline set in during the 1980s, so much so that kestrel numbers have fallen by around 30% in the last 25 years. We do not really know the answer but intensive farming practices are no doubt connected. Small mammals are not doing as well as they once did. We continue to nibble away at their ideal habitat. There is not so much rough grass on farmland and harvesting has become more efficient. Conversion of rough grazing to arable land and the practice of stubble burning are not conducive to a healthy population of voles and mice. The removal of dead trees from hedgerows results in a shortage of nest sites although the kestrel takes readily to nest boxes.

There is often a three to five year cycle in kestrel numbers that is linked to the population of short-tailed voles. Numbers are highest in good vole years in rough upland grassland. In peak vole years some pairs breed only a few metres apart in small shelter belts. Mortality can be high in harsh winters, particularly among juveniles.

Kingfisher

A streak of electric blue across the salt pans of the Newtown estuary on a crisp December morning reminds me that the green woodpecker has a rival for Britain's most exotic bird. It is in the winter months that the kingfisher leaves its frozen inland habitat for the milder surrounds of the salt marsh. When perched, the orange belly, white cheeks and dagger-like bill of the kingfisher are most conspicuous. As it manoeuvres down the muddy creeks with a fast direct flight and a sharp ringing call, all that can be glimpsed is a flash of iridescent blue.

The kingfisher is an attractive bird with most unattractive nesting habits. It nests in tunnels in the riverbank excavated with its strong bill. The young need over a dozen small fish a day and the nest soon becomes filthy, fouled with fish bones and excrement. The slimy entrance hole is not difficult to find! When fishing the kingfisher hovers like a hummingbird if no suitable perch is available. A telltale plop can be heard as it dives into the water. The kingfisher returns to its perch with a spiny fish such as a stickleback. It then proceeds to beat and juggle the fish in its beak in order to position its meal correctly for swallowing.

During the 19th century the kingfisher suffered serious persecution. It was shot by water keepers who perceived it as harmful to young fish stocks. There was a thriving trade in stuffed specimens and the feathers were used for both fly tying and the adornment of ladies' hats. At the turn of the century came protection and a resulting increase in numbers. A further setback was introduced with industrial pollution. The kingfisher's prey, very small fish, are susceptible to water pollution. As industrial pollution abated in the second half of the 20th century, agricultural run-off, particularly from animal waste slurries and liquor from silage clamps, poisoned the food supply. In addition the kingfisher was poisoned directly as it accumulated toxic chemicals from its prey.

Of all British birds the kingfisher is worst hit by harsh winter weather. Thousands starved to death in the cold winters of 1962-63, 1978-79 and 1981-82. There was one breeding pair every one and three quarter miles along the upper reaches of the River Thames in 1961. This had fallen to one pair every 20 miles in 1964. Nature has a way of restoring the balance and so the kingfisher has two to three broods of six to seven eggs a year. The kingfisher is very territorial and it chases the young away after they leave the nest. In this way many young birds starve or drown before they have mastered the art of fishing.

In the modern day the kingfisher has to cope with disturbance from human leisure activities, regrading of vital riverbanks and the removal of riverside trees that act as perches. Dry summers do not come along without hazard. Water quality declines and when the flow dries up not only are food supplies threatened but also the risk of predation increases as there is no protective water beneath the nest hole.

All this being said, prospects look good for the kingfisher. Global warming bringing milder winters, better control of pollution and sympathetic drainage all augur well for this charming bird. Although the Waterways Bird Survey showed the kingfisher down 7% since 1970 and still recovering from those hard winters, the 1999-2000 Wetland Bird Survey count was the largest ever recorded. Following a series of mild winters, around 4,500 pairs currently nest in Britain.

Stable

Kittiwake

In one way the kittiwake is most deserving of the name seagull but in another it seems unfair to classify it as a member of the gull family. Unlike other gulls it is a true bird of the sea, only coming ashore to nest on high craggy cliffs. For much of the year it roams the open ocean, moving deep into the north Atlantic during the winter months. In a similar fashion to the shearwater it is a master of the elements and flies with a steeply banking action in rough weather.

The kittiwake is a seagull of charm and beauty as opposed to most other aggressive scrounging gulls. It is a bird of taste that feeds on small sand eels and will never countenance foraging on a refuse pit. Its snow-white head contrasts the delicate grey of the body and its gentle facial expression gives rise to an almost dove-like appearance. It is a loving bird that greets its mate affectionately as it flies into the nest from the sea. Unlike other gulls it builds an elaborate cup-shaped nest providing the young with a secure home on the narrow cliff ledges. A visit to a kittiwake colony is a noisy affair. The steep cliffs echo with incessant wailing 'kitt-ee-wayke' calls.

In the 19th century the kittiwake was shot for sport in its breeding colonies. In addition its wings with their distinctive black tips became a popular item in the plumage trade. An improvement in its fortunes took place following the introduction of the *Seabirds Protection Act* in 1869, and from 1920 to 1970 the population increased at around 3.5% per annum assisted by a growth in the offshore fishing industry.

Since 1980 there have been reports of overall declines although there have been pockets of success such as in south-east England, where 80 pairs nested in 1969 and 3,760 pairs were counted in 1987. The important Shetlands colonies halved in numbers from 1981 to 1997 and between 2000 and 2001 the kittiwake population index fell by nearly 18%, to the lowest level recorded since monitoring began in 1986. Food availability, particularly during the breeding season, must play an important role in this decline. A substantial reduction in fish discards from the trawling industry has played its part but a decline in the availability of sand eels is almost certainly the key factor as demonstrated in the Shetlands. The North Sea sand eel fishery has now been closed and this coincided with some recovery in breeding success.

Unlike the guillemot, that dives deeper and feeds on medium sized sprats and sand eels, the kittiwake takes smaller fish from or near the surface. It is now thought that because of the absence of larger predator fish these small sand eels spend less time near the surface thereby curtailing the kittiwake's main food source. The guillemot has access to a wider range of prey species and as a result their numbers are currently increasing.

Another key factor contributing to the decline in kittiwake numbers is predation. Great skuas are moving further south and are increasing in numbers on the kittiwake's stronghold islands.

Decrease

Knot

A sociable wader that winters with us in smallish numbers at Newtown is the knot. It is an amazing long-distance traveller that migrates around the world from the high Arctic to as far away as Australasia. The bird can lose 80% of its body weight on such a flight. Its aeronautical displays are legendary. It forms very tight flocks that twist and turn in the sky like columns of smoke; colour changes are spectacular in the sun as one minute the dark upper parts are glimpsed and the next, the white bellies. On its breeding grounds it performs a delightful display flight, similar to that of the greenshank, whereby the male rises 100ft on rapidly beating wings and then circles downwards, piping loudly as it descends.

The knot does not have the same presence on the ground that it has in the air, except perhaps in the breeding season. It is bigger and plumper than a dunlin with a shorter bill. It congregates in large numbers on the mudflats feeding on small cockles and other molluscs. The knot is a gregarious bird that feeds grey shoulder to grey shoulder with often thousands of other birds. On its nesting grounds the dull grey plumage is transformed into a rich reddish colour.

There are around 250,000 knot wintering in Britain today. It prefers the large sandy estuaries of the west coast such as the Ribble estuary and Morecambe Bay. Numbers have halved over the last 30 years largely due to a run of unusually cold springs and summers on their breeding grounds in Greenland in the early seventies. In 1971-72 over 400,000 birds wintered in Britain. Birds that nest in Siberia pass through Britain on their way to west Africa. Canadian breeders make their way down to the southern hemisphere.

During the autumn moult most of the British wintering population gather on the Dutch Waddenzee. Wader counts for 1999-2000 show a definite shift in wintering knot numbers from our west coast estuaries to the east. As winters become increasingly mild it is likely that more and more waders will winter in the east, benefiting from the productive sediments and being nearer to their northern breeding grounds. Perhaps some birds are remaining on their Waddenzee moulting grounds for the winter and not bothering to make the journey on to Britain.

The knot's strange name may well be derived from its low, quiet call, *'knutt'*.

Decrease

Lapwing

There is no more thrillingly evocative sight or sound than that of the lapwing display-ing over its territory in springtime. The flight is characterised by a sudden dive as the bird twists and turns like an aircraft out of control. As it corkscrews it utters a series of cat-like calls and the large square wings, which deliver this immense agility, clap like sailcloth when a yacht tacks into the wind.

The lapwing is a vociferous bird. When an intruder enters its breeding ground it dashes down at the offending party, uttering a series of 'wheezes' and 'whoops'. The bird fiercely defends its family against predators. An old gamekeeper on North Uist in the Outer Hebrides once described the lapwing to me as *'brave as a lion'*. The lap-wing's call can be heard at all hours during the nesting season; to listen to its eerie wailing cry when wandering on the marshes at the dead of night is a chilling experi-ence.

WH Hudson, writing a century ago, described the lapwing as a *'familiar bird to most persons.'* Sadly this is not the case today. One of the few places you can expect to enjoy displaying lapwing is on upland pasture or beside a river estuary. Large flocks of immi-grant birds from Scandinavia or Eastern Europe will over-winter with us, but resident nesting birds have fallen by over 50% in the last 15 years. Few birds epitomise the demise of farmland species more than the lapwing.

The lapwing had a chequered history in the 19th century. A combination of farming improvements, particularly the drainage of marginal land, and egg collecting, led to a

decline in numbers that was only halted by the Pro-tection Act of 1926. Lapwing eggs, with their dark rich yoke, were considered a great delicacy – much more so than eggs of the black-headed gull. This encouraged frenzied egg collecting; in the 1820s a single collector might take 2,000 a season and 2,500 were sent from the Romney Marshes to the Dover market in one year.

As a result of protection recovery was rapid until the post-war agricultural revolution. Over the past 50 years there has been a catastrophic decline in numbers. The lapwing's favoured habi-tat is a classic mixed farming patchwork, with tillage for nesting and adjacent pasture for rearing their chicks. The rotational farming system was common practice before World War II. The agricultural improvements that followed had a number of consequences for the lapwing.

Most importantly, today, tillage is dominated by the autumn sown cereals and oil seed rape, with the amount of intermixed grassland having declined. Springtime ploughing used to provide the lapwing with the perfect habitat for nesting. Today's autumn-sown crops are too tall for lapwings at nesting time as they require all-round vision. In 1962, autumn tillage accounted for only 22% of all tilled land in England and Wales – today the figure must be nearer 80%. Over the post-war period, increasing mechanisation with the repeated rolling and spraying of land has had a devastating effect on rearing success.

The same gloomy story applies to areas under grassland management. The lapwing normally avoids silage fields, which are treated with quantities of inorganic fertilisers. These give rise to a denser, faster growing sward that allows multiple mowings. The lapwing then tends to move onto permanent pasture, and with increased stocking levels its nest and eggs are more prone to trampling by sheep and cattle.

Lowland Scotland and some upland areas in northern England still harbour lapwing strongholds where farming systems retain a higher proportion of spring tillage and damp unimproved grassland. In the south of England the importance of wetland bird reserves to the survival of the lapwing should not be underestimated.

Dangerous Decrease

# *Lesser spotted woodpecker*

Perhaps it is not so surprising I have never consciously seen a lesser spotted wood-pecker. Not only is it a shy and elusive species but it is also becoming increasingly rare. It lives high up amongst the small branches of deciduous trees and rarely ventures lower than 10 metres from the ground. As it is no larger than a sparrow it is easily overlooked. It frequents well-timbered country, avoiding conifers, and has a particular liking for spinneys, orchards, cemeteries, parks, and alder river valleys. Unlike its close cousin, the great spotted woodpecker, it is thinly distributed across southern Britain, rare in the north and absent from Scotland. Its drumming 'song' is more prolonged and high-pitched than the larger bird and the first hint of its presence in spring is often a soft *'pee-pee-pee'* call.

A decline of over 75% in the last 25 years is of particular concern as its demise does not coincide with a period of cold winters. Being a small bird it is susceptible to harsh conditions such as experienced in the winter of 1962-63. The population rose soon after, increasing rapidly during the spread of Dutch Elm disease in the 1970s. The dead woodland trees provided an abundance of invertebrate food, which in turn triggered a spill-over onto farmland as a growing number of infected hedgerow elms provided additional feeding opportunities.

During the 19th century the lesser spotted woodpecker was most common in south-west England. Substantial localised decreases were noticed in Somerset and Hereford-shire around the mid-20th century with the grubbing out of many mature cider or-chards. As Dutch Elm disease died away in the 1980s and the availability of dead wood shrank, so the lesser spotted woodpecker declined across southern Britain. The great spotted woodpecker, on the other hand, managed to maintain a healthy degree of sta-bility, aided no doubt by its adaptability to garden feeding. Before the Dutch Elm epi-demic BTO records show that elms were one of the most important nesting trees for the lesser spotted woodpecker.

So why this frightening decline? Factors affecting woodland birds are much less ob-vious than those relating to farmland populations. The reduction  in the area of mature broadleaf woodland, the loss of non-wood-land trees like elms, an under-supply of dead wood with improved management practices and an increase in woodland isolation have all contributed to this tiny woodpecker's demise. A new Woodland Bird Project has recently been set up to study the changes in wood-land bird populations and the effects of such factors as deer-brows-ing together with the resulting impact on vegetation structure.

Dangerous Decrease

# *Lesser whitethroat*

One May Bank Holiday at Newtown I woke at 4.30am to enjoy the dawn chorus led by a blackbird and a nightingale. As dawn broke and the volume increased, the rattling song of a lesser whitethroat became a central part of the chorus. Its song consists of a loud far-carrying note that is repeated five or six times. Sir Edward Grey wrote in *The Charm of Birds*: *'its song to me is associated with warm days in June and July: it is a monotonous repetition of one note and suggests the syllable "sip" repeated several times.'*

The lesser whitethroat likes taller, denser growth than its close cousin the common whitethroat. A pair returns every year to our hawthorn bank in Derbyshire where they frequent the secluded undergrowth of bushes and straggly hedges. The lesser whitethroat is a shy bird by nature and has no song flight. It skulks in thick vegetation and is extremely difficult to spot. The male has prominent dark ear coverts giving it a masked appearance. It has a pink flush to its white underparts and is greyer above than the common whitethroat with no rusty fringes to its flight feathers. The lesser whitethroat is less abundant than its cousin and Britain represents the western edge of its breeding range. It has the most restricted breeding distribution of our warblers, aside from the Dartford warbler, and is largely located in the south-east, although there has been some recent expansion in Scotland, Devon and north Wales.

Although numbers have fluctuated over the years they remained stable from the 1960s to the 1980s. There has however been a worrying decline in the 1990s with the Common Bird Census showing a 20% fall from 1994-2000. Farmland habitat has been degraded over the past few decades by the grubbing out of hedges and mechanical trimming. Current changes in agricultural practices, with grants being directed towards environmental protection by way of Stewardship Schemes, should be beneficial to this species in the future.

The lesser whitethroat is more likely to be influenced by climatic changes in its winter quarters or along its migration route than by events on its breeding grounds. It migrates through the eastern Mediterranean down the Nile valley to Sudan and Ethiopia. As it winters north of the Sahara the lesser whitethroat escaped the ravages of the 1968-1969 Sahel drought; however there have been substantial rainfall deficits in north-east Africa since the 1970s.

Decrease

Linnet

The linnet is one of the most charming British birds both on account of its song and looks, which is no doubt the reason why it was so popular with the Victorian cage-bird trappers. In the 19th century the linnet was often scarce around big cities as thousands were sold into captivity. There is no more delightful sight than a cock linnet with its delicate pink crown and breast perched on top of a gorse bush in full yellow flower. The linnet also gifts us an enchanting soft musical song that consists of a series of fast fluty whistles, 'twangs', warbles and trills.

The linnet is primarily a bird of lowland England and is replaced in the Highlands by the twite. I am lucky enough to enjoy the linnet's company all year round as it is a partial migrant that winters well to the south of its nesting grounds, many birds moving down as far as Iberia. It is a common bird at Newtown in the winter months where it frequents the scrubby gorse bushes on the edge of the coastal salt marsh. In summer the linnet moves north to breed with us in Derbyshire and small colonies build their nests in low thick blackthorn bushes on the warm southward facing side of the valley. If we are lucky a pair will occupy a gooseberry bush in our walled garden.

In the 19th century the linnet suffered on two accounts. Its persistent twittering song made it one of the most sought after cage-birds in Victorian England. As the agricultural revolution gathered pace the linnet lost more and more of its favoured habitat, scrubby marginal land. Protection from trapping was introduced in the 1880s and a recovery took place over the next 50 years during the prolonged agricultural recession when the linnet benefited from the neglect of farmland. In addition new nesting sites presented themselves with the planting of extensive coniferous forests and the appearance of scrubby margins alongside motorways and old railway lines.

The linnet population started a drastic decline in the 1970s. It is a species that depends on the availability of weed seeds for its survival and the introduction of chemical herbicides proved disastrous. Weeds such as chickweed and fathen became scarce and mortality through starvation occurred especially amongst first year birds. As spring

sown corn fell from favour so the winter stubbles disappeared, as did the huge flocks of foraging finches. By 1980 surveys were demonstrating a big fall in linnet numbers in areas dominated by tillage whereas the population was more stable on grassland. The steep decline in the 1980s may also be due to more intensive agricultural practices in the linnet's Iberian winter quarters.

Thankfully numbers have stabilised in the last 15 years. Many acres of farmland have more recently been given over to oilseed rape. The seeds became a favoured food source for the linnet and it feeds in the rape fields as soon as the seed is formed in June. To the delight of many the linnet has recently moved into gardens where it finds an abundance of weed seeds and suitable nest sites.

Dangerous Decrease

Little egret

July is not the month to expect the exotic in Exbury gardens. The dancing yellow carpet in Daffodil Meadow beside the Beaulieu river has disappeared as suddenly as it arrived in March. The blaze of colour generated by the rhododendrons and azaleas faded in June; but today, in high summer, above the canopy of oak, pine and cedar, a small white heron floats over the gardens like a huge moth.

Over the last decade the little egret has become a familiar sight in the Solent. It is now part of the landscape in the Newtown estuary and can be seen tiptoeing through the muddy channels sporting its neat 'Chinese pigtail' and dagger-like bill. The first documented evidence of a little egret in Britain was in 1926, but it was not until the 1990s that these small herons began arriving in any numbers. Counts rocketed and a national survey in 1999 found well over 1,500 in Britain.

Little egrets are now more numerous than grey herons on most estuaries in Britain. The egret has many characteristics of the grey heron but is more interesting to watch. It is a more active feeder than the heron and as such can be observed chasing small fish through the shallows. Although usually a silent bird, the egret's cry is a heron-like croak, and its nest is likely to be found under the protective umbrella of a heronry. The first record of a breeding pair in Britain was at Poole Harbour in 1996.

The little egret has been expanding northwards along the French Atlantic coast from its Mediterranean heartland since the 1980s. It is an adaptable and mobile species that is no longer persecuted for its feathers. The majority of European egrets used to migrate back to the Mediterranean for the winter but a recent series of mild winters has led to many over-wintering in north-west Europe. Numbers in Britain peak in September.

Substantial Increase

# Little owl

Around Easter time our valley in Derbyshire echoes with the territorial calls of the male little owl, a far-carrying *'whoo-ee'*; the females shriek back eerily in reply. These charming owls like open countryside containing parkland, orchards, hedgerows and copses. They commonly nest in deciduous trees and have a particular liking for pollarded timber. Little owls can be observed in daylight hours sitting on telephone wires or in a favourite tree which may often betray their nesting site.

The little owl is not a native British bird and was successfully introduced into the Kent and Northamptonshire countryside between 1870-1880. A population explosion took place between 1910-1930. It was reported in Yorkshire in 1925 and confirmed breeding in Scotland in 1958. Expansion slowed in the 1940s when a succession of severe winters took their toll.

A decline set in around the late 1950s which coincided with the organochlorine pesticide era when poisoning from seed dressings spread up the food chain. The cold winters of 1961-63 compounded the effects of the toxic chemicals. Thereafter little owl populations have remained reasonably stable with three to five year cycles of peaks and troughs. These cycles closely track those of small rodent prey such as fieldmice and voles. When rodent densities are high clutches are large and more pairs attempt to breed.

Before the Great War little owls suffered from persecution by gamekeepers. Recent research has demonstrated that earthworms and insects form a large part of their diet, with small birds only being taken in the nesting season.

Little owls have suffered at the hands of modern agriculture and there are fewer present today in the intensively cultivated areas of East Anglia and Lincolnshire where old farm buildings and hedgerow trees have been lost, both of which provided favoured nesting sites.

There are around 9,000 pairs in Britain today and the CBC survey shows a small decline of 8% over the past 25 years.

Stable

# *Little tern*

I associate this dainty little bird with high summer on the Solent. The little tern represents our smallest, nimblest tern and is a joy to behold as it pauses and hovers with fast flickery wingbeats over the inshore lagoons of the Beaulieu and Newtown estuaries. Unlike the larger terns that tend to feed out at sea, the little tern has a preference for fishing in dykes and brackish ditches of coastal marshland. The rapid chattering calls are heard long before the bird can be identified by its size and distinctive yellow bill.

The little tern is the rarest of the 'sea swallow' family in Britain after the roseate tern. It winters in the rich fishing grounds of the west African coasts, returning to its breeding territory in April. Numbers declined rapidly at the end of the 19th century with persecution from egg collectors and the millinery trade. The UK population probably peaked in the 1930s and then declined to around 1,600 pairs in the 1960s, largely due to human disturbance. With special protection from the RSPB and other conservation bodies, numbers rose and have now stabilised at around 2,000 pairs; in recent years a moderate decrease has been witnessed.

The little tern nests outside the vegetation zone on sand and shingle close to the sea and, consequently, the nest is often washed away by high tides or covered with sand in strong winds. The location of the nest also makes it highly vulnerable to disturbance by holidaymakers. Conservation bodies have successfully taken remedial steps whereby the nest is raised artificially or individual nests are moved up the beach. Many colonies are now policed by wardens or protected with fences and notices that explain to the public the damage their presence may cause. In this way a colony on the beach at Great Yarmouth grew from five pairs in 1977 to over 200 pairs in 1990.

Little tern colonies tend to be small, averaging around 30 pairs. Breeding sites are not as dense or compact as those of other terns. The little tern is less aggressive than its

larger cousins and is more liable to predation from crows and even kestrels. Concentration into fewer, larger sites is also a cause for concern as high densities attract the more dangerous predators at the top of the food chain. In 1990 the Gronant colony in Wales failed completely due to fox predation.

There is at present no evidence to show that a food shortage is a problem for the little tern, as is the case with the more maritime Arctic tern.

Decrease

 *Long-tailed tit*

The long-tailed tit is one of our most delightful birds. Its appearance, nest and family grouping are charm personified. If it was not for its three-inch tail, this tiny pinkish acrobat would be Britain's smallest bird.

While standing under the canopy of mature woodland during a pheasant drive or tucked into a hedge trying to flight a pigeon, I have often been surprised by a noisy family of long-tailed tits playing 'follow my leader' in search of precious insect life. Each family grouping maintains a winter territory. They are very vulnerable to cold weather and it is this social unit that allows them to survive the harsh conditions of the winter months. Long-tailed tits roost together and forage together, keeping in touch through a series of high pitched '*si-si-si*' call-notes that allow them to be heard long before they are identified dancing through the undergrowth.

Unlike other members of the tit family, the long-tailed tit has not until recently frequented the garden bird table and as such suffers when natural foods are scarce. A hoarfrost that persists for a few days can be fatal. Lengthy periods of glazed frost prevent access to the insects needed by these small birds. In the prolonged glazed ice conditions of 1916-17 up to 90% of the population probably perished. In the extreme winter conditions of 1946-47 fewer birds died owing to the absence of freezing fog.

Over the past 25 years, long-tailed tit numbers have remained stable and if anything increased slightly. There were some sharp declines in the 1970s with the advent of cold winters, particularly in the harsh winter of 1979 when there were prolonged periods of hoarfrost. Farmland areas demonstrate sharper peaks and troughs, no doubt due to the fact that woodland provides a more sheltered habitat.

If I had a prize to give for nest building I would give it to the long-tailed tit. The nest represents a wonder of ornithological architecture. The oval-shaped, domed nest contains up to several thousand feathers and spiders' webs. It can be placed low down in a thorn bush or high up in the fork of a tree. Many nests are raided by woodland predators such as jays. Losses are high with perhaps only a third of all pairs success-fully rearing young, however this is counterbalanced by the laying of large clutches of up to a dozen eggs.

Stable

Magpie

The magpie and the fox have a good deal in common. They are highly successful predator/scroungers; they enjoy a catholic diet and are mobile and adaptable. Both are sedentary and territorial in nature, and force their offspring to seek their own territories in the autumn. These characteristics have been responsible for the magpie's success story, with their numbers increasing in excess of 75% over the past 25 years.

The magpie represents the most persecuted member of the crow family, which makes its success all the more remarkable. It is omnivorous, eating invertebrates in the summer and plant material in the winter. In the springtime it has a weakness for the eggs and fledglings of other birds, both game birds and songbirds, and as such has always attracted the attention of gamekeepers.

Magpies were exterminated in Norfolk before World War I and it was only after the two wars, with a substantial reduction in gamekeepering, that overall numbers began to recover. After World War II they began to spread into suburban areas taking advantage of the rich pickings available in parks and gardens. On the outskirts of towns they are largely free from persecution. Although their nests are bulky and conspicuous they are often placed deep in thorn bushes and difficult to access.

A decline set in during the late 1950s in eastern England and other agricultural districts, attributed to the unrestricted use of organochlorine chemicals, hedgerow removal and the ploughing of old grassland. Big increases were then seen in the 1960s with the banning of toxic chemicals, and a spread into urban areas began to take place. The latter was facilitated by the magpie's unspecialised diet, but city centre trees are essential for nesting sites.

By the mid-1980s magpie numbers stabilised, probably with the introduction of the Larsen trap. The Larsen is a highly effective means of trapping territorial birds in the mating season. Larsens have become popular with many ordinary country folk who perceive the magpie as the enemy of songbirds. Anyone who has watched a magpie systematically hunting a hedgerow in the nesting season knows that they can take a terrible toll on our garden birds. Their numbers having already been devastated by modern farming practices.

The magpie has a harsh, chattering, machine-gun-like call that gives away its presence long before it is seen in flight.

Substantial Increase

Marsh tit

It was not until 1900 that the marsh tit and the willow tit were identified as two different species. As with the chiffchaff and the willow warbler the best form of differentiation is song. The willow tit is slightly chunkier with a pale patch on its wing and a sooty black cap as opposed to the glossy one of the marsh tit but at any sort of distance they appear identical. The softer *'chick-abee-bee'* and *'pitchu'* calls of the marsh tit are often to be heard around the bird table whereas the more grating, nasal, *'tchay-tchay'* calls of the willow tit are more characteristic of woodland habitat.

The names of these two members of the tit family are misleading. Although both are woodland species, willow tit habitats are often damper than those of marsh tits. The marsh tit prefers deciduous woodlands with mature trees, parkland and wooded gardens. The willow tit can be found in a variety of woodland including conifers where it uses its finer bill to access pine needles and as such breeds at the northern end of the two birds' range. The marsh tit nests in natural holes whereas the willow tit excavates its own hole in soft rotten wood and as such is found in damper, marshier places.

Both birds have declined seriously over the past 25 years along with other woodland species such as the lesser spotted woodpecker. A succession of cold winters in the middle of the 20th century may have led to the extinction of small populations of the willow tit in the Highlands. The decline of the marsh tit began in the 1960s, being steepest in the 1970s, at a time when the blue, coal, and great tits were all increasing in numbers. This has led many people to assume that the marsh and willow tits are losing out to competition from other members of the tit family for food and nesting sites.

It is more likely that both species have been affected by a general deterioration in the quality of their woodland habitat. Research has demonstrated that their decline has been driven by low annual survival as breeding productivity has improved. As more and more woodland is professionally managed, drainage is undertaken and dead wood cleared and burnt, thereby decreasing their invertebrate food source and the number of potential nesting sites. The enormous increase in the number of deer across the country has a detrimental effect on woodland ecology. Both marsh and willow tits forage on insects and spiders in summer and berries in winter and increased browsing by deer is destroying the woodland shrub under-layer.

The willow tit's decline has been sharper than that of the marsh tit. This could result in part from nest site predation by other tit species. The willow tit excavates its own hole, which is a time consuming business. If it has to commence the process all over again the optimum slot for best breeding success soon passes. Blue tits and great tits do not just seek abandoned cavities but have become used to watching the excavating activity of their more industrious cousins and seizing these such tailor-made sites.

Dangerous Decrease

 # *Meadow pipit*

If there is one British bird we can excuse for having a persecution complex it is the meadow pipit. It is a victim of the merlin and hen harrier on the heather uplands and a favoured host of the cuckoo in many areas. This heavily streaked 'little brown bird' is the commonest breeding songbird of the uplands. It is an adaptable bird that frequents a variety of habitat: rough grassland, heathland, salt marsh and young forest. Historically it bred widely across Britain but today it is commoner in the north, particularly above altitudes of 1,500ft. The meadow pipit is a partial migrant and as such in winter moves south to the lowlands and further on to the Continent.

Although the meadow pipit is a relatively nondescript bird with a thin, weak, *'tsip'*, call note it does perform a redeeming territorial song flight whereby it glides earthwards with wings half open and tail spread displaying distinctive white outer tail feathers. Anybody who has walked the moors will be familiar with this little bird that on being flushed from the ground, flits on a short distance before rising again.

There is a charming passage in *The Charm of Birds* where Grey describes encounters with 'the tit lark' in the heather:

'they are very common in heather country and though so small and, except when in song flight, so insignificant in their ways, they evidently have a strong scent. To the nose of a pointer or setter, a moor must seem pervaded with the smell of meadow pipits and when grouse are scarce a dog will vary the monotony of finding no grouse by pointing a meadow pipit or "tit lark" as it is often called. The scene is only too well known to everyone who shoots over dogs. The pointer becomes rigid and earnest as if a covey of grouse were in front; the guns, if there are two, draw together and advance each side of the dog, which, encouraged by the keeper, moves forward with intense caution. At length a "tit lark" flits unconcernedly out of the heather, the dog relaxes and wags its tail in a deprecating manner, as if asking us to excuse the joke since it is such a small one; and then, as if doubtful how the joke be taken, starts off again in quest of the scent of grouse. Thus in one way or another the little meadow pipit mixes itself with memories of Highland sport.'

The meadow pipit has recently become much scarcer in the lowlands, particularly on the heavy clay soils of central and southern England. The Common Bird Census monitored a significant decline during 1985-86 but it is perhaps too simple to put this down to agricultural intensification alone. Of course much marginal land has been lost to cultivation and grassland converted to arable. In the north considerable areas of rough grazing have been lost to afforestation although the deep ploughing and thin cover is greatly favoured by the meadow pipit in the early years. Eighty per cent of the British population leave the country to winter in south-west Iberia and the winter of 1984-85 was unusually severe in southern Europe. In addition Britain experienced cool, wet summers in the late eighties. The meadow pipit is entirely dependent on small insects for its diet and as such will be vulnerable to poor weather conditions.

Decrease

Merlin

In the winter months at our home in Derbyshire I see this agile, dashing little falcon, that is no bigger than a mistle thrush, streaking low down the roadside ditches. The merlin is a raptor of open moorland where it feeds on small birds like meadow pipits. When its prey departs in the autumn so the merlin moves down to farmland and the estuaries where food will be abundant. The male is a slate grey and the larger female, brown. Their call is a rapid chatter, 'ki-ki-ki-ki'.

During the 19th century the merlin was unfairly persecuted by gamekeepers who snared this supposed predator on pole traps. It was also sought after and killed by collectors of stuffed birds. A slow steady decline set in from the 1900s, becoming most marked from 1950 to the 1980s. The acceleration in 1950 was due to the application of organochlorine chemicals in pesticides. The winter movement of the merlin to coastal farmland where it preyed on flocks of seed-eating finches meant it was exposed to the risk of accumulating toxic residues. When these chemicals were banned in the 1960s the merlin for some inexplicable reason did not recover as quickly as the peregrine or sparrowhawk. Was it something to do with its size?

The continuation of grouse shooting is vital for the future success of the merlin. It is a ground-nesting bird of the open moorland and as such is susceptible to both mammalian predation and the destruction of its habitat. Today the merlin is no longer persecuted on its moorland home, except by foxes and stoats if the moor is not well keepered. Landlords and gamekeepers alike enthuse about their nesting pairs. On a well managed grouse moor the heather is burnt in strips that provide a combination of deep old heather that provides perfect nesting habitat and a patchwork of short young heather where the merlin will find its prey. In addition sheep numbers are strictly controlled with the assistance of stewardship schemes and forestry that encourages vermin is not allowed to encroach the moor.

Since the 1980s the merlin population may have doubled in Britain to around 1,300 pairs. The breeding performance has improved since the 1960s because of the declining influence of organochlorine chemicals. The merlin has also made increasing use of forest-edge habitat for breeding, particularly in Northumberland and North Wales where it uses old crows' nests high up in trees. The breeding success of these tree-nesters is more productive suggesting the dangers of predation to ground-nesting birds.

Substantial Increase

Mistle thrush

There can be no more appropriate local name for the mistle thrush than 'storm-cock'. Not only does it have connotations of power and strength but it also suggests an association with inclement weather. The bird song year can be said to commence with the mistle thrush. On a wet and windy day in early January this large thrush will choose an exposed perch and sing his heart out.

The rendition represents a truly uplifting performance. No other bird sings in such conditions and so early in the year. The song is reminiscent of the blackbird although not as fluty. Edward Grey thought *'there was boldness and mildness as well as sweetness in the tone'* and that *'there was weather in his song.'* WH Hudson wrote in his *British Birds*: *'He is not of the winter singers that wait for a gleam of spring-like sunshine to inspirit them, but is loudest in wet and rough weather; and it is this habit and something in the wild and defiant character of the song, heard above the tumult of nature, which have won for him the proud name "storm-cock"* '.

The mistle thrush is an early nester. The nest is often placed in the fork of a tree and without the benefit of leaf cover is highly exposed. Grey said of the storm-cock's nest, *'you never find it, it finds you'*. Mistle thrush numbers have declined by 43% in all habitats over the past 25 years with the greatest falls on farmland. Predation by carrion crows should not be discounted as a contributing factor. As large estates have been split up there are fewer gamekeepers in today's countryside. Carrion crows take young chicks as well as eggs, and have never been so prolific as they are today. I have watched a mistle thrush defend its nest against an attack by a party of crows. It bravely fought off the intruders with as much gusto as a lapwing dive-bombing a hungry hen harrier.

Modern changes in farming practices have contributed to the decline of the mistle

thrush but perhaps not to the same extent as the song thrush. The mistle thrush, like the song thrush, consumes terrestrial insects but supplements its diet with berries and fruit in the autumn and winter months. It has an ability to forage widely and territories are much larger than those of the song thrush. Clutch sizes have always been larger in areas where pasture predominates over cereal growing.

The mistle thrush is one of the few birds that benefit from silage-making as mowing provides a sudden flush of invertebrates previously unavailable because of long grass. Silage-making, which devastates ground-nesting birds, usually involves two cuts rather than the one for haymaking.

In cereal-growing areas a big switch to autumn sowing was taking place in the late 1970s and early 1980s, which greatly reduced the area of spring tillage. This represented an important food source during the nesting season. Many younger, less dominant birds find it difficult to survive their first winter, particularly if conditions are harsh, because of the limited food available. Over-wintering fieldfares and redwings provide unwelcome competition for berries. During a more prosperous period for farming, some thirty years ago, farmers actively flailed their hedges (in addition to grubbing them out), thereby destroying a vital source of hedgerow fruit. This period, interestingly, coincided with a decline in mistle thrush clutch sizes.

Decrease

Moorhen

One of the most evocative sounds of an early spring morning by any expanse of water is the liquid croak, '*kurruk*', of the moorhen. The presence of this pretty bird, with its scarlet comb and bright red base to its yellow bill, will enliven life on any small pond. It is a highly strung species that scampers away across the lily pads at the first sign of an intruder. It will take refuge underwater, raising its bill just far enough above the surface to enable it to breathe. The moorhen is highly territorial and as such will pick a fight with any neighbouring bird. It swims with jerky movements, flicking the white flashes on the side of its tail as a warning to others to keep their distance.

The moorhen is an adaptable bird that will colonise any sort of small pond, stream or lake. It prefers canals to rivers yet can be found on any slow-moving water, only being absent from unproductive acidic upland waters that do not provide enough plant matter for food or emergent vegetation for nesting. The moorhen quickly settled in to new habitat provided by man in the form of canals and gravel pits.

Like many other water birds and insect feeders the moorhen is very vulnerable to cold winters. During the harsh winter of 1962-63 it lost 50% of its breeding population. Numbers recovered almost immediately as, with many birds that suffer in this manner, the moorhen has a capacity to rear two to three broods a year.

The CBC survey shows a 20% fall in the moorhen population over the last 25 years. This no doubt reflects a series of cold winters in 1978-79, 1981-82 and 1986-87. The population fluctuates with no long trend although small declines have been seen on farmland over this period. Intensive farming techniques such as improving drainage on low-lying land, piping ditches and the filling-in of farm ponds are at the root of this decline.

Although the population appears to be reasonably stable at the present time the CBC survey demonstrates an 8% fall over the past five years. This may well result from increased predation. Nests are very vulnerable to thieving crows and stoats early in the year when the platform is conspicuous due to a lack of bank-side vegetation.

The moorhen has unfortunately become the staple diet of the feral mink. These ruthless killers have escaped from captivity and spread across the country. There is no better example of this than in the Outer Hebrides. Fur farms were established on Harris in the

1950s and the first feral mink recorded in 1969. By 1988 there were estimated to be 7,500 female mink on Lewis and Harris. Prior to their arrival 60 pairs of moorhen bred locally but by 1982 they were extinct.

Decrease

Mute swan

There is no more graceful sight in nature than a male swan swimming against the current of a crystal clear Hampshire chalk stream. These elegant, powerful birds can become very aggressive if an intruder approaches too close to the family group. The angry swan, hissing loudly, surges across the water with arched wings, breast thrust forward, and its head curved back. The swan has no need for song, its mere presence acts as a territorial statement. It is a bird that occurs on all types of water and can be found from urban parks to the Outer Hebrides. It is only restricted by a need for subaqueous vegetation and a long take-off in flight.

The swan became semi-domesticated in medieval times when it was valued as an ornamental bird and farmed for food. Swan keeping declined in the 16th century when the introduction of the turkey and greylag goose provided a substitute for the swan as a luxury food. For centuries the Crown controlled ownership of the swan population and assigned licences to noblemen and to City Guilds. Swan keeping finally died in the 18th century and today only two livery companies, the Dyers and the Vintners, own swans outside the monarchy. Ownership now only applies to the Thames and every July the cygnets are rounded up and marked in the 'Swan-upping' ceremony.

In the 19th century swans survived on private waters and it was only recognised as a truly wild bird in the 20th century. With the introduction of gamekeepers, poaching declined in England and the swan spread out into the wild. Today there are around 19,000 swans in Britain and 7,000 breeding pairs. Many swans do not breed until their third or fourth year and can be easily recognised by their pink bills as opposed to the bright red ones of the mature birds.

The first half of the 20th century saw a dramatic increase in the swan population reaching a high of over 25,000 birds in 1960. It was in the late fifties that national surveys were commenced following complaints from the farming community that the swan was becoming a pest by way of grazing on young corn and fouling meadows. It was soon recognised that the very opposite was happening and a sudden decline in swan numbers had taken place, so much so that between 1961 and 1965 the swan population decreased by 25%. The cold winters over this period had no doubt taken their toll as had disturbance by pleasure craft and collisions with overhead wires.

A further survey was undertaken in 1978 which reinforced the decline since the 1950s with the most pronounced falls taking place on the Thames, Trent and Warwickshire Avon. It was quickly discovered that swans were suffering from the huge increase in coarse fishing over the recent decades, four million people participating by 1970. Lead weights were ingested along with the grit needed in the digestive process. The lead was absorbed into the bloodstream that in turn affected the neuromuscular system. This resulted in death by starvation. Of 94 dead swans on the Thames examined from 1979-1981, 60 died from lead poisoning. It was thought 3,500 died annually from lead poisoning.

Mute swan populations have increased progressively on both CBC and Wetland Bird Survey (WBS) plots since the late eighties when it became law that anglers' lead weights were replaced by non-toxic alternatives. A succession of mild winters has also assisted the substantial increase in numbers.

Substantial Increase

Nightingale

The nightingale is at the northern limit of its range in Britain and is one of our rarest songbirds as well as being our best performer. Contrary to popular belief the nightingale did not sing in Berkeley Square; the culprit was probably a robin under a street lamp. At Newtown in the Isle of Wight three pairs keep to their traditional nesting grounds and return in mid-April to the same patch year after year. The cock birds arrive 10 days before the females and defend their territories with delightful song. At the little stone bridge below the village on a warm still spring evening one bird answers another with a series of rich and fluty notes.

What makes the nightingale's song so special? It is the power and variety of the notes that places the nightingale at the top of most people's list. The song starts with a series of soft pipes and whistles and builds up to a crescendo of machine-gun-like 'choc-choc' notes. The period of song is short, maybe terminating by the end of May. The nightingale sings by day as well as night with the best performances reserved for dawn and dusk. William Wordsworth had no doubts about the power of its song:

'O Nightingale! Thou surely art
A creature of a "fiery heart":–
These notes of thine–they pierce and pierce;
Tumultuous harmony and fierce!'

Sir Edward Grey was struck by the physical impact of the song: *'notes of an energy, force and dominance with which none of the others can compare'*. He did however prefer the sweetness of the common blackbird's song. He wrote in *The Charm of Birds*: *'the nightingale's song has compass, variety and astonishing power; it arrests attention and compels admiration; it has onset and impact; but it is fitful, broken and reckless: it is a song to listen to, not to live with.'*

Nightingale numbers probably peaked in Britain around 1950 when birds became scarce in western and central counties of England. A bird was once recorded breeding as far north as Boroughbridge in Yorkshire but most nightingales are found south of a line from the Wash to the Severn. The majority of the 5,000 pairs today breed in the south-eastern counties, which coincides nicely with the presence of our remaining coppiced woodland.

The nightingale is a shy, inconspicuous, ground-feeding bird that takes insects from the leaf litter. It requires dense bushes down to ground level and frequents thickets of blackthorn, dog rose and brambles. Old-fashioned coppiced woodland provides the perfect habitat for the nightingale, particularly during the middle stages of growth from years five to eight. This is the time when thick undergrowth is present around ground level yet it is not too dense for light and warmth to penetrate the woodland floor. Sadly this form of forestry management has increasingly been replaced by the planting of conifers.

A 1990 British Trust for Ornithology survey reported a decline in nightingale numbers over the preceding decade of just below 10%. Modern forestry has taken its toll as has intensive agriculture. Damp areas favoured by the nightingale have been drained, hedges removed, spinneys felled and scrubby land cleared. The rapid spread of roe and fallow deer in the south of England has destroyed much of the thick ground cover needed by the nightingale.

Climatic changes are important to a bird at the northern limit of its range and the cold wet springs 50 years ago played a part in the nightingale's post-war decline. It likes warm dry anticyclonic weather in April and May and the advent of global warming should be a positive pointer for the future. Wholesale trapping of the nightingale on the Continent for food and the caged bird trade is now thankfully disappearing.

Decrease

Nightjar

The nightjar is a secret and mysterious bird of our southern heathlands. In the daytime, taking advantage of its brilliant camouflage, it lies motionless on the ground or perches along a branch. In the twilight it appears like Dracula, a shadowy profile twisting and turning as it catches insects in its gaping bill. Old shepherds referred to the nightjar as 'the goatsucker.' It was thought this strange bird alighted on the grazing animals and feasted on their milk.

I once shared a dinner table with a nightjar. We were enjoying a summer holiday on Corsica and one night we dined on the hotel terrace. A male nightjar, identifiable by its striking white wing spots, wheeled over our table throughout the meal, chasing its own dinner of moths and flying insects.

Most years I hear their remarkable churring song on a summer's evening in the New Forest. The pitch of the churr changes as the nightjar turns its head from side to side when perched along a branch. It is a mechanical sound and nobody hearing it for the first time would believe it came from a bird. Sir Edward Grey wrote in *The Charm of Birds*: *'It is of that class of stationary, soothing, continuous sounds, such as the hum of a threshing machine, or the noise of waves on the shore heard at a distance, which dispose us to sit still and listen indefinitely.'*

Acidic heathland areas on sandy or gravelly soils in southern England and East Anglia are the nightjar strongholds in Britain. More than 50% are found in Hampshire, Dorset, Sussex and Surrey while 20% frequent the Norfolk Brecklands and the Suffolk sandlings near the coast. A long term decline set in during the 1930s that finally bottomed out 50 years later; a survey in 1981 recorded just over 2,000 calling males. The substantial decrease in their numbers was caused by the fragmentation of their heathland habitat through scrub invasion, forestry planting and reclamation for agriculture and housing.

Between 1950 and 1980 we lost 40% of our heathland in the south of England to housing, afforestation, agriculture, airfields and golf courses; remaining areas have been degraded by burning and overgrazing. Sympathetic forest management is vital to the success of the nightjar. A further survey undertaken in 1991 showed a 50% increase over the prior decade due to the availability of young forest habitat as plantations have been felled and replanted. At Minsmere, numbers fell as their favoured habitat was encroached by birch scrub. The RSPB then set about a thinning programme, creating clearings and spraying the bracken; within a short time nightjar numbers increased.

The nightjar arrives late from its winter quarters in east Africa, usually by mid-May. Global warming is important to a species that normally produces two broods. Cool springs delay the start of the nightjar's first clutch. A second clutch is only possible if the first clutch is commenced before the second week in June. With warmer weather and the introduction of professional forest management the nightjar is staging a significant recovery.

Increase

Nuthatch

The nuthatch is a real garden favourite. It is at the same time noisy, aggressive, beautiful, acrobatic and provides plenty of entertainment at the bird table. It also enjoys a remarkable repertoire of call-notes. The two most common are a high-pitched, clear reeling call and a double noted *'chuit chuit'*. Hudson describes the latter in his *British Birds*: *'he has another call not so loud and piercing but more melodious: a double note, repeated two or three times, with something liquid and gurgling in the sound, suggesting the musical sound of lapping water.'*

This pretty woodpecker-like bird, which dresses in a combination of buffs, blue-grey and chestnut, took to the 'bird table boom' like a duck to water. Here it demonstrates its unique ability to climb down tree trunks by feeding on the peanuts upside down while simultaneously flashing its dagger-like bill at competing great tits. Unlike the woodpecker, the nuthatch has a soft tail, which it does not use for support when foraging on a tree trunk or nut dispenser.

The nuthatch has another endearing characteristic. It is not the most creative of nest builders and refuses to excavate its own hole. The nuthatch is however an accomplished plasterer and reduces the entrance to its nest hole with mud, which keeps out larger birds and predators such as starlings and weasels. The presence of mud on the front of your nest box around the entrance hole is a reliable way of detecting a nuthatch in occupation.

The 19th century witnessed a serious contraction in numbers across Scotland and the north of England. The nuthatch even deserted the London parks and it was suggested that atmospheric pollution which covered the trees with soot had driven them out. Over the last 50 years they have steadily clawed their way back with a rapid increase taking place in the mid-1970s, so much so that in the last 25 years numbers have increased by 115%.

It is perhaps all too easy to link their expansion to the outbreak of Dutch Elm disease. An abundance of rotting wood no doubt helped, but the nuthatch is a surface feeder and the larvae of scolytid beetles lie beneath the bark. What is more, by the mid-1980s most dead and infected elms had been felled, yet nuthatch numbers kept on increasing.

The key to their astonishing success may well lie with the huge increase in garden feeding over the same period. Historically these birds feasted on the beech mast crop, and poor years coincided with short term fluctuations in their numbers. Anybody who has observed a nuthatch at the bird table knows they store food for the winter. They fly off with a nut lodged in their beak and are back again in a trice. They can empty a dispenser in hours. The nuthatch is a very territorial and sedentary bird whose fortunes have been transformed by garden feeding. If the beech mast crop is thin they head straight for the peanut dispenser, thereby ensuring a hoard of nutritious food for the winter months.

Substantial Increase

Osprey

Twice a year I am lucky enough to enjoy the company of these charismatic birds. The osprey returns to its nest site in the Highlands of Scotland in the spring. It has spent an exotic winter break in tropical west Africa. When salmon fishing on the river Spey in May I am often joined by an osprey stalking a meal of young sea trout. This large raptor, with its distinctive white underparts, is unmistakable as it quarters the river with a slow flapping flight. Its call is a high-pitched cheeping cry like that of a young game bird.

The osprey moves south in August and although an uncommon sight on migration, individual birds will stop off enroute to fish in lakes and reservoirs in England. Every year without fail we receive an autumnal visit from several birds in the Newtown estuary on the Isle of Wight where they fuel up on flatfish for the long journey south.

WH Hudson, writing in his *British Birds* at the turn of the 20th century, informs us that even then ospreys were strictly protected in their summer haunts. They had been persecuted for well over a hundred years, and with vision he wrote: *'That the osprey will remain permanently as a member of British avifauna is scarcely to be hoped.'* By 1916 this fish-eating raptor was extinct in Britain, thanks to the rapacious activities of egg thieves, skin collectors and river keepers.

The osprey returned to breed in the Cairngorm region of Scotland in the early 1950s with a particularly well publicised pair nesting at Loch Garten in 1955. Under the protection of the RSPB the family prospered and, along with the avocet, became a symbol of conservation in Britain. In 1980 over 50 pairs bred in Scotland. That number has now doubled and the 75% that are successful normally raise two young birds each.

Ospreys have recently been released at Rutland Water and it is hoped they will soon start breeding again in the Midlands. They have begun to colonise the Lake District. Ringing recoveries demonstrate that on migration to Africa, many Scottish birds are shot or collide with overhead wires, however local birds are continually being augmented by Scandinavian ospreys. Despite ongoing nest protection schemes, egg thieves continue to persecute the osprey with an average of 10% of the clutches being taken every year. Happily the Scottish population increases annually with pairs building in new areas to which they return the following season to lay eggs. The osprey has yet to recolonise the north-west Highlands, and insufficient fish stocks may be an explanation for its absence.

The osprey's nest usually takes the form of a bulky platform of sticks built in the top of a Scots pine. On the conservation front much effort has gone into rebuilding storm-damaged nests. The provision of artificial eyries in safe locations where there are plentiful fish stocks is now considered one of the best ways of helping the birds to further increase.

Substantial Increase

Oystercatcher

The oystercatcher, otherwise known in days gone by as the 'sea magpie', guarantees to enliven a quiet day on the river. These birds are both colourful and noisy. As I wade downstream after that elusive salmon, the oystercatchers tear up and down the river in pairs, twisting and turning while at the same time piping loudly. With their distinctive black and white plumage and long orange bills they are the most conspicuous of our wading birds.

The oystercatcher was historically a coastal bird breeding on shingle, sand or salt marsh although as early as the 18th century they began to move inland. At the beginning of the 20th century there was a marked spread into the countryside when the gravel margins of slow-moving rivers and reservoirs were colonised. Breeding numbers increased steadily during the 20th century with some local declines due to persecution, particularly in the south. Between 1956 and 1974 25,000 birds were shot in England and Wales to protect the supposed interests of shellfishermen.

A dynamic expansion took place during the decade 1975-85 when agricultural land along river valleys but away from water was colonised. In winter oystercatchers are exclusively coastal and feed on cockles and mussels. The inland breeders have adapted to a broader diet of earthworms and leatherjackets. These farmland birds have advanced their normal breeding time by over a month to meet the peak abundances of such soil invertebrates.

Recent surveys have shown a small decline in Scottish numbers with an increase in nest failure rates. Earlier nesting, encouraged by general global warming, leaves the birds susceptible to late snaps of adverse weather. The oystercatcher's spread inland into 'wilder areas' no doubt leaves them more vulnerable to predators such as foxes and crows. An interesting theory was put forward some years ago that predators of eggs and chicks such as shore-breeding gulls had triggered a genetically based behavioural change in oystercatchers to breeding inland.

In the south of England breeding oystercatchers are becoming more confined to nature reserves as a result of human disturbance along the coastline. The *New Atlas of Breeding Birds* suggests that their dramatic expansion in the north was caused by behavioural change rather than human pressure. An important advantage that the oystercatcher enjoys over other waders is the habit of bringing food to their chicks. This means they are not geographically restricted as far as nest sites are concerned. Ringing studies have demonstrated that oystercatchers live for many years. With limited persecution at the current time, it may just be that their own success and the resulting population pressures have pushed the oystercatcher inland.

Substantial Increase

Peregrine

There are few more charismatic birds in Britain than the peregrine falcon. A stooping peregrine, reaching speeds of over 100mph, is one of nature's most exciting offerings. I am lucky enough to enjoy the peregrine over most seasons of the year. In the spring an increasing number nest in the local Derbyshire quarries. In the winter months there is certain to be a pair working the Newtown estuary. A frenzied pack of waders bursting out across the mudflats announces the raptor's presence. In the late summer I often fish for seatrout on Jura in the Inner Hebrides, a beautiful wilderness that for centuries has been a stronghold of the peregrine. As we sail out into Loch Tarbert we pass 'the Narrows' where on an inaccessible ledge the peregrine raises its family year after year. It is an eagerly awaited bonus to catch a glimpse of this chunky falcon, bluish-grey above and heavily barred underneath, uttering its shrill cry above the green waters of the sea loch.

The peregrine has an interesting and well-documented history. It has made a spectacular recovery from the low point in its fortunes around 1960 when it was down to under 400 breeding pairs. There are three times this number nesting in Britain today which represents approximately 30% of north-western Europe's breeding population.

The peregrine has always been highly prized by falconers and was protected by severe penalties from the Middle Ages. As a result numbers remained stable until the middle of the 19th century when they began to be persecuted by gamekeepers, especially on grouse moors. A recovery set in after World War I with a dramatic fall-off in

the number of gamekeepers. The feral pigeon is an important part of the peregrine's diet and in 1940 emergency legislation was introduced by the Air Ministry to protect homing pigeons that were used to carry messages. Over 600 birds were killed in this fashion and the English peregrine population fell by 50% of their pre-war level.

The lowest point in the peregrine's history came in 1963 when only 16% of the British population bred successfully. This resulted from the introduction of toxic organochlorine chemicals in pesticides during the late fifties. The peregrine, being at the top of the food chain, killed prey that had fed on contaminated seeds. These substances built up in the bird's body tissue and led to egg shell thinning and breeding failure. To make matters worse, as the peregrine became scarce it occupied the attentions of chick thieves and egg collectors.

Toxic chemicals were banned and by 1980 numbers were back to pre-war levels. Ever since the peregrine has prospered and is now reported breeding in lowland Britain on such diverse sites as cooling towers, pylons and high-rise flats. A few isolated areas like the far north of coastal Scotland have not recovered fully from the effects of poisoning. Pollutants affecting the local peregrine population were no doubt acquired through the marine food chain. Peregrines are still illegally persecuted on grouse moors. They certainly kill a large number of mature grouse but I do not put them in the same predator category as the hen harrier. Grouse tend to go down in the heather at the sight of a peregrine rather than lifting enmasse off the hillside as is the case in the presence of a harrier.

Substantial Increase

Pied wagtail

One of the most popular spring visitors to our home in Derbyshire is the pied wagtail. It announces its presence by 1st March with a loud high-pitched *'titchzikk'* call from the top of one of the farm buildings. It is quite tame and has enormous charm, particularly when feeding its young on the lawn. Here it shows its great agility, dashing around after insects, with bobbing tail and sporting a bold, black and white plumage. The pied wagtail becomes part of the family during the summer months, its nest being placed in a cavity on the roof over the back door of our house.

The pied wagtail demonstrates a halfway stage between a resident and a migratory species. Northern breeders in Britain move to the south of the country in winter while southern birds migrate to France and Spain. Its breeding range is confined to Britain and it is replaced on the Continent by the white wagtail. The wagtail is a specialist in catching winged insects and in the winter it moves down to the coast or urban areas. It will set up a territory near water where there is a rich source of insects or even forage on tarmac roads. It can be located in almost all areas except woodland and its adaptability to habitat and nest sites explains its wide distribution.

During the 20th century the pied wagtail declined in certain localised areas. Improved hygiene around farms and the development of underground sewerage resulted in local reductions in insect prey. It has also declined in areas where farming has become totally arable. A change from mixed farming to arable results in fewer livestock and insect-rich ponds being filled in. Not surprisingly pied wagtails are scarce in eastern England and more abundant in the north and west. A substantial increase in numbers has been witnessed in the Western Isles of Scotland over the past 25 years.

The real enemy of the pied wagtail is a harsh winter. The population took several years to recover from the cruel winter of 1962-63: following it, pied wagtail numbers fell to one third of their 1962 level. Population levels rose in the seventies with a series of mild winters but fell back again during the winter of 1981-82 when periods of continuous freeze were witnessed. Winter mortality is related to the duration of unbroken periods of frost. Although the CBC survey shows a 23% decline over the past 25 years, resulting from two particularly harsh winters, pied wagtail numbers have now stabilised.

Stable

Pintail

The jewel in a glittering crown of wintering birds at Newtown is the pintail. In November a small group of around thirty birds arrives in the creek below Newtown bridge and will remain until March. The pintail drake is our most elegant British duck sporting a glorious plumage pattern. It is unmistakable with its chocolate head, white breast and long pointed tail. The jet-black under-tail is complemented by orange-buff wing bars and yellow-buff patches on the rear flanks.

As a breeding bird in Britain the pintail is scarce and widely scattered. They are difficult to monitor as they give up nest sites after a few years and move on, the reason being virtually unknown. The pintail was first recorded breeding in Inverness-shire in 1869. It expanded slowly, moving north to the Orkneys and colonising north Kent in 1910. One hundred years ago Loch Leven was the only regular breeding site. They frequent wet pastures and low-lying marshland, the nest often being concealed under a tussock. Nesting numbers may have reached a peak of approximately 100 pairs in the 1960s but since then there has been a decline to around 40 pairs. The decline is almost certainly associated with the gradual disappearance of inland wetland sites due to drainage. Late flooding of low level marshy sites is a threat to breeding birds and may be a reason for desertion. A small feral population has certainly built up elsewhere across England with escapees from collections breeding successfully in the wild.

Wintering pintail are widely scattered in small groups as at Newtown. British numbers remain healthy at 25,000 to 30,000 birds with large concentrations of over 5,000 birds on the Mersey, Ribble and Dee estuaries in the northwest. The British wintering population arrives from Siberia, Scandinavia and Iceland and has increased steadily over recent years. Pintail feed on hydrobia (small snails) in the estuary mud and have recently developed night flighting into stubbles, potato and beet fields. They also upend in shallow water and take a variety of seeds.

The biggest threat to our wintering pintail comes from landclaim. Reclamation of their estuarine habitat for such projects as tidal barrages results in the destruction of their feeding grounds. Sites such as the Mersey and the Dee urgently require designation as Special Protection Areas.

Decrease

 *Pochard*

I will always associate pochard with Blenheim Lake; standing on the Grand Bridge on a frosty January morning and spotting a tight flock of buoyant colourful ducks well out in the deeper water. The pochard is a handsome bird with a chestnut head, black breast and greyish body. This particular gathering appears to consist entirely of drakes. Some appear asleep with their heads tucked under their wings. In amongst this flock of pochard, perhaps 50 strong, a handful of black and white tufted ducks bob gently on the water.

The male pochard leaves its breeding grounds in Eastern Europe before the female and arrives at its winter quarters earlier than its mate. By the time the females arrive in western Europe the more northerly sites are full of males so the females are forced to move on. The drakes also feed in deeper water further from the shore and being larger stay submerged longer and dive deeper. In this way many winter flocks are segregated by sex and do not compete for the same food source. The drake's call is a wheezing whistle whereas the female produces a growling '*kurrr*'.

The change in habitat at Blenheim Lake is interesting as it reflects the requirements of the pochard. The Queen's Pool, on the Woodstock side of the Grand Bridge, was dredged in the 1950s, creating deeper water and much thick reedy vegetation was cleared away. The old habitat was tailor made for breeding pochard that like shallow, well vegetated lakes. The new habitat with its deeper water is ideal for winter flocks of diving duck. On 10th December 1947 a count on the lake revealed seven tufted duck and no pochard. Twenty-seven years later on the same date 102 pochard and 73 tufted duck were present. Until the 1970s one or two birds bred with a maximum of 13 pairs in 1939. There has been little proof of breeding since 1974.

The pochard is a scarce breeding bird in Britain with a maximum of 600 pairs. It was first recorded breeding in 1800 and the population grew slowly throughout the latter part of the 19th century, largely restricted to East Anglia. There are strongholds in the

Norfolk Broads, the north Kent marshes and the Essex marshes. Unlike the tufted duck it has not taken advantage of man-made sites like gravel pits and as a result has not expanded its breeding range. A primary reason lies with the fact that these expanses of water tend not have the required cover around the margins. The pochard does not build on dry land but rather close to or actually on the water and therefore needs dense stands of vegetation in which to nest. In addition 85% of the pochard's food is represented by plant material such as seeds and weed whereas the tufted duck has a broader diet.

The nesting population is slowly increasing in Britain yet the Wetland Bird Survey shows a 15% decline in wintering pochard numbers over the past 25 years and a 5% fall over the last 10. This is almost certainly the result of a series of milder winters. The pochard does not come as far west as it once did and winters on the Continent in greater numbers. An average of 35,000 birds over-winter in Britain each year.

Stable

Puffin

The puffin is one of Britain's most charming and popular birds and not only because of that huge, brightly coloured bill. It has great character. When standing beside its burrow it appears confident and self-important. Macaulay wrote: '*it seems to be conscious of its own beauty, cocking its head very smartly and assuming a great air of majesty.*' Once airborne the reverse is true and insecurity sets in. The puffin circles the sky with rapid wing beats like a little doodlebug, always aware of the predatory intentions of the skuas and black-backed gulls. When returning to its subterranean home with a beak full of sand eels it crash lands, avoiding harassment from a hungry herring gull, and scampers clumsily down its burrow.

The puffin spends most of the year far out in the North Atlantic feeding on plankton. It comes ashore to breed in a few large isolated colonies together with other members of the auk family. It is a difficult bird to monitor as it lays its single egg at the bottom of an old rabbit hole on a grassy slope often decorated with sea campion and pink thrift. The island colony is a hive of activity as the puffin takes off with deep growling calls in search of small fish. It dives as deep as 50ft and uses its wings vigorously, making it a formidable underwater predator.

A substantial decline in the British puffin population took place in the first half of the 20th century, especially amongst the colonies of southern England and Wales. It was thought that sea temperature rises might have diminished the amount of available fish prey, which were then further reduced by over-fishing. Other local factors certainly came into play such as pollution from oil spills, predation from rats and sea-birds, human interference and erosion. Few now nest on the Welsh island of Grassholm, which lost its peat through erosion nearly a century ago.

In the latter half of the 20th century good increases were recorded in northern and eastern colonies. A spectacular increase took place at the Isle of May in the Firth of Forth from ten pairs in 1950 to 12,000 in 1984 but then adult survival declined and the increase halted. This could well have been linked to the industrial harvesting of small fish for processing into meal. The sand eel fishery in the North Sea has now been severely restricted, which could well explain recent increases at eastern colonies at the Isle of May, the Farne Islands and Coquet Island. All members of the auk family have benefited from their ability to dive deeper than other seabirds and take a wider variety of fish sources.

St Kilda still remains the largest colony where puffins filled a vital role in the 19th century economy. Upwards of 25,000 birds were taken by way of rods and gins each year for food and feathers. Numbers here have dropped and although the puffin seems currently to be thriving at many colonies more research will be needed into their feeding habits. It is a bird with a northerly distribution and continued global warming may not suit them in future years.

Stable

Raven

The raven, with a wingspan the size of a buzzard, is the world's biggest crow. Its deep croaking call is evocative of wild remote landscape. Much to my surprise I heard this hoarse barking cry at my home in Derbyshire for the first time in 2002; it is now also to be heard over the Newtown Estuary in the Isle of Wight. This demonstrates conclusively that after a century of contraction to the north and west of the country the raven is confidently expanding into old hunting grounds. The raven is the consummate scrounger of high sheep country. Its big problem is finding enough food. It forages the hill for carrion but also is an adaptable bird with a broad diet.

In the 17th century the raven, along with the red kite, was a common scavenger in London's streets. At the beginning of the 19th century the raven bred in every county across Britain. By the end of the century it had been lost to lowland England through persecution with the last pairs disappearing from Sussex, Essex and Kent between 1890 and 1895. Numbers rose after World War I with a reduction in gamekeepers and it expanded into the south-west, Welsh Borders and southern Scotland.

Declines of over 50% took place from Northumberland through the Scottish Borders from 1950–80 for a combination of reasons. Improved sheep husbandry and widespread afforestation took their toll but the decline was exacerbated by the introduction of toxic chemicals like dieldin. Similar falls were witnessed on Speyside, probably as a result of poison baits put down by sporting interests. The raven is unlikely to reoccupy much of lowland England because of a local conversion from livestock husbandry to arable farming.

The highest densities are found in mid-Wales, Snowdonia and the Hebrides. There was an 80% increase in raven numbers in Snowdonia in the latter half of the 20th century. Craggy nest sites were plentiful and over-wintering sheep numbers increased significantly. On the lower ground the raven population remained stable at a reduced density. There was a scarcity of secure nest sites and the ravens that nested in trees made themselves more susceptible to persecution. With enclosed farms there is less carrion as the farmers tend to dispose of dead animals. The Hebrides and the west coast of Scotland have the benefit of providing both sheep and deer carrion; in addition on a deer forest the raven shares the gralloch with the golden eagle and a multitude of ravenous hooded crows after the deer has been shot.

The seven-year Breeding Bird Survey (1994-2000) shows increases in the raven population of up to 100% in England and Scotland but based on small samples. Bearing in mind the devastation that took place in eastern Scotland a few decades ago both areas start from a low base. With limited persecution in today's environment the raven is certainly expanding its range in England and no doubt making a comeback in the north-east. This will be counterbalanced in the future by tight EU restrictions on the disposal of dead animals, thereby limiting the supply of carrion, in addition to a general downturn in unprofitable sheep husbandry as the subsidies are removed.

Substantial Increase

Red grouse

There is no more exciting game bird than the red grouse. The downwind flight of a grouse is erratic and furiously fast. A really successful grouse shot must have the reactions of a fighter pilot. Ironically the British grouse population owes its welfare and indeed its continued existence to the shooters. The grouse is a truly wild game bird that is unique to Britain and it cannot be reared in captivity. Its moorland habitat must be preserved and carefully nurtured. Landowners who shoot their moors are first and foremost conservationists and without grouse driving our heather uplands would disappear as quickly as our southern heathlands did in late Victorian times.

The red grouse has recently been 'amber listed', meaning that the UK grouse population has declined by between 25% and 49% in the last 25 years, primarily as a result of the degradation and loss of its moorland habitat. High up in the hills the grouse feeds exclusively on a diet of heather. It is a very hardy bird and its head to toe feathering allows it to withstand atrocious weather conditions. The grouse has declined steadily since Edwardian times. A lack of moorland management over the two World Wars took a heavy toll, as has the more recent afforestation of the uplands and overgrazing by sheep and deer. Thousands of acres of heather have been lost to conifers, rough grass and bracken. Professional gamekeepering is essential for a healthy grouse population. Predators such as foxes, hooded crows and stoats must be kept under control and the heather must be burnt on a rotational basis to allow the fresh young shoots to appear. Around 10% of the moor should be burnt a year in random strips allowing the grouse to nest in the cover of old heather and feed in the young heather.

Langholm, in south-west Scotland, is one of the best known moors, holding the record for a day's grouse bag when eight guns shot 1,260 brace in 1911. It is now better known for the joint raptor study, started in 1990 by the Game Conservancy Trust. The purpose was to study the effects of hen harriers on the grouse population and the landlord undertook to give raptors special protection on the moor. The report concludes that although hen harriers prefer to feed on meadow pipits and voles which are found on more grassy moors, they also take large numbers of grouse. This can have a serious effect on the overall population in years when grouse stocks are cyclically low. During 1995 and 1996, when birds of prey numbers were high at Langholm, it was estimated they killed 30% of adult grouse during the winter, 30% the following summer and about 40% of all grouse chicks. It was calculated that over this two year period August grouse numbers at Langholm would have been four times higher had raptors been absent. By 1999 grouse stocks were so low that gamekeepers were re-deployed elsewhere and all attempts at driven shooting were abandoned; at the same time harrier numbers declined significantly, because of a lack of food.

The local red grouse population fluctuates over a four to six-year cycle linked to the dynamics of infection by a nematode parasite. It is possible to alleviate this condition by dosing netted birds with vermicides. Climate change in the form of wetter summers and milder winters provides the ideal conditions for strongyle worm survival. These worms live in the gut and if counts rise too high the condition of the birds deteriorates and in due course they die. The grouse also suffers from sheep tick and associated tick-borne diseases, principally louping-ill. Sheep living on tick-infested moorland need to be treated with tick-killing pesticides.

The red grouse has a dramatic territorial display whereby the cock bird leaps into the air with spread wings and then descends steeply calling 'go-back, go-back, go-back'.

Decrease

Red kite

When driving back home to Derbyshire I often select the M40 motorway rather than the more direct M1 route knowing my journey will be enhanced by the aerial antics of a burgeoning local population of red kites on the Chilterns. Once an extremely rare bird in England, the red kite has made an extraordinary comeback. Along with the avocet they have become a symbol of conservation in Britain.

Red kites were reintroduced into England in 1992 and the Chiltern birds have prospered ever since, so much so that a dozen birds can be seen from the motorway at any one time. Their effortless, agile flight is a joy to behold. They circle their hunting grounds on slim bowed wings using a long forked tail that seems constantly twisted for steerage. Red kites are the consummate aerial raptor. They are always on the wing searching for carrion and small mammals and give away their presence with a shrill buzzard-like mewing as they soar over the wooded countryside.

Until the 18th century red kites were widespread in Britain to the extent that they were common scavengers in medieval London, encouraged by the lack of rubbish disposal facilities. During the 19th and 20th centuries the population dwindled. By the 1930s there were only a handful of birds left in their heartland in central Wales.

Red kites became harshly persecuted with the advent of game shooting; in addition their tail feathers were highly prized for the production of fishing flies. As farm hygiene improved fewer animals died and those that did were buried; this resulted in less carrion for the kites. They were extinct in England by 1870 and ceased to breed in Scotland by 1890.

Their fortunes improved slightly during World War II and by 1954 there were around 20 pairs breeding predominantly in the high hill country of Wales. Then, over the next decade came two setbacks, myxomatosis and the introduction of organochlorine pesticides. The rabbits disappeared and toxic chemicals found their way down the food chain resulting in greatly reduced breeding productivity.

With the banning of these chemicals a slow increase took place in the late sixties with the population rising by 5% a year. Egg collectors and abnormally wet springs causing chick mortality continued to present problems. By 1990 there were approximately 60 pairs in Britain, still concentrated in the high open sheep walks and hanging oakwoods of central Wales.

Then came the RSPB reintroductions into England and Scotland in the 1990s using Continental birds. This resulted in a period of explosive growth as kites prospered on the more productive open countryside. By 1999, 350 pairs were breeding in Britain producing roughly the same number of young; come 2010 there may well be 2,500 pairs breeding in Britain.

The only real concern today lies with illegal and accidental poisoning. Poison baits for crows and foxes containing illegal substances such as strychnine have been responsible for killing one third of the kites in north Scotland. In addition highly toxic rodenticides have been introduced because of the resistance of rats to warfarin. Birds scavenge the dead bodies and pick up the poison.

Substantial Increase

Red-breasted merganser

The saltings on the Newtown estuary were used for salt production until the 1930s. In the winter months the two redundant reservoirs are often frequented by a small group of handsome yet strange looking ducks with snake-like necks and spiky heads. The red-breasted merganser drake has a dark green head complete with an untidy double crest. The female is brown and grey with a distinctive white bar on her wings. The red-breasted merganser is a sawbill duck that takes small fish and eels and as such has been much persecuted over the years. It is entertaining to watch as it dives energetically and stays submerged for long periods.

The red-breasted merganser received protection under the 1981 *Wildlife and Country-side Act* and their numbers have increased substantially over the past 25 years; the Wetland Bird Survey demonstrates a 20% increase since 1990 alone. It still suffers from both illegal persecution and licensed control but continues to flourish. From April to February 1990 418 were reported killed in Scotland and with the enormous increase in the number of coastal fish farm installations, the potential for conflict is high.

By the 1880s the red-breasted merganser had a wide breeding range in western Scotland and the islands. The next 30 years saw a major phase of increase and expansion to the east

and south. Movement into counties like Aberdeenshire saw persecution from ghillies and gamekeepers who perceived it as a danger to salmon and trout fisheries. Even so it continued to flourish and birds that bred in the more inaccessible coastal waters were less affected by shooting and nest destruction than those that bred inland.

The bird is a maritime species that breeds around the Scottish coasts, whereas its close cousin the goosander nests on the upper reaches of rivers. The goosander's nest is easier to find as it builds in tree holes unlike the red-breasted merganser that nests on the ground. By the 1950s the latter had started to breed in England, establishing itself in the Lake District and then on into the Peak District by the 1970s. It also spread into north-west Wales where a recent decline in the number of inland nesting birds may denote competition from the increasing goosander population.

In winter the red-breasted merganser prefers salt water and visits estuaries all along the coast of Britain. In the nesting season it is very much a Scottish bird. Over 2,000 pairs breed in Britain of which 90% nest in Scotland. The British winter population can reach as high as 11,000 when resident birds are joined by those from Scandinavia.

Substantial Increase

Redpoll

In the 1890s Sir Edward Grey had a weekend cottage on the banks of the River Itchen near Winchester. Just below the ruins stands a little bridge that leads to the water-meadows. Here Grey would contemplate the beauty of a chalk stream and watch the waterfowl feeding in the crystal clear waters. A solitary alder tree bends over the river at the far side of the bridge providing a shady pool for a lazy brown trout. It was amongst these frosty branches one Boxing Day morning that I chanced upon my first redpoll.

I was alerted to its presence by an unfamiliar fast rattling call. A solitary bird with a distinctive crimson patch on its forehead was demonstrating tit-like acrobatics on the slender twigs. It is unusual to come across a single bird as these sociable little finches are often found in the company of siskins, feeding high up in alder trees or joining other buntings on the winter stubbles. Small flocks of redpolls undertake noisy, undulating and looping display flights during which they emit their metallic twittering calls.

The redpoll population in Britain has undergone several sharp fluctuations over the past 100 years. It increased in numbers around 1900, breeding in our widespread damp woodlands, and then declined in the 1930s for no known reason. It is a bird of our northern woods and forages on the seeds of conifers, alder and birch. As such it is easy to understand why numbers multiplied again in the 1950s. They began to take advantage of the post-war boom in conifer plantations and then spread northwards into the birch woods and southwards into field hedgerows and gardens.

The late 1970s witnessed a sharp fall in their numbers. The redpoll likes the pre-thicket stage of conifer plantations and by this time the post-war plantings were becoming less suitable as they matured. In addition the proportion of birch found in lowland Britain declined. Birch developed rapidly in most woods following wartime felling and reached its peak in the 1960s and 1970s. Other tree species have since grown enough to compete successfully and replace birch. Damp alder woods have disappeared as woodland has been drained and the climate has warmed. In southern Britain agricultural intensification has resulted in losses of hedgerow trees.

In Arctic latitudes redpoll populations fluctuate in size via an eruptive strategy depending on the availability of birch and spruce seeds. Maybe these movements occur on a smaller scale in Britain linked to the supply of birch seeds. In the 1950s it is thought that local stock invaded and colonised dune afforestation in the Netherlands and the coastal plantations of Denmark.

Dangerous Decrease

Redshank

The redshank is a neurotic bird that constantly bobs its head in a nervous fashion. It is easy to understand why this vociferous wader is known as the 'sentinel of the marshes'. When disturbed on its wild salt marsh habitat it explodes into the air screaming a warning to other birds. Its song is a melancholy musical triple piping call, *'tu-hu-hu'*. The shrill piercing pipe is so evocative of bleak open places that the very sound is enough to precipitate goose pimples and to bring exciting wildfowling memories flooding back. The redshank is a slim, elegant bird with long scarlet legs and, although inconspicuous when feeding at the tideline, its attractive white rump and wing bars are very distinctive in flight.

The fortunes of the redshank in Britain over the last 200 years have been closely linked to the farming industry. Periods of agricultural intensification have led to steep declines in redshank numbers. The redshank mostly frequents coastal habitats and breeds on the middle and upper salt marsh. It also used to breed inland in lowland river valleys that were flooded in winter and on rough grazing land in upland valleys. There was a huge contraction in breeding numbers during the first half of the 19th century with the expansion of cultivation and the boom in Victorian drainage.

The 1880s witnessed a cutback in farmland drainage as a result of a deepening agricultural recession. Numbers then began to recover and the redshank spread westwards. With the outbreak of World War II there was a huge increase in land brought under cultivation. Pasture was converted to arable land and grassland was more heavily stocked. A further expansion of farmland drainage, aided by substantial government grants,

meant that the redshank population once again declined, so much so that over the past 25 years numbers have fallen in Britain by 30%. Perhaps the wheel is about to turn again. There is hope for the future now that there is more emphasis placed on 'greener farming' with grants being directed towards environmentally sensitive schemes. Drainage must be restricted, overgrazing relaxed, water tables raised with pools and shallow flooded areas created on coastal grazing marshes.

Despite a serious decline inland, the redshank continues to breed successfully in coastal areas. There are still threats to its survival in specific habitats. The spread of spartina grass in our southern estuaries deprives the redshank of feeding habitat. Predation on the Hebridean machair has also become a worrying problem in recent times. This sandy coastal plain represents a fertile breeding habitat for many species of wader. During the nesting season their eggs are vulnerable to a rapidly increasing number of marauding mink and hedgehogs that have been released or escaped from captivity.

Decrease

Redstart

Around the third week in April, a song can be heard at dawn from a treetop outside my Derbyshire bedroom window that I initially mistake for a chaffinch. On sleepy reflection the notes are less robust than those of a chaffinch and the sweet song has some of the characteristics and quality of that of a warbler. Its call-note is a plaintive *'hooweet'*. The handsome cock redstart has arrived from West Africa. Sir Edward Grey wrote: *'the redstart's is a thin song but there is something brisk and wild in its tone that gives distinction.'*

The redstart derives its name from the Anglo-Saxon word *'staert'* that means tail. The cock redstart, with russet tail, black, red and blue-grey plumage, adds colour to the spring migration; indeed, it is one of the most beautiful British birds. The redstart's eggs are a lovely greenish-blue like some other hole-nesting birds. Its movement is delightful to watch as it flits from branch to branch catching insects with a flycatcher-like flight. Along with the pied flycatcher and wood warbler the redstart is a bird of the western oak woods with strongholds in Wales, the Pennines and the Lakes. It is commoner in pasture-dominated regions where stone walls form field boundaries and hedges retain old trees, both providing ideal nesting sites.

The redstart population has been subject to a history of periodic fluctuations mainly caused by events in its African wintering grounds. It winters in the Sahel zone on the southern fringe of the Sahara desert. An increase in numbers during the 1950s coincided with a return to normal levels of Sahel rainfall following the drought of the late 1940s. Numbers peaked in 1965 following a period of high rainfall only to crash in the early seventies when Sahel conditions deteriorated further and the redstart population in Britain fell by three-quarters.

Since the 1970s redstart numbers have recovered faster than other Sahel species such as the whitethroat and it appears the redstart was relatively unaffected by the 1984 drought. Circumstances within Africa therefore may not be the only factor controlling redstart numbers. Intensive agriculture inhibits its expansion in lowland and eastern Britain as mixed farming, characterised by a patchwork of hedgerow trees, has become a thing of the past. We do not really know the reasons for its success over the past 25 years. There is plenty of good habitat in the west of Britain. There has been an enormous increase in nest box provision in the recent past. The redstart will take to artificial nest sites but not as readily as other species. It is more likely that the boom in garden boxes has freed up natural woodland nest holes as great and blue tits have moved on. Many nest boxes are today placed in woodland locations to encourage pied flycatchers.

Substantial Increase

Red-throated diver

There is no more evocative sound of Jura, in the Inner Hebrides, than the goose-like cackle of the red-throated diver. This beautiful island wilderness provides the perfect habitat for the 'rain-goose'. Whenever the locals heard its deep, quacking call, it was thought rain was on the way; a safe bet for the west coast of Scotland!

The red-throated diver can take off on a shorter run than other divers and so chooses small remote pools and lochans way up on the hill for its nest site. It commutes down to the sea for its meal and can be identified as a speck in the sky and by its mournful call. In flight, that is straight and fast, the body is pencil slim and the wings slender.

There are as many as 1,500 pairs breeding in Scotland today. The ready availability of nesting sites explains why 50% breed in the Shetlands. In the 19th century this diver was badly persecuted by collectors. The 20th century saw a range expansion into the Caithness Flows and the Western Isles and more recently into south-west Scotland and the west Grampian region.

In the winter months the red-throated diver travels south and fishes out at sea around the coasts of Britain. The winter population rises to 10,000 as birds move in from Iceland, Greenland and Scandinavia. The Moray Firth is an important moulting site.

The population has undergone a moderate decline over the past 25 years. Increasing nest failure rates at the egg stage in the Shetlands have offset recent range expansion. Although the future looks healthy and secure for the red-throated diver it does face a number of threats that should not be overlooked; the two biggest being human disturbance and pollution.

Hill walkers can indirectly cause nest failure. If a diver is disturbed at its nest site it may well fly off from the loch and not return for half an hour or so. During that time the eggs are susceptible to predation by gulls, crows and, in the Shetlands, skuas. Foxes are a problem on the mainland and there was a definite fall-off in diver numbers during the

1940s when there were fewer gamekeepers on the ground. There are no foxes on the Western Isles.

Marine pollution, particularly oil spillage from tankers, is the diver's worst enemy. During the eight winters from 1971-78, 418 divers were found ashore as part of an RSPB Beached Bird Survey; of these 247 were oiled and 201 of those oiled were red-throated divers. Other threats include drowning in fishing nets, declining fish stocks, loss of nesting sites to forestry and nests lost to flooding.

Decrease

Redwing

The redwing rides shotgun to the fieldfare. It represents one half of the winter thrush population that arrives on our shores every autumn from the Continent and is invariably found feeding in the company of fieldfares. The redwing is the smallest of our thrushes and has a distinctive red underwing and prominent eye stripe. It is an altogether more delicate bird than the fieldfare with a thin, high pitched call note, *'see-ih'*. Like the song thrush it is very susceptible to cold weather and when the ground is frozen for long periods the redwing perishes in large numbers. Its food is the same mixture of fruit and invertebrates as taken by the fieldfare. The grubbing out of hedgerows has an adverse effect on this small thrush in harsh winters as hawthorn berries are an important source of food.

The redwing has developed further as a breeding bird in Britain than the fieldfare. It was first recorded nesting in Sutherland in 1925 and since the 1950s has become a regular breeder in the Highlands. Scottish birds usually breed in birchwood or scrub with easy access to damp patches for feeding.

There are two distinct populations that visit Britain each year. An Icelandic race migrates to our western shores, which is a darker and larger bird. A Scandinavian race is then found to the east of the country. The main population in the Highlands is to the north of the Great Glen and this colonisation could be connected with an eruption of the Scandinavian population. The redwing is very sensitive to changes in the weather and is constantly moving south in a nomadic fashion. Individuals may winter in widely different areas in successive years.

In the 1970s breeding numbers remained static at several dozen pairs and then in the eighties there was a sudden increase to nearly 100 pairs. It has been suggested that this rapid growth was caused by migrants returning from south-east Europe and being displaced to the Highlands by easterly winds.

The Scottish breeding redwing has a most distinctive song usually performed from a prominent perch. It consists of a series of descending fluted notes that can be heard at a considerable distance.

Increase

# Reed bunting

The cock reed bunting, with its distinctive black and white head, is a particularly handsome bird. When surprised in some favoured damp habitat, it flits away in a characteristically jerky flight and displays its prominent white outer tail feathers.

The brief repetitive unmusical song is delivered from a prominent song post such as a young willow tree. The reed bunting's great gift, like that of his cousin the yellowhammer, is to sing late into the summer when others are silent. Sir Edward wrote in the *The Charm of Birds*:

'in spite of his noble appearance the reed bunting has rather a paltry song: it suggests to me the ascent of steps, the first two or three being mounted sedately and the last taken trippingly. In the plenitude of song in May and early June the reed bunting's contribution would not be missed, if he happened to be absent or silent, but in July by a chalk stream I should miss him very much; there he prolongs the season of song.'

When WH Hudson was writing his *British Birds* 100 years ago he wrote: *'the reed bunting, although by no means an uncommon bird, is not nearly so common as either the corn bunting or yellow hammer.'* He would no doubt be shocked to learn today that the corn bunting has all but disappeared from the English countryside. The reed bunting has also suffered and declined by 60% over the last 25 years. By the time Hudson was writing the widespread drainage that occurred on farmland had deprived the reed bunting of a large amount of suitable habitat.

As with many ground-feeding seed-eaters, reed buntings find it hard to cope with extensive snow cover and the bad winters of the early 1960s had an adverse effect on numbers. The reed bunting population then quickly recovered to the extent that an interesting ecological expansion took place. It spread from its typical wetland habitat into drier areas such as hawthorn scrub, chalk downland and coniferous plantations. A sharp decline followed in the 1970s (along with other seed-eaters such as the linnet and the sparrow) coinciding with an increase in the use of herbicides for weed control. On farmland reed buntings forage on weedy patches among crops and at the base of hedges. 'Clean fields' and a lack of winter stubbles due to autumn sown crops have given rise to a scarcity of food over the toughest period of the year.

Recent research shows that declining survival rates of young fledged birds may be responsible for the fall in numbers. Dominant mature birds will have first claim on limited farmland food sources. Greater numbers of reed buntings are now visiting bird tables in suburban gardens during the winter months.

Reed warbler

The reed warbler is tied as tightly to its phragmites reed habitat as the red grouse is to the heather moorlands. Over 90% of the reed warbler population nests in such reedbeds. This plain brown migrant is a shy bird that rarely breaks cover and most of the daylight hours are spent singing low down in the thick vegetation. When we had a house in Blenheim Park I spent many happy hours sitting by Bladon Water listening to its gentle churring song.

Sir Edward Grey captures the atmosphere perfectly in a charming passage from *The Charm of Birds*:

'as the new reed beds grow green in May the reed warblers come and make their presence known. The time to listen to them is on a fine day in June, when there is just enough breeze to make a slight rustling in the tall reeds that blends with the continuous singing of the birds. Then we know the world in which reed warblers live, and we feel the spirit of it.'

The song that is usually performed from a reed stem is not as harsh as that of the sedge warbler. It is less varied and more rhythmic.

Historically the reed warbler bred in the south and east of Britain. It is a late arrival that fares better in the warmer, drier south where the reedbeds are of superior quality. It will thrive in low-lying areas like East Anglia and the Romney Marshes where the countryside is bisected by reed-filled dykes. With a general improvement in the climate the reed warbler spread westwards along the Welsh coast and northwards through Cumbria in the 1970s and 1980s. It may well have benefited at the expense of the sedge warbler. In Kent reed warblers are increasingly breeding outside their normal reedy environment, in arable fields, scrub and hedgerows, all classic sedge warbler habitat. The reed warbler's winter quarters lie well to the south of the Sahel zone in Africa and as such are not affected by drought to the same extent as the sedge warbler.

With the advent of warmer summers the future looks set fair for the reed warbler. A proliferation of gravel pits and small nature reserves have provided many extra breeding sites. A word of caution is needed as the phragmites habitat is a vulnerable one and without ongoing conservation reedbeds can be encroached by willow and alder scrub. In addition cuckoo predation has increased substantially leading to nest failure. 'Reed warbler cuckoos' are more successful at rearing young than other hosts and such nests taken over by cuckoos have more than doubled over the last few decades. The reed warbler nest is deep cupped and cylindrical to ensure the contents are not spilled when the wind causes the reeds to sway; the reed stems are used to bind the nest together.

Ring ouzel

In the 1970s I would go and stay with friends in Arkengarthdale at the top of Swaledale. May is a glorious time to visit the Yorkshire Dales. Skylarks perform from the heavens, curlews call happily and the tiny lapwing chicks scamper through the white grass beside the dusty road. We would take picnics in a small gill containing a few bushes and stunted trees up behind Punchard farmhouse. It was on this remote rocky hillside that I first met with the ring ouzel. A sweet, piping song came wafting down the hill, audible above the sound of the bubbling stream. With the help of binoculars I saw what I thought was a blackbird perched on a stony ledge, but this particular bird had a white crescent around its neck.

This shy member of the thrush family is often referred to as 'the mountain blackbird.' It winters in the Mediterranean and reaches our shores in mid-March, arriving on its northern nesting grounds a month later. It feeds on snails and worms and requires access to short grass for foraging such as enclosed pasture or sheep walks, and is absent from acid moorland due to low earthworm densities. In early autumn like other thrushes it turns to fruit and berries.

Ring ouzel numbers declined steadily throughout the 20th century. The population fall has gathered momentum in recent years, for which there is no obvious reason. In the early part of the century the ring ouzel retreated from the Highlands, southern Scotland and south Wales. In the 1970s it disappeared from the southerly limestone areas of the Peak District supposedly as a result of encroachment by hill walkers and more intensive farming. Some credence may be given to the disturbance factor as the ring ouzel is a timid bird and modern farming practices are unlikely to have degraded its mountain habitat. Likewise I think one can discount the effects of afforestation in the uplands, as the ring ouzel frequents steep valleys and rock outcrops not suited for trees. Bracken that provides valuable nesting cover has never been so common on our hillsides.

There is no suggestion that the ring ouzel has suffered in its winter quarters, thus the most likely cause of its demise may result from climate amelioration and associated competition from the blackbird and mistle thrush. As our climate has warmed the blackbird has expanded its territory north and to higher altitudes. The blackbird is a dominant species as the song thrush has discovered to its cost in our suburban gardens.

Dangerous Decrease

Ringed plover

One of the most evocative sounds of the shoreline is the liquid *'too-lee'* cry of the ringed plover. On hearing its soft call I am immediately transported to a sandy Hebridean beach fringed with seaweed and shingle. Here, I have watched this little wader feeding for hours at a time with that characteristic plover 'stop-go' gait. It pauses, bobs its head and then scampers off over the sand in search of small insects. Once airborne, the ringed plover is conspicuous by its white wing bar. It often bunches together in a compact group with a low, direct flight across the water. It receives its name from the black and white rings around its neck.

In the 19th century the ringed plover bred on any coastal frontage with a pebble beach. In several areas it established thriving inland colonies. By 1900 over 400 pairs bred in the Breckland rabbit warrens and in the Highlands it would move miles inland to nest by lochs and rivers. A widespread decline in the coastal population took place between the wars as a result of the growth of tourism and a dramatic increase in the human use of our coastline. Caravan sites and bungalows sprang up all along the coast and by the end of the 1960s the ringed plover had disappeared from Cornwall.

Since the 1950s the ringed plover has demonstrated remarkable adaptability allowing range expansion. It moved behind seawalls onto agricultural land and into power stations and oil refinery complexes. Drawn by the enormous increase in the numbers of gravel pits and reservoirs it moved inland where breeding success has been higher. Along the coastline it survives locally through conservation; in Hampshire and Sussex 70% of breeding ringed plover are located in reserves with wardens.

Although the ringed plover has benefited from range expansion there has been an increasing trend to breeding failure at the egg stage resulting from both human interference and predation. Eggs are so well camouflaged on coastal shingle that they are

easily trampled on. In 1990 it was thought that the machair grassland in the Outer Hebrides held 40% of the British ringed plover breeding population estimated at 8,500 pairs. The recently released hedgehog has caused havoc amongst the machair nests. The hedgehog is an even more notorious egg thief than the carrion crow on our southern shingles.

The British ringed plover population has probably shown a small overall increase over the past 25 years; however the past decade has witnessed a sharp decline in wintering birds. Normally three times as many birds winter in Britain as breed locally. Numbers have decreased mostly in the south and west of Britain suggesting that climate change has been behind the downturn in numbers. As winters become milder increasingly large numbers of birds will winter in the east or even on the Continent, being that much nearer their breeding grounds in Scandinavia and northern Europe.

Stable

# *Robin*

The robin is our national bird. It comes out top in any poll including William Wordsworth's when he wrote:

'Art thou the bird whom man loves best,
The pious bird with the scarlet breast
Our little English robin?'

Its pretty red breast and confiding nature make the robin a true favourite. There is no more charming experience than gardening with a dumpy little cock robin sitting on the wheelbarrow, the very same wheelbarrow that, once back in the garden shed, could well house its leafy nest.

Yet it is the robin's song that gives us the most pleasure. Apart from a short break in July, it sings all year. It is all too easy to be deceived by those innocent looks but the robin is an aggressive bird that vigorously defends its territory with song in the winter months. The song is a plaintive warble. There is little doubt that it is the source of the celebrated *'Nightingale sang in Berkeley Square'*, as robins often sing at night in cities, stimulated by the artificial light of street lamps. In the countryside he is the last to cease in the evening, even outstaying the song thrush. Sir Edward Grey wrote of a difference between the spring and autumn song of the robin. In *The Charm of Birds* he felt it was more vigorous in the spring and it whetted his appetite for the approaching warblers and the joys of summer to come.

In the silent autumn period Grey thought the song sounded thin and acid, prompting the coming of winter. Hudson wrote the reverse in his *British Birds*:

'His song indeed, never seems so sweet and impressive as in the silent and dreary season. For one thing, the absence of other birds and voices causes the robin to be more attentively listened to and better appreciated than at other times, just as we appreciate the nightingale best when he sings darkling, when there are not other strains to distract the attention. There is also the power of contrasts – the bright, ringing lyric, a fountain of life and gladness in the midst of a nature that suggests mournful analogies – autumn's decay and wintery death.'

Historically the robin was a woodland bird, as it still is in continental Europe, with a special liking for dense vegetation. It enjoys a broad diet from insects to berries, which are mostly taken on the ground. Over the past 200 years it has successfully colonised farmland hedgerows, town parks, and suburban gardens. As a result of its adaptability the robin population has remained very stable with a 15% increase over the last 10 years. This rise coincides with a period of milder weather. Harsh winters have the biggest influence on the robin population, although their ability to rear two to three broods a year means decreases are short-lived. Farmland is not a major habitat although robins do use mature hedgerows as a woodland substitute. Hedgerow removal as part of intensive arable farming will invariably lead to local declines.

Increase

Rook

The springtime cawing from the village rookery is as quintessentially English as is the bobby on a bicycle or the pub beside the cricket field. We have a small rookery at our home in Derbyshire and I guard it jealously. There is an old ritual superstition that when the rooks leave the landowner leaves his home. Our rookery is situated in three sycamore trees and represents a satellite community to the three larger rookeries further down the valley. As such our birds start building a few weeks later around the middle of March. The rook is one of the earliest British nesters and returns to the rookery by the end of wintery February, fuelling an anticipation of warmer days to come. At the time of building the chorus from the treetops can be deafening as the rook becomes extremely contentious and seems to delight in stealing the neighbours' nesting materials.

The recent history of our local rookery closely parallels the welfare of the British rook population over the past half-century. When we arrived in Derbyshire 15 years ago there were 22 pairs nesting in four trees. Seven years later lightning took out one of the trees and the number of nesting birds crashed to three pairs. Today nests are back into double figures. Several hundred years ago rooks were considered pests, no doubt because of their liking for newly sown corn. Young rooks were considered a delicacy and were shot at the rookery for food. During the late 19th century it became widely recognised that the rook was a beneficial bird in that it consumed huge quantities of agricultural pests such as leatherjackets (the larvae of daddy longlegs). Rook numbers increased generally into the 20th century until 1950 when a 25-year decline set in. A British Trust for Ornithology (BTO) survey held in 1975 confirmed a fall from 1,413,000 nests in 1945 down to around 800,000.

The rook frequents agricultural land and there is little doubt that the change in farming practices over the period was responsible for their demise. The rook prefers a mixed farming system with the balance slightly in favour of pasture and grass/clover leys. The second half of the 20th century witnessed an intensification of farming with a move towards increased arable cultivation. At the same time a move away from spring sowing to autumn sowing meant that a ready supply of earthworms was no longer available over the nesting season. It is interesting to note that the most dramatic decline in rook numbers took place in the cereal growing areas of eastern England. The timing of this decline coincided with the peak use of organochlorine seed dressings in cereal growing areas. Grain has always been a favoured element in the rook's diet, and the intake of toxic chemicals caused egg shell thinning which in turn reduced hatching success.

Since the banning of these toxic pesticides rook numbers have steadily increased and a repeat survey undertaken in 1996 showed a recovery of 40% on 1975 numbers. Rooks have also benefited from the recent general demise of farming industry with the resulting return of arable land to grass. Feeding opportunities away from farmland, such as landfill sites, outdoor piggeries and more carrion on roads may also be responsible for their recovery.

Although the loss of a single tree in our own rookery caused a sharp decline in nest numbers, Dutch Elm disease was not a cause of the rook's decline in the 1960s. Dutch Elm disease came later in the mid-seventies. Rook numbers were then beginning to pick up and in any case they quickly adapted to using other rookery sites containing such trees as ash and oak.

Increase

 # *Sandwich tern*

The Sandwich tern is a misnomer. The bird took its name from this ancient Kentish town after it was first recorded there in 1784. There is no colony at Sandwich today, the nearest being located at Dungeness or in the Thames estuary.

The Sandwich tern is one of the earliest migrants to arrive in the Newtown estuary on the Isle of Wight. It can be seen in late March with the first chiffchaffs. It does not nest at Newtown but flies over from the mainland to fish for sprats and sand eels in the estuary. The Sandwich is the largest of our terns. It has a slower and more powerful flight, dives into the sea from a greater height and flies further to feed. It has a distinctive shaggy black crest and black bill with a yellow tip. In flight it appears much whiter than the greyer Arctic and common terns. Its rasping *'kirrick'* call is harsher than that given by the smaller terns.

In Britain the Sandwich tern occurs in very localised colonies, the main sites being the Farnes, Coquet Island, Blakeney Point and the Sands of Forvie in Aberdeenshire. It is an unpredictable bird that will desert a colony on a whim and move on. Persecution and egg collecting eradicated the species on Coquet Island and Holy Island in the 1870s but protection afforded on the Farnes allowed it to thrive locally. The British population then slowly increased with numbers nearing 15,000 pairs around 1980.

The Sandwich tern is often found nesting in association with black-headed gulls on sand and shingle bars. The protection against predators derived from these aggressive gulls more than outweighs the loss of some eggs from the tern colony. The black-headed gulls usually steal eggs from deserted clutches. There is always a lurking danger from fox predation or oil spillage because Sandwich terns nest in a small number of large colonies.

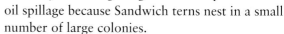

Although the Sandwich tern is very mobile and moves from one breeding site to another it does seem overall numbers have declined by as much as 15% in Britain since their high nearly 25 years ago. This is particularly true of Scotland where the Firth of Forth colony has been abandoned. They also left the Sands of Forvie colony but many terns have now returned. It is thought the killing of birds at their winter quarters in west Africa may be important in limiting numbers. The RSPB is currently trying to reduce the incidence of trapping in Ghana.

Sedge warbler

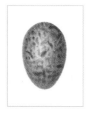

While staying at Sandwich Bay last summer for the British Open I walked out onto the Deal links for an early morning 'fix' of skylark song. In the event it was the cheerful chattering song of a sedge warbler that caught my ear. The reclaimed water meadows with their complex of small ditches provide the perfect habitat for this energetic little migrant. The sedge warbler spends much of its time hidden in the thick, rank vegetation emitting a jumble of harsh grating notes. It will then suddenly leap into the air in courtship display like a whitethroat with quivering wings and outspread tail.

The sedge warbler is an active and fidgety bird. It will sing at night and impersonate the songs of other birds. Edward Grey wrote of the sedge warbler that it was *'the comic spirit among birds'*. He thought its distinctive creamy eye-stripe gave it *'a jaunty look'* and *'its demeanour and movements very lively'*. Its song is very similar to that of the reed warbler but harsher in tone; it is less restricted to reedbeds than the reed warbler and can be found in any thick cover, not necessarily near water.

The sedge warbler population peaked in the middle 1960s and then suffered a serious decline in 1969 following a drought in its sub-Saharan winter quarters. There is no evidence to suggest that the fall in numbers has resulted from a downturn in breeding success. BTO research has in fact demonstrated that variations in population size are related to adult survival rates that in turn are dependent on changes in rainfall at its African wintering grounds. The Sahel and other adjacent savannah zones are used for feeding prior to migration.

The sedge warbler is less colonial than the reed warbler and therefore easier to census. Rainfall patterns in west Africa over the last 30 years are evident in the sedge warbler indices. In years of normal rainfall floodplains develop around the Niger and Senegal rivers providing wetland for the arriving migrants. Following failure of the rains in 1983 it is estimated that only 5% of adult birds survived. With the more recent easing of drought conditions the decline witnessed in the 1970s and 1980s has now stabilised and sedge warbler numbers are clawing their way back. In its British breeding grounds drainage of wetlands and general agricultural intensification has accounted for some local declines.

Increase

Shelduck

The shelduck is one of the few birds of the salt marsh, together with the redshank, that is present all year round. It is the largest British duck, goose-like in shape, and is the exception to the rule that females are more drably coloured than males. Close to they are the most colourful bird of the estuary with sharp clear lines of black, white and chestnut plumage. They are easily identifiable at long range and stand out a dazzling white on the mudflats where they feed on the ebb and flow of the tide searching for molluscs. The characteristic call given by the female is a deep cackling; the drake whistles.

The shelduck became virtually extinct in parts of England during the middle of the 19th century as a result of persecution. It breeds in almost any hollow but has a particular liking for rabbit burrows. When rabbits were farmed, up until the 19th century, shelduck competed for space in the warrens and were eradicated entirely in the Norfolk Breckland. At the beginning of the 20th century local increases in Scotland also became evident in southern England and this in turn led to a wider expansion in their breeding range.

More and more shelduck have been colonising inland sites like the New Forest and the Trent Valley and wintering numbers have increased steadily since 1965. The causes

of this distribution change may have been a saturation of original estuary sites. Shelduck are very territorial and defend their feeding areas aggressively. When they nest in colonies breeding productivity declines. Egg dumping leads to desertion and internal fighting leaves the ducklings more open to predation from large gulls. More dispersed populations have a significantly higher fledging success than crowded ones and this may have caused the move inland.

Every year in July a high proportion of the 10,000 British breeding pairs fly off to the German Waddenzee to moult, although an increasing number are moulting in UK sites like Bridgwater Bay. Legislative protection both at home and at their German moulting grounds has been a major factor in population increases as has a series of mild winters. The freezing temperatures of 1978-79 increased the total wintering population in Britain from 38,000 in December to 68,000 in January.

The last few years have witnessed a worrying decline in wintering shelduck numbers and we really do not know the reason. It is a very difficult duck to monitor as it lives on the open salt marsh and breeds down inaccessible burrows. Are our local breeding birds suffering from a lack of food supplies in their estuarine habitat or perhaps experiencing increased predation from feral mink? The latter would seem more likely than the former. It is possible that moulting birds are not returning in past numbers from the Waddenzee because of mild winters.

Decrease

 *Short-eared owl*

On a typically damp, foggy, November day on the Acton moor near Allendale, three owls with long rounded wings rise from a reedy gill and proceed to quarter the hill. They flap buoyantly across the moor like enormous moths, eerily disappearing from time to time into the mist.

A large pack of grouse explode from the heather in terror; they need not worry, for these are not deadly hen harriers but rather a small group of short-eared owls, recently arrived from the Continent in search of their favourite dish, the short-tailed vole.

The short-eared owl is often seen in daylight, and is a very specialised predator whose presence is dictated entirely by the availability of prey. The owls have an uncanny ability to detect a plague of voles. An abundance of these small mammals will inevitably draw in owls, and result in large broods at nesting time. Nests are placed on the ground in thick heather where their occupants present a threat to grouse chicks in the late spring and early summer. As a result the short-eared owl has been persecuted by gamekeepers over the years. The mere presence of these owls on the hill will cause panic and disturbance amongst the local grouse population.

Every year the breeding population of short-eared owls is augmented by a substantial autumnal immigration from the Continent. Numbers again depend on the vole population and can fluctuate between 5,000 and 50,000 birds. The UK breeding population is likely to be in the region of 1,000 to 5,000 pairs. Short-eared owls increased in Britain after the war, with fewer gamekeepers on the hill, and more importantly with the spread of young coniferous plantations in the uplands. These plantings provide the ideal habitat for voles. Grazing animals are fenced out and the long grass encourages the small mammal population.

The future does not look bright for this diurnal owl, and numbers have fallen over the recent past. As forestry has become less viable fewer new plantations are laid down. In addition the post-war plantings are long since mature, with a heavy canopy, which does not provide suitable habitat for small mammals. Drainage of inland marshland may also contribute to local declines.

The short-eared owl has a most attractive display flight in the spring when it circles its territory with an exhibition of noisy aerobatics, including a booming song and a clapping of wings.

Decrease

Shoveler

The drake shoveler, with its distinctive combination of chestnut, green and white, should lay claim to being one of our most beautiful birds if it was not for that grotesque bill. The large, heavy bill is specially adapted for feeding on the surface and picking out seeds and tiny crustaceans. The bill has serrated edges, like the teeth of a comb, through which the shoveler sieves the water and filters its food.

At my home in Derbyshire I used to keep a small wildfowl collection on the largest of my ponds and the shoveler occupied top place in my affections. It had an individuality of its own. At close quarters it looked different and of course it had a unique method of feeding. The female could be relied upon to produce two broods and the nest, which was some distance from the water, was always notoriously difficult to find.

The shoveler is found exclusively on brackish and fresh water as it needs shallow, muddy waters on which to feed. It frequents rich lowland lakes with plenty of shoreline vegetation. It nests in rough pasture or marshland adjacent to open water. The nest is well concealed in tall grass or other thick cover. It is a shy and silent bird with the occasional 'quack' emanating from the female.

During the 19th century the shoveler only bred regularly in East Anglia and southeast Scotland. It began to expand around the turn of the century when an element of protection was introduced by way of the *Preservation of Wildfowl Act* in 1876 and the *Wild Birds Protection Acts* of the 1880s in which the shoveler was specifically listed.

The last 50 years have witnessed a period of increase for breeding pairs in Britain where the Ouse and Nene Washes in East Anglia are favoured sites. In 1950 there were 50 breeding pairs on the Ouse Washes and this had risen to over 300 pairs by 1975. A maximum of 1,500 pairs now breed in Britain.

An increase in breeding birds has reflected an increase in wintering birds with a peak of 10,000 mostly originating from Russia. The British breeding population moves south to southern France and Spain for the winter. It is thought that the general rise in numbers of British shoveler stems from a succession of warmer summers.

The Wetland Bird Survey shows a 100% increase in shoveler numbers over the past 25 years with a smaller 10% rise over the last 10. There are some local areas where the birds are declining due to drainage and changes in agricultural practice. At a reservoir in Essex there were 15 pairs breeding in 1960 but this had been reduced to a pair by the late eighties. Silage was cut up to the edge of the water leaving little rough pasture for nesting. Many nests can be disrupted by spring flooding in the Ouse Washes and local drainage has seriously affected breeding birds in the north Kent marshes.

Substantial Increase

Skylark

I know of no more uplifting experience than to walk the limestone tops in Derbyshire on a spring day under an umbrella of skylark song. The sustained warbling song of the skylark can last for over five minutes and is delivered while the bird is a speck in the sky. It is performed both as the skylark ascends vertically and while it descends. George Meredith wrote:

> 'He rises and begins to round,
> He drops the silver chain of sound,
> Of many links without a break,
> In chirrup, whistle, slur and shake.'

The skylark has been immortalised by poets for generations. Wordsworth called it *'pilgrim of the sky'* and Shelley referred to it as *'blithe spirit'*. Can one imagine the English countryside without skylarks? The skylark used to be the most widely distributed bird in Britain and the 12th most numerous, yet in the mid-1970s a steep decline set in which lasted for a decade before the population stabilised.

The mixed farming practices of the 19th and early 20th centuries suited the skylark and it thrived despite being caught and caged, killed and eaten. It was netted on the South Downs and exported to France as a delicacy. In 1854 alone 400,000 were sold in the London markets. At a dinner held to celebrate the opening of the Forth Railway Bridge in 1890 a pie was served containing 300 larks.

The post-1950 agricultural revolution spelt disaster for the skylark. Rotational farming was phased out and replaced by regional specialisation. The skylark needs a sparsely vegetated habitat in order to flourish. In the pastoral west of Britain it prefers undisturbed pasture and young grass leys and in arable areas it frequents spring-sown cereals. It feeds on grain and weed seeds and will even graze the leaves of winter wheat. In some areas the skylark is considered an agricultural pest as it forages on sugar beet seedlings.

Historically population densities were higher in regions dominated by cereals and root crops than in pastoral areas. The increase in winter-sown cereals has been the main reason for the demise of the skylark. Vegetation height in the spring restricts opportunities for late season nesting. If the crop height exceeds 50–60cm it will not be suitable as a breeding habitat. Winter-sown cereals also reduce over-winter survival as there are few stubbles for foraging. The application of chemical herbicides results in cleaner ground and a lack of important weed seeds over the winter months.

In pastoral areas the skylark suffers heavy nest losses in silage fields. Intensive fertilisation leads to a dense sward, fewer weed seeds and earlier and more frequent mowing of meadows. Ongoing reform of the Common Agricultural Policy will help the skylark recover. One-year rotational set-aside, where the previous crop is left as stubble, has provided a foraging ground for skylarks and non-rotational set-aside consisting of grasses adds welcome nesting habitat.

Dangerous Decrease

Snipe

There is no more evocative sound than a snipe 'drumming' over its territory in spring. It takes me back to warm spring evenings on the South Uist machair when, in the early 1980s, I would go up to the Hebrides for a few days to help a friend with the lambing.

'Drumming' is not a song as such because it has nothing to do with the snipe's voice. Sir Edward Grey called it '*a joy sound*'; as the male plunges through the air with his colourful tail feathers outspread, the two outer tail feathers vibrate in the wind to produce the sound mechanically. Grey wrote in the *Charm of Birds*:

'the flight has a very happy appearance, but the 'drumming' seems to be performed by the bird in order to find vent for an exuberance of spirit that cannot be expressed by flight alone. The sound is that of a bleat rather than a drum, and in some places the snipe is called "air goat" in consequence.'

The snipe is a secretive and mainly solitary bird that takes off in an evasive zig-zag flight and emits a loud rasping '*scaap*' call when distressed. It feeds at night, probing for earthworms with its long bill, and like the woodcock flights into its feeding grounds at dusk.

The UK snipe population witnessed a decline in the early 19th century associated with extensive drainage of the countryside. This trend then reversed with agricultural recession, which lasted until the 1940s. The last fifty years have seen a widespread decline in snipe numbers over lowland Britain due to pasture improvement, a loss of damp grazing land and the general switch to arable farming.

A discussion paper by the RSPB, *The Reform of the Common Agricultural Policy – New Opportunities for Wildlife and the Environment* (July 1988) includes the following paragraph:

'Snipe are highly vulnerable to drainage because they need the water table to be within twenty centimetres of the soil surface. Breeding is invariably disrupted, if it starts at all, in drained grasslands. Snipe have disappeared from many breeding sites, particularly in the southern counties. A high proportion of the remnant population of about 3,700 pairs nesting on lowland wet grasslands in England and Wales now depend on a handful of protected sites. In the UK it is estimated that 50% of lowland fens, valley and basin mires, and 60% of lowland raised mires, have been lost or significantly damaged over the last thirty years. It is also estimated that the area of fens has been

reduced by 99% since 1600.'

A shooting ban would be of little assistance to our resident population. Every autumn our resident birds are augmented by migrants from areas around the Baltic. It is estimated that the total number that pass through north-western Europe at this time is in the region of 20-30 million birds. In Britain snipe migrate down the west coast via the Outer Isles and on to southern Ireland, always keeping just ahead of freezing conditions in which they are prone to starvation.

Dangerous Decrease

Song thrush

I cannot contemplate a garden without a song thrush. There is no more enchanting sight than this handsome heavily streaked bird hopping across the lawn and cocking its head to one side in search of a worm. Then there is the thrill of that exquisite nest. A unique, mud-lined cup which harbours five sky blue, black-spotted eggs. Finally, this little thrush gifts us a wonderful persistent song that we can enjoy for so many months of the year. The repetition of each loud phrase prevents confusion with the blackbird and makes it one of the easiest garden songs to recognise. Robert Browning wrote: *'That's the wise thrush; he sings each song twice over, lest you should think he never could recapture the first fine careless rapture!'* The song thrush commences his song in the garden early in February and fires anticipation of the soft months ahead. Lord Tennyson captured the spirit of the thrush's song when he wrote:

'Summer is coming, summer is coming,
I know it, I know it, I know it.
Light again, leaf again, life again, love again,
Yes, my wild little poet.'

Sir Edward Grey felt that although the thrush was not in the same league as a blackcap or nightingale, no bird put more effort into its performance. He wrote:
'Probably if birds were to be regarded as endeavouring to please us by song, the thrush should be put first among British birds. He does not rank in the very highest class for quality, but he certainly comes high in the second class. His is undoubtedly a major song and owing to the number of thrushes, their persistent singing and the many months in which they are to be heard, we hear more of their song in the South of England than that of any other bird, except the robin. In song, the thrush seems to be working very hard to please and he succeeds. His song, too, can give a very pleasant impression of quiet contentment as well as exultation. Along with the robin the song thrush is always the last performer on a summer's evening and will happily continue in the dusk.'

WH Hudson wrote in his *British Birds*:
'His evening music always seems the best, but the effect is probably due to the comparative silence and the witching aspect of nature at that hour, when the sky is still luminous, and the earth beneath the dusky green foliage lies in deepest shadow.'

One of the greatest tragedies in British wildlife over the past 25 years is that song thrush numbers have declined by as much as 60%, and we do not really know the reason why. Although song thrushes are very vulnerable to cold winters, this reason alone is not sufficient to explain their continuing decline. Winters over the past 15 years or so have been relatively mild. At the start of the 20th century song thrushes outnumbered blackbirds in all habitats, but over the last 50 years the situation has reversed and the blackbird is now the dominant species. The blackbird has the advantage of utilising a wider range of food. The song thrush relies on earthworms as its staple diet but in early summer will move on to pupating caterpillars. Snails and slugs become an important source of food only when other foods are difficult to obtain, for example in late summer when the weather is very dry, and in winter when the ground is frozen.

The use of garden pesticides to kill molluscs has probably been overemphasised in the song thrush's decline. Recent research by the RSPB is pointing to a series of dry summers combined with widespread drainage of agricultural land as the main causes of the song thrush's demise. On farmland the thrush struggles to make enough nesting attempts each summer to keep the population stable. As the soil dries out thrushes move into damp woodland to feed. If there is a shortage of woodland in a particular area, they move onto farmland where in mid-summer earthworms and snails are difficult to find.

As a result of intensive agriculture, fields have been drained and hedges, which provide damp shaded areas, have been grubbed out. The predominance of autumn-sown crops leaves little spring tillage on which the thrush can feed at a time when food sources are naturally scarce. If the thrush has only one late brood as a result, it means that the chances of young bird survival throughout their first winter are greatly lowered. These young first-year birds simply will not be experienced enough to cope with a scarcity of winter food.

In the last few years there has been a rise in song thrush numbers which has coincided with a series of wet summers. This would tend to support the RSPB's theory that a decline in food sources resulting from global warming has been responsible for fewer nesting attempts. With further dry summers forecasted, the future for the 'wild little poet' looks bleak.

Dangerous Decrease

Sparrowhawk

The sparrowhawk is a most efficient killer, the scourge of woodland birds, and more recently garden birds. It preys by preference on birds, as the kestrel does on mice. Its long tail and broad 'Spitfire' shaped wings give the sparrowhawk great agility, which it uses to devastating effect with dashing surprise attacks along hedgerows. It is not a vociferous bird and tends to lead a secretive life, spending much of the day perched up in thick cover. Its harsh *'kek-kek-kek'* call is usually heard at nesting time when the incoming male calls out to the female on the nest.

The heyday of the sparrowhawk would have been in the medieval period when there were no gamekeepers and the countryside enjoyed a much denser cover of woodland. In Victorian and Edwardian times gamekeepers killed anything with a hooked beak. Sparrowhawks were shot indiscriminately. The advent of the Great War and the break up of many of the big estates in its wake offered the sparrowhawk a reprise. Numbers rose steadily until the mid-1950s. The following decade witnessed a catastrophic decline, so much so that in 1966 only one pair was reported nesting in my native Derbyshire.

The reason for their decline stemmed from the introduction of organochlorine pesticides in agriculture such as DDT, aldrin and dieldrin. These were taken in sub-lethal amounts by seed-eating and insectivorous birds and then accumulated to a lethal level by predators such as the sparrowhawk higher up the food chain. The insecticide DDT led to shell thinning and egg breakage with a drastic downturn in breeding success. The more toxic chemicals such as aldrin and dieldrin were introduced later and actually poisoned many adult birds. The local declines in the sparrowhawk population were always greater in areas with a predominance of tilled land. Since these lethal

chemicals were banned some 40 years ago, there has been a 250% increase in sparrowhawk numbers. Today the population has probably stabilised.

But what of the sparrowhawk as a predator? There is no doubt that it is a ruthless executioner of songbirds. Although it is quite wrong for gamekeepers to persecute sparrowhawks, there might be a case for their control again at some future point. The RSPB publishes research that shows tit populations growing alongside increasing sparrowhawk numbers and concludes that these raptors do not affect songbird populations. It should not be forgotten that tits feed in trees and are not affected to the same extent by modern farming practices as are seed-eating birds. Many of our songbirds are in serious decline and predation by sparrowhawks compounds the problem. A classic example of this is the hedgerow-loving bullfinch. Recently bird tables have encouraged the sparrowhawk into the garden. As a rule it is the smaller cock sparrowhawk that concentrates on the peanut-feeding tits, but members of the declining thrush family and other garden favourites are also victimised.

Substantial Increase

Spotted flycatcher

This inconspicuous, relatively silent, plain, little brown bird is so unobtrusive that many people fail to realise it has established a territory in their garden. It arrives at our home in Derbyshire each year like clockwork, just in time for the Cup Final. It is the last of the summer migrants to reach our shores, appearing around the middle of May, its presence invariably being betrayed by a thin, squeaky call-note.

The spotted flycatcher has enormous charm. Its upright posture and big, brown 'spaniel eyes' make it the most human of our garden birds. Its name is a misnomer as the spots are in fact 'designer stripes'. The spotted flycatcher loves to build in a creeper on the wall of a building yet it can be as creative in its choice of a nest site as the robin. At our home it often builds its nest snugly behind the rusty hinge of a barn door. As one nears the nest it flits off, demonstrating a restless energy that makes it such a successful predator of insects. When feeding it is a master of aerobatics. It occupies a favourite perch and darts out to capture its hapless prey with an audible snap of the beak.

Whereas a decade ago we might have had three pairs of spotted flycatchers around our house and buildings, today we only have a solitary pair. Numbers in Britain have been falling drastically in all habitats and the Common Bird Census reports an 80% decline over the past 25 years. Ringing recoveries point to declines taking place either after fledging or before the first breeding season and research has shown that declines in breeding performance have not been implicated in the spotted flycatcher's decline. Factors affecting its decline in Britain appear to be broadly based, influencing populations in all habitats and regions equally. These environmental factors could affect the spotted flycatcher in Britain before migration or during their journey across Africa and in their wintering grounds.

The spotted flycatcher winters in South Africa well to the south of the Sahel. However, it has to cross the Sahara twice a year and a substantial decline in its population coincided with the failure of Sahel rains in 1983-84. The spotted flycatcher has the smallest fat reserves of any of our African migrants and hence it feeds at oases en route.

If drought reduced the number of insects at these feeding grounds, the spotted flycatcher might be affected more than other species that rely on a similar food source. Interestingly, unlike the whitethroat, spotted flycatcher numbers did not crash during the disastrous 1968-69 Sahel drought.

Conditions on the spotted flycatcher's nesting grounds in Britain are more likely to be behind its decline. Although we are in a period of global warming we have been experiencing a series of cooler, wet, early summers. The availability of insects is affected by air temperature and if May is a warm month research has demonstrated that the spotted flycatcher breeds earlier and has more and larger broods. Likewise, the drier late summer weather that we are currently experiencing might decrease the availability of flying insects at a vital time, immediately before migration. Recent research in Scotland has shown that modern agricultural practices, especially the use of pesticides, are behind the general decline in insect life. The more intensive the farming, the fewer insects for birds. The spotted flycatcher has a 'wait and pounce' approach to feeding. Perhaps there is just not enough prey for the young birds to build sufficient strength and to perfect the art of flycatching before they set off on the hazardous journey south.

Dangerous Decrease

Starling

If I were to ask the man in the street for his views on the starling he would probably say it was uninteresting, scruffy and very common; he would be wrong on all counts. The starling is not one of our more accomplished songsters yet it has a varied and charming repertoire of whistles, trills, rattles, clicks and wheezes. Its real party piece is to mimic other birds. At springtime in Derbyshire I have often thought I was listening to a curlew in the big meadow or a green woodpecker in the park, only to find a solitary starling perched on the chimney giving a cheeky imitation. It is a social bird that can also provide entertainment in a group. A roost of starlings, once a common sight, can number a million birds. A swarm of starlings going to roost in a big city just before dusk is one of nature's wonders; the noisy host drifts and wheels across the sky like smoke.

It is easy to undervalue the starling's beauty. More often than not it is depicted as a rather plain, unhygienic bird that fouls many of London's celebrated landmarks such as Trafalgar Square. In the spring the male starling is a beautiful specimen with an iridescent purple-green and blue plumage spangled with white. The starling does build a very scruffy nest, always in a hole, but makes up for it by laying a delicious sky blue egg and being a most conscientious parent.

Until the middle of the 19th century the starling was a rare bird. In Scotland it was only breeding in the Western Isles and Caithness. The latter part of the 18th century witnessed a period of severe winters. The new century brought climate amelioration and new methods of animal husbandry. Urbanisation presented the starling with a wealth of new nesting sites and the combination meant the bird spread rapidly across Britain. Adaptability was the key to its success and an ability to live on a variety of foods: invertebrates in spring, fruit in summer and seeds in winter. Close-cropped grassland is a favoured habitat and there was much forest clearance in Europe in the 19th century.

Analysis of the Common Bird Census data shows that the starling population has dropped by nearly 70% in Britain since 1962. Suburban and urban populations are declining to a lesser extent than those on farmland habitats where livestock-based areas have been hit hardest. Research has shown that starling breeding performance has improved over the last 40 years, probably because of warmer springs; however over-winter survival rates amongst first-year birds has fallen and is almost certainly responsible for the overall decline in population.

The Breeding Bird Survey demonstrates that starling densities are 2.5 times as great in pastoral as compared to arable habitat. It is thought that the general intensification of grassland management has impacted adversely on starlings. The area of pasture has decreased by 10% since 1970. Soil and ground-dwelling invertebrates, particularly leatherjackets and earthworms, are the main prey of starlings, and soil cultivation reduces their numbers. In a quest for increased yields, the use of fertiliser promotes taller, denser swards in which starlings will have greater difficulty foraging. As a result of fertilisers and modern machinery there has been a dramatic shift from hay making to silage making since 1970 and associated cutting and rolling markedly reduces the number of invertebrates. The total area sprayed with insecticides has increased tenfold since then. In hard weather starlings feed on surface-dwelling invertebrates, and modern 'worming' drugs such as ivermectin result in a lack of insect life in dung. Starlings often forage around pig and cattle breeding stations; pig numbers in Britain have declined and more cattle are kept indoors.

Suburban and urban habitats hold 60% of the starling breeding population. Starlings require a cavity to nest in and some short grass fields close to the nest. In the autumn first-year birds move away from the family home onto agricultural habitats. A greater decline in survival in western Britain may result from a shortage of habitat into which juveniles can disperse in addition to a shortage of food; for example upland afforestation may have reduced habitat availability. Nesting attempts in urban situations appear to produce fewer young; it is not known whether lawns, parks and sports fields provide lower quality food resources.

In the winter the British breeding population of starlings is augmented by millions of birds from the Baltic region. Surveys demonstrate that their numbers have declined 45% since 1970.

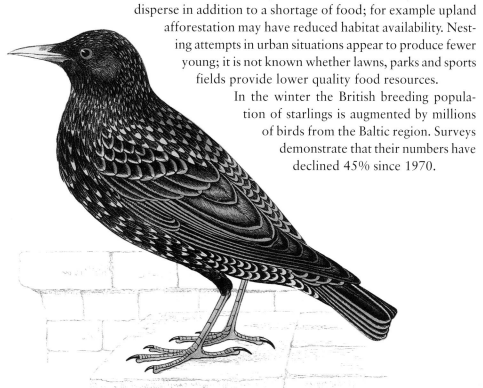

Dangerous Decrease

Stone-curlew

There is a delightful entry in Edward Grey's *Cottage Book* for 22nd May 1902 that reads thus:

> *'I went with Dorothy on Tuesday to be shown a stone curlew's egg – we spied and stalked and crept and saw a stone curlew standing by a ragged lonely whin bush on the down like a sentinel. As we got nearer it trotted off with the skip of a ghost in the evening light, passed the nest and disappeared. In the nest we found one egg and one young bird hatched since the day before which lay flat and uttered. Both the egg and the bird are coloured to match chalk flints that have been a long time among the mole heaps.'*

The stone-curlew is a 'wader' of dry heaths. It frequents sandy soils with a high proportion of chalk and flints against which it is perfectly camouflaged. It needs large open spaces where grass is kept low by grazing and where bare ground is found, hence its two main strongholds in Britain today are the Norfolk Brecklands and the chalk downs of southern Britain. It becomes active at dusk, sitting immovable and invisible in the daytime on the stony ground, and has a large yellow eye adapted for nocturnal habits. Its wild curlew-like cries are heard at night, particularly when flocked up on migration to Spain and north Africa.

When Grey made his entry in the *Cottage Book* the stone-curlew was well on its way to becoming a breeding rarity in Hampshire. A decline had set in before the end of the

19th century with the loss of heathland to arable farming. The farming slump of the 1920s caused a temporary increase in some areas but the stone-curlew had disappeared from Yorkshire by 1938. By this time there was a maximum population of 2,000 pairs in Britain, a figure that had fallen to 140 pairs by the 1980s. A serious contraction began in the 1940s with the conversion of much marginal land and grass to arable.

The decline in mixed farming and of spring-sown crops adversely affected the stone-curlew by reducing the availability of sparsely vegetated sites and short pastures rich in invertebrates. Mixed farming practices provided lay pastures rich in insects close to tilled land suitable for nesting. Areas of once short grassland have become too tall and dense with the introduction of fertilisers. In the 1950s the introduction of myxomatosis and a lack of demand for low quality grazing caused a further deterioration in the stone-curlew's natural habitat. Today two-thirds of the population nest on arable farms in spring-sown crops.

As a result of RSPB research and the introduction of conservation programmes under Countryside Stewardship Schemes stone-curlew numbers rose to 233 pairs in 1999. Many nests are destroyed by the rolling of cereal crops in the spring together with the inter-row hoeing of root crops. With the co-operation of the farming community, nest protection by RSPB field wardens has recently produced increases in breeding success. The management of stone-curlew habitat, particularly with regard to grazing pressure, is vital to its future success. On one Breckland reserve rabbit grazing is encouraged and the area enclosed by a fence.

Decrease

Swallow

It is always exciting to glimpse the first swallow in early April; its arrival, together with that of the willow warbler and cuckoo, stirs anticipation of the 'golden time' ahead. Yet it is in the autumn that I really appreciate this elegant, acrobatic, long-distance commuter. In the quiet mellow days of September, when all that is heard is the acid song of the robin or maybe a weak farewell from the chiffchaff, hundreds of swallows gather noisily on the telephone lines for the 'off'. Whether at home in Derbyshire or high up on the heather moorlands the scene is the same. It is one of frenzied activity as swallows twist and turn above the farm buildings uttering their harsh *'tswick'* call-note, or glide serenely past the grouse butts on their long journey back to South Africa. This sudden burst of activity reminds me that winter is just around the corner and takes me back to my childhood; that sad, empty feeling before returning to school after the extended summer holidays.

Even though over five million swallows perch on our telephone wires each autumn, enveloped in a chorus of soft, fast, twittering warbles as they contemplate their flight south, their numbers have dropped alarmingly over the past 25 years. The swallow spends six months of the year in South Africa. Not only do they have to overcome the perils of a return journey but they also seem to be experiencing a very different set of problems in their summer and winter quarters.

Swallows are linked closely to man and natural nesting sites like caves and hollow trees are no longer used. They moved into chimneys and old mine shafts and then on to traditional farm buildings. Modern farming methods with renovations in farm build-ings and improved hygiene have been partly responsible for the swallow's decline in Britain. Nesting sites have disappeared and their food source has dwindled with the introduction of insecticides and a fall in livestock numbers. A change from mixed farming to arable has not helped the swallow's fortunes. Many farms in the south have gone out of dairy farming. Drugs used to worm those remaining cattle result in sterile cow

pats. The result is a drastic cut in insect numbers. Swallows prefer large flies like bluebottles, horseflies and dung beetles, all associated with farm livestock. An increase in urbanisation has compounded the problem as swallows are not at home in towns; they need wide open spaces complete with grazing animals, where they can sweep low for insects.

A lack of nest sites and improved farm hygiene cannot in them-selves explain the large fall in numbers, and problems in their winter quarters may be more significant. The most hazardous obstacle on their migration is the Sahara. Also, swallows can be easily hit by a cold wet snap in the autumn while traversing Europe. Once they arrive in South Africa the biggest danger is drought, which reduces the supply of insects. Since 1978 the Transvaal and Cape Province have been experiencing extreme periods of drought. This neatly tracks the swallow's decline in Britain. A prolonged drought will cause many birds to arrive back in the north in poor condition, which will in turn impair breeding performance.

Swift

There is no more fascinating British breeding bird than the swift. Like Henry Douglas-Home 40 years before, I used to enjoy them on balmy summers' evenings while at school at Eton in the 1960s. I would sit dreamily at my window and watch them wheeling, diving and screaming past the science schools and my house, South Lawn. The long sickle-shaped wings suggest that the swift is the most aerial of our birds. Its minute feet are too frail to support the body weight and the swift never perches or alights on the ground except by accident.

The swift's breeding ecology is very sensitive to weather conditions as its diet is made up wholly of aerial insects. As a result the swift spends the shortest time of any migrant in this country, usually arriving at the end of April, and the young leave for central Africa as soon as they are out of the nest. The chicks hatch at staggered intervals, thus ensuring at least the oldest survive, and if weather conditions are poor and insects in short supply they become torpid for long periods; the young may take seven weeks to fledge in cool conditions. Radar has revealed that a British swift is capable of making a round trip as far as the Baltic in a single day to gather flies. The swift will ascend as high as 10,000ft, buoyed up by currents of rising air, in order to sleep on the wing at night. Ringing has proved that the swift can live for up to 15 years and if so will have reached four million flying miles in its lifetime.

The swift nests exclusively in buildings, usually under the eves of taller, older houses where the nest sites are more than five metres above the ground. The swift approaches from below, scampering into a hole in the roof, and then leaves by falling out. Declines were reported in the early part of the 20th century because of the adverse effects of aerial pollution, particularly sulphur dioxide, on its food supply; then came the *Clean Air Acts.* The swift is a difficult bird to census because of its colonial nesting habits and an ability to travel hundreds of miles to feed. Since the Breeding Bird Survey was commenced in 1994 a decline of around 20% has been registered for the swift.

Modern housing does not provide suitable nest sites and the swift is being excluded from nesting holes by restoration and demolition work. Better roof maintenance is driving the swift's decline. A survey in a small area of Northamptonshire demonstrated an 80% decline between 1978 and 1998. In his book *The Birdman,* Henry Douglas-Home relates how he successfully introduced nest boxes for swifts at his home in the Borders. Builders and home-owners will have to be educated as to how to help the swift before it is too late.

Decrease

Tawny owl

Unlike the barn owl the tawny owl is heard but not seen. As children we were all brought up with the *'tu-whit, tu-who'* of the tawny owl in a most misleading fashion. The call in fact represents a duet and not a single bird. The male utters its eerie *'hoo-hoo-hoo'* and the female replies with a piercing *'kee-wick'* cry. This chorus reaches a crescendo in February when owls are establishing their territories.

The tawny is our most widespread and numerous owl. It is nocturnal in its hunting habits and highly territorial and sedentary. Its density on farmland is closely correlated with the density of farmsteads. It is often found in mature trees and copses around houses. At home in Derbyshire I sometimes disturb a tawny roosting in a laurel by the walled garden. As this is a woodland bird camouflage in the form of its brown plumage is an important commodity. Daytime roosts can often be discovered by the incidence of mobbing from small birds.

Tawny owl numbers fell during the 19th century due to the activities of zealous gamekeepers. The population increased during the 20th century with fewer gamekeepers and warmer weather. The CBC index peaked in 1972 and has remained fairly stable since. The tawny owl has proved more resilient than other birds of prey. It was less affected by the severe winter of 1962-63 than the barn owl and also suffered to a lesser degree from the introduction of organochlorine pesticides than did the sparrowhawk.

The key to the tawny's success lies with its adaptability. It has a much broader diet than other owls, which allowed it to move out of woodland into parks and gardens.

Its catholic diet also prevented it suffering on farmland in the same way as the barn owl. In suburban areas the tawny owl kills small birds such as house sparrows and on farmland takes a higher percentage of invertebrates such as earthworms. In years when supplies of small mammals are low the tawny lays small clutches; it has an uncanny way of assessing the likely food supply at the beginning of each year. It may not breed at all in years of food shortage. Chicks hatch at two-day intervals so if food is short the biggest chick eats the smallest. Nests are usually located in a tree hole or in a disused crow's nest.

There are around 20,000 breeding pairs in Britain. Breeding rates and chick survival have been fairly constant since the 1972 peak, probably due to the banning of toxic chemicals in pesticides. Sparse distribution in the fens of eastern England reflects a shortage of nesting sites and an absence of woodland. In 1993 research found evidence of a contraction in the species range and the Common Bird Census demonstrates a decline of around 10% over the past 25 years. This may have been caused by the effects of agricultural chemicals on the owl's small mammal diet. A new generation of rodenticides were introduced when rats developed a resistance to warfarin.

 *Teal*

The handsome little drake with his chestnut head and metallic green eyestrip is one of our most charismatic ducks. His musical fluty call is as evocative of a wintery estuary as the whistle of the wigeon or the yelping cry of the redshank. The teal is a shy bird that nests on the edge of boggy moorland pools. The nest is difficult to find as it is placed in thick vegetation from which the ducklings rarely venture far.

The best place to enjoy teal dashing about the sky is on an estuary in midwinter. Our small English resident breeding population of around 2,000 pairs is joined in the winter by over 130,000 immigrant birds from Scandinavia and the Baltic countries. The two most important wintering sites are the Somerset levels and the Mersey estuary. This tiny duck is very susceptible to cold winters and is always moving south in front of harsh conditions. The teal is much prized by the sportsman both for its acrobatic flight and the quality of its meat. Shooting has little effect on over-wintering numbers.

In Britain we have been witnessing an increase in wintering birds, but at the same time our resident numbers have been decreasing. The destruction of habitat for breeding teal, primarily by land drainage, began in the 19th century. This caused their withdrawal from lowland areas in the south and began a long-term retreat to upland areas in the north, which has continued to the present day. Pollution and increased human disturbance have also affected this shy duck, which frequents densely vegetated wetlands.

Since the 1960s there has been a worrying range contraction in the north, principally due to extensive afforestation. Tax breaks were introduced in the 1960s for planting forestry. As a result a considerable amount of 'lochan habitat' in the flow country of

Caithness and Sutherland was planted. Afforestation has also been responsible for a decline in breeding teal numbers. Forestry consumes considerable quantities of water, which in turn reduces river flow. This leads to a build-up of sediment on the riverbed. Boggy pools are drained and rivers become clogged up, not just with sediment but also with vegetation stimulated by fertiliser run-off from plantations.

Developing tree cover on the teal's moorland nesting grounds increases the abundance and diversity of predators, which in turn affects the duck's breeding success and adult survival.

Decrease

Treecreeper

It is Easter Sunday and we are enjoying the benefits of a high-pressure system. Easter is early this year and late March has brought glorious spring sunshine. The treecreeper has sung incessantly all weekend as it flits about its business from one mature tree to the next. Grey referred to the song as *'a very sweet wisp of sound'*, and at first had much trouble confusing it with song of the goldcrest. The treecreeper's song ends in a powerful flourish which is the most satisfactory way of distinguishing it from the goldcrest's equally thin high-pitched rendition.

I will never forget sighting my first treecreeper. It was on the trunk of a chestnut tree in Blenheim Park. It reminded me of a mouse. Sir Edward Grey's description in *The Charm of Birds* says it all:

'It is a very attractive bird; the slender bill suggests a humming-bird; the back is a rich arrangement of brown colours; the under parts are silvery white, and the body has a delicate rounded curve from head to tail as it searches the tree trunks.'

The treecreeper always works its way up a tree trunk and then with weak flight progresses to the bottom of the next mature tree and repeats the process. We have a custom-built nest box for the treecreeper at our home, which has never been used. One year I found its nest 50 yards away in a tiny crevice wedged between a gritstone gate-post and a garden stone wall.

The treecreeper is a sedentary resident bird and as such is hit by cold wet winters. Numbers have been reasonably stable since the 1970s with declines that correlate closely to poor winter weather. Research has shown that temperature alone is not the decisive factor. The treecreeper is an arboreal species and as a result long periods of freezing rain or of glazed frost may be threatening. The last cold wet winter was in 1978-79. This gave rise to prolonged ice coating of tree trunks and associated branches and as a result numbers fell dramatically. Although the Common Bird Census shows a decline of 25% from a peak in the mid-seventies, treecreeper numbers have recently been stable with no particular long-term trend.

Stable

Tree sparrow

Over the past 15 years at our home in Derbyshire, the spotted flycatcher has declined noticeably, the whinchat and the pied flycatcher come and go, yet only the tree sparrow has completely disappeared. It must have been 10 years ago when I last saw this plump little bird hopping around under the bird table. It is very similar to its close cousin, the house sparrow, and must have gone unnoticed in thousands of gardens across the country. The tree sparrow is smaller than the house sparrow, has a black patch on its white cheek and sports an all brown cap. It chirrups like its relation but its voice is higher-pitched and more metallic. As a smaller and weaker species it appears to be unable to compete with the house sparrow and therefore tends to be excluded from urban areas and occupies a more rural niche.

The tree sparrow population has crashed since the late 1970s, so much so that it is one of the most threatened species in Britain. It should be said that numbers have plummeted in the past and risen again. After high population levels at the turn of the century there was a marked decline until the 1950s, only for numbers to rise again in the late 1960s. The tree sparrow is a seed-eating bird and its decline could have been linked to the agricultural recession; however the resurgence in farming took place much earlier during World War II. The long-term fluctuations in tree sparrow numbers are very difficult to explain, particularly as numbers remained high over the organochlorine pesticide era from 1955-1965.

A characteristic of the tree sparrow is that once-thriving colonies suddenly dwindle and die. Although it is largely a sedentary bird, from time to time considerable population movements take place. There was a massive increase in numbers in 1958 and many areas of Britain in which the tree sparrow had disappeared were mysteriously re-colonised. An upsurge of this nature in the British population could be caused by eruptions from Europe following high numbers on the Continent.

A report from the BTO demonstrates that breeding performances of the tree sparrow have improved as population sizes have fallen suggesting that decreases in productivity are not responsible for the overall decline. A lack of insects for nestlings in the modern agricultural landscape may not be such a problem as thought in some quarters. The real problem lies with a lack of food over the winter months for first-year birds. Tree sparrows used to flock up on stubbles with other seed-eating birds like the linnet and corn bunting over the harshest months of the year. A move to autumn sowing over the last 25 years reduces the availability of weed seeds and scattered grain in stubble

fields. The widespread use of herbicides in weed control has made matters worse.

The introduction of set-aside, financial inducements for spring-sown crops and the provision of nest boxes all offer the tree sparrow a ray of hope for the future.

Dangerous Decrease

273

 # Tufted duck

The tufted duck is the most widespread and best known duck in Britain after the mallard. It can become very tame, where it is protected, as anyone who has visited St James's Park in London will know. The drake is a glossy black and white with a prominent crest from which it takes its name. It is a gregarious duck that often mixes with pochard and coot on large lowland lakes and reservoirs. The more acid waters of the uplands are avoided.

A pair will occasionally arrive and nest at one of my ponds in Derbyshire. The rather dull brown female, when disturbed, utters a deep growling call on take-off. I once managed to approach within yards of the family feeding on the reedy water. The lively little ducklings reminded me of buoyant bumblebees as they dived beneath the surface and bobbed up like corks. They learn to dive within days of hatching and feed themselves immediately on midge larvae.

The tufted duck, unknown as a breeding species in Britain at the beginning of the 19th century, is now our most common diving duck. Around 7,500 pairs nest in Britain and in the winter months numbers are swollen by up to 60,000 birds from Iceland and northern Europe. The wintering population has increased threefold since the 1960s.

The availability of food and habitat are behind this success story. Eighty percent of

the tufted duck's diet takes the form of animal matter such as molluscs, crustaceans and insects with the balance made up by plant material. The spread of the zebra mussel, first released in 1824 at the London docks, is thought to have greatly assisted the spread of the tufted duck.

The first pair bred in Yorkshire in 1849 and in Scotland a pair was reported nesting at Loch Leven in 1875; five years later more than 100 pairs were breeding at the latter site. *The Wild Birds Protection Acts* of the 1880s had a beneficial effect on range and numbers by enforcing a closed season on shooting.

The tufted duck was quick to make use of artificial habitat such as reservoirs and gravel pits. It frequents sites with small islands where refuge is found from foxes. Unfortunately a much worse threat awaits this duck with the spread of the feral mink. The tufted duck nests later than most other ducks from mid-May through to mid-July. The denser vegetation during the summer months provides welcome cover from predation by crows and magpies. The mallard by contrast lays its first clutch as early as February; that is little short of suicidal.

Substantial Increase

Turtle dove

The turtle dove is the smallest and slimmest of our pigeons and the only European dove that migrates to breed with us in Britain. In days gone by its deep, soft, lazy song in early May was eagerly awaited by country folk in the south of England. In the middle of the day in high summer the only song to be heard aside from the wheezing of the yellowhammer was the soothing croon of the turtle dove, usually performed from within dense cover.

In the early 1980s, when we used to visit my parents-in-law's house at Bramdean in Hampshire, the turtle dove would feed on corn with the bantams outside the kitchen window. It is richly coloured, with a pink chest and neat patterns of black and light orange-browns on its upper parts. When disturbed it departs in a fast, low flight with rapid wingbeats. I was lucky to enjoy this pretty little dove at close quarters when I did, for it has experienced a catastrophic decline in numbers in recent years. The CBC reports a 75% loss over the past 30 years.

The turtle dove is a lowland bird that is always associated with agriculture and needs open ground for feeding. It spread across southern England in the 19th century as new methods of arable cultivation were developed. There was a further upsurge in the early decades of the 20th century that coincided with the agricultural recession which encouraged weedy conditions. The staple diet of the turtle dove is weed seed. Most birds feed their chicks on insects but the turtle dove and linnet do not. Weed seeds have become a rarity in the modern farming routine.

Although intensive agriculture is the principal culprit behind the turtle dove's demise, two other factors come into play that are working against any possible revival in numbers through 'set-aside' schemes. Every year thousands of turtle doves are shot on migration in countries such as France and Spain; over 100,000 are shot annually in Malta alone. Turtle doves winter to the south of the Sahara in the Sahel scrub zone and the savannahs of Senegal and Gambia. The increased desertification of the Sahel and the loss of scrub and forest must be working against the turtle dove in its winter quarters. However, turtle dove numbers did not crash in the 1970s as did the whitethroat and redstart populations. Winter flocks of doves in west Africa have become more mobile and this may well have reduced the effects of drought.

Ornithologists first noticed that the turtle dove was declining in the 1960s when it started disappearing on its south-western, western and northern margins, interestingly all grassland areas. A study in the early 1960s showed that over 90% of all feeding by turtle doves was on weedy hayfields and clover leys. Then in the late 1970s and the early 1980s came the dramatic switch from hay to silage and with it earlier and more frequent mowing together with the application of improved herbicides and fertilisers. Early mowing limits seeding by grassland herbs and the use of fertilisers results in a loss of plant diversity as less dominant grasses are suffocated by the dense sward.

The turtle dove's favourite weed on arable land is fumitory that used to be found on any light, dry and disturbed soils. Other favoured weeds are fat hen, chickweed, charlock and redshank. With the widespread use of herbicides these weeds are increasingly rare on British farmland. The turtle dove now consumes cultivated seeds but these are only available at harvest and this is too late for the breeding cycle. Research has also shown that the nutritional value of cultivated seeds is less than weed seeds. Spilt corn available at grain stores means birds congregate at fewer sites and are more vulnerable to predators such as sparrowhawks.

In the 1960s the turtle dove laid three clutches of eggs as opposed to 1.5 today. There is currently a reduced availability of nest sites as more and more tall, overgrown, thorny hedges are grubbed out in the interests of higher agricultural yields.

Dangerous Decrease

Wheatear

One of the first signs of spring in Derbyshire is a colourful, fidgety bird with a blue-grey back, buff underparts and a prominent white rump, flitting along the roadside drystone walls. It is early March and the wheatear has just arrived from tropical Africa. It draws attention to itself by its loud *'chak'* call-note and a constant nervous energy. The wheatear is the first in a long list of migrants to reach our shores every year, even outstripping the chiffchaff by a week or so.

The wheatear has an interesting history in Britain. It is a bird of open country frequenting heaths, sandy coastlands and heather upland. It nests under boulders, on scree slopes, in stone walls or even in rabbit holes. A century ago it bred widely across the country using the latter for nest sites on the chalk downland. It was on this very habitat that this charming little 'chat' was snared in its thousands by local shepherds. The wheatear was considered a delicacy on the Victorian dinner table. It was recorded in the 19th century that a shepherd on the South Downs caught up to 1,000 a day using a horsehair noose and about 22,000 were taken annually around Eastbourne at the end of the 18th century.

Over the past 100 years there has been a substantial contraction in wheatear numbers in lowland Britain as a result of habitat loss. Since the initiation of the Breeding Bird Survey in 1994 the wheatear population has fallen by 6%. There are few breeding birds now south of a line from the Humber to the Severn. The wheatear today nests in open upland above 1,000ft where there is short turf resulting from sheep and rabbit grazing and an abundance of insects.

A real decline in numbers was noticed in the 1930s. The great agricultural recession had been running for many years and much marginal land was taken out of production, short turf being replaced by scrub. During World War II the ploughing of marginal land led to the wheatear's virtual extinction on the southern downlands. Following on in the 1950s the advent of myxomatosis meant that much downland habitat deteriorated due to a reduction in rabbit grazing. On the Suffolk heathlands afforestation contributed to habitat loss and wheatear numbers fell from 800 pairs in 1947 to 50 by the 1960s.

Some 55,000 pairs breed in Britain today. It is possible that drought in the Sahel desert hit wheatear numbers in the recent past. Migrating birds have to pass through this inhospitable area en route to Britain from Africa. On the Welsh island of Skokholm the wheatear population dropped from 20 pairs in 1971 to eight pairs in 1973 over a period of severe drought. There was then a steady increase until a decline in 1984. It was at this time that the Sahel experienced a complete failure in its rainfall.

Decrease

Whimbrel

The whimbrel is the consummate English passage migrant. It is a long-distance traveller that winters in tropical west Africa and drops in on our estuaries to refuel en route to its northern nesting grounds in Iceland and Scandinavia. May is the best time to see the whimbrel at Newtown on the Isle of Wight. The first clue to its presence is invariably the rippling, whinnying call that gives the whimbrel its country name, 'seven whistler'; a cry that is so evocative of wild open marshland.

The whimbrel makes a more leisurely return journey down the east coast of England. It is not as timid as the curlew and one August Bank Holiday I got within yards of a whimbrel feeding on the greens of the Deal golf course in Kent. The whimbrel is dumpier than the curlew, having a shorter bill and quicker wingbeats. At close range bold striping is visible on its head.

The whimbrel is the ecological replacement for the larger curlew in higher latitudes and is at the southernmost limit of its breeding range in Britain. The two birds overlap in the Shetlands, the whimbrel nesting higher up on the hillside and the curlew frequenting damp meadows down on the coast. The whimbrel prefers to nest in short sward moorland or heathland and often on gentle slopes that provide a degree of protection against predators.

In the 19th century whimbrel eggs were considered something of a delicacy and

collected by the Shetland islanders. It was noted that numbers were decreasing rapidly in the 1870s and by 1880 the whimbrel had ceased breeding on Orkney. In 1900 it was estimated there were only 30 pairs in Britain, all on Shetland. By 1964 the population had doubled and a survey completed in 1994 produced 480 pairs nesting on the Shetland Islands with Fetlar proving the most densely populated island site. Although the whimbrel has probably been under-recorded it was estimated at this time that an additional 25 pairs bred mainly on Lewis and St Kilda.

It has been suggested that cooler, wetter summers have been the reason for the big increase since the 1970s yet until the passing of the *Wildlife and Countryside Act* of 1981, the curlew and whimbrel were both a legitimate quarry for shooters. Reclamation of moorland and maritime heathland by the crofters for agriculture has historically been a threat to the whimbrel population. At the current time an increasing number of SSSIs are affording protection to a larger and larger percentage of the Shetlands' nesting birds.

The whimbrel is susceptible to predation on its nesting grounds from great skuas and black-backed gulls now that offal discard from the offshore fishing industry is in such short supply. Predation accounts for nearly 50% of egg losses and chicks under 10 days old are particularly vulnerable.

Like the greenshank, the whimbrel executes a beautiful song-flight on its nesting grounds. A steady climb on beating wings is followed by a glide when it emits a curlew-like bubbling trill.

Substantial Increase

Whinchat

This pretty little spring visitor often shares my summer holidays in the north of Britain. Whether in the sand dunes of Seahouses on the Northumberland coast or on the bracken-clad, raised beaches of Jura in the Hebrides, a harsh *'tac-tac'* call alerts me to the presence of a whinchat. The word 'chat' is derived from the imitation of the sound of two pebbles being struck together. The whinchat's song is a robin-like warble. It assumes a snappy upright pose when performing from a prominent song post within its territory. It is a nervous bird that constantly bobs its body and flicks its wings. The whinchat is attractively streaked on its back and sports beautiful buff plumage on its underparts, the best form of identification being a striking white eye-stripe.

We used to play host to a pair in some rough grassland at the bottom of our valley in Derbyshire. One year the farmer moved some cattle in to eat off the coarse tussocks and the whinchat disappeared. This experience has been mirrored across the country as numbers have declined steadily over the past 70 years. Declines have been particularly marked in lowland England due to a loss of marginal farming habitat. The whinchat used to breed freely on rough pasture, waste ground and railway embankments. A general tidying-up of the landscape has resulted in the destruction of much of its favoured habitat. Grass is cut earlier, herbicides reduce weeds and fertilisers produce a denser sward. Roadside verges are now mown for traffic safety and many railway embankments have become overgrown with dense scrub.

The depths of the agricultural depression in the 1920s and 1930s presented the whinchat with an abundance of favoured habitat as neglected pastures were colonised by small hawthorn bushes. The post-1940 revival converted much land to arable, which provided unsuitable habitat for the whinchat. There was a localised recovery in the 1960s as increased areas of young forestry were planted and a further setback in the 1970s when farm subsidies were introduced for land improvement by the EEC Today the whinchat has all but disappeared from the Midlands, Thames Valley and the Suffolk and Kent coasts. Its distribution is largely unchanged in Scotland, Wales and north-west England. The whinchat is more of an upland bird than its close cousin the stonechat, which frequents lowland and gorse-clad heath.

The whinchat is a trans-Saharan migrant yet there is little evidence that it has been hit by drought in its winter quarters. The whinchat's winter survival is higher than the resident stonechat and consequently it only has one brood that is commenced in May soon after its arrival on our shores.

Decrease

Whitethroat

The tiny stream which feeds the duck ponds at my home in Derbyshire is bordered by an untidy hedge of willow and hawthorn. It is in this low bushy wasteland that the whitethroat makes its summer home, having arrived from its African winter quarters in late April.

Warblers are busy birds and the whitethroat is the most restless of them all. The cock whitethroat bounces and dances up from the undergrowth, singing his scratchy song, then drops down again like a stone. He will readily display his smart plumage from a perch on top of a hawthorn bush. At this moment, as he performs his sweet song, his white throat and grey cap are quite distinctive.

The whitethroat's song is as jerky as its flight. I have often heard it described as irritable or bad tempered. Sir Edward Grey wrote in *The Charm of Birds*: *'the song is fussy, as if the bird is in a hurry or slightly provoked. Sometimes the tones and manner suggest scolding.'* Grey concluded: *'the prevailing impression the whitethroat gives is that of excitement and happiness, and its animation and vitality are a pleasant feature in the places it chooses to inhabit.'* It is a bird that is often associated with thick ground cover and its old country name, 'nettlecreeper', reflects one of the whitethroat's favourite nesting sites.

The whitethroat winters in the Sahel thorn scrub zone on the southern fringe of the Sahara. The winter of 1968-69 saw massive mortality with a severe drought in the Sahel when nearly 80% of the previous year's breeding stock failed to reappear in Britain. The whitethroat reached a low point in 1974, following which numbers stabilised and then slowly recovered. There were other low points in 1983-4 and 1991-2 but numbers have now increased by in excess of 40% over the last 25 years. The population has still not recovered completely from the 1968-69 crash.

Scrub supports over 50% of whitethroat nests. Its ability to use low cover was well illustrated by a BTO study of farmland birds in which it was one of the very few hedgerow species not adversely affected by severe hedge-cutting. The whitethroat would however have suffered from the widespread removal of hedgerows that took place after the war, particularly in arable areas of the east and the south.

Increase

Wigeon

I have always found the whistling call of the wigeon as evocative of wild watery places as the piercing piping cry of the redshank. Our home on the Newtown estuary in the Isle of Wight is only 70 miles from London yet the thrilling whistle and purr of the wigeon envelops us 24 hours a day over the winter months. The wigeon is a highly gregarious and beautiful duck, the drake attired in a stunning array of yellow, chestnut and pink.

Britain lies at the southern edge of the wigeon's breeding range with around 500 pairs of which 75% nest in northern Scotland. The wigeon colonised Britain during the cooler climate of the 19th century, the first breeding record being in Sutherland in 1837. The first English nest was found in Yorkshire at the turn of the 20th century. There has been little breeding expansion over the past 50 years, with recent southerly records no doubt representing escapees from collections.

The wigeon prefers to breed adjacent to small moorland lochs and tarns or on islands where the nest is well concealed in a grassy tussock. Historically the biggest colony was at Loch Leven, where brood survival was low due to a shortage of sheltered shorelines that harbour an abundance of insects. In Iceland it has been proved that emerging midges are an important food source during brood-rearing. In Sutherland and Caithness, broods are commonly found along streams and at their convergence with lochs, where they feed on insects and rich plant life.

The number of wintering wigeon in Britain has been increasing steadily since the 1970s and today represents over 30% of the entire north-western European population. Around 200,000 birds move south from Russia and northern Europe to winter in Britain, 60,000 alone on the Ouse Washes and at Lindisfarne. On coastal mudflats wigeon are closely associated with brent geese where they feed on eel grass. When the zostera was reduced by disease, wigeon began to diversify their habitat. They moved inland, taking advantage of new gravel pits and reservoirs, and began feeding on stubbles and winter wheat, in addition to pasture on flooded fields next to the coast.

This adaptability lies behind the success of wintering wigeon in Britain. Seventy percent of these birds utilise nature reserves where there is little shooting. Their continuing success depends on the availability of undisturbed estuarine habitat and water management schemes.

Increase

Willow warbler

The fishing lodge at Knockando on Speyside is surrounded by a young plantation of birch and Scots pine interspersed by clumps of thick heather. As I lie in bed at dawn the garden rings with the song of amorous willow warblers.

Willow warblers arrive in England around the 1st April although unfavourable north-east winds can delay their appearance into May. They are widely distributed and can be found in some of the most isolated places in Britain as long as there is scrubby cover present. I can quite understand why Edward Grey referred to this warbler as '*the everlasting bird*'; in some locations their songs never seem to cease. He wrote:

'*the song is particularly pleasant as well as frequent. It is a succession of slender and delicate notes, forming a completed sentence, which is repeated again and again at intervals. The notes have an endearing quality of their own. They suggest something plaintive – as if the bird was pleading. A cadence as soft as summer's rain has occurred to me when listening to the song which is particularly touching. The impression made on a human listener by these plaintive notes is one of intense sadness: the tone is pathetic; there are tears in the voice.*'

Unlike its close cousin, the chiffchaff, which prefers mature trees and feeds higher in the vegetation, the willow warbler frequents scrub, small bushes and trees. Both birds are very similar in appearance, as are their domed nests, yet the willow warbler builds on the ground and the chiffchaff just above ground level.

Although the willow warbler is our most numerous summer visitor it only ranks tenth in the national league table of abundance. During most of the 20th century willow warbler numbers remained stable with some local swings. An interesting concept was recently put forward suggesting that migrant species exploit the gaps left behind by resident species. Interestingly, willow warblers were at reduced levels in the 1970s when resident species prospered following a series of mild winters.

CBC surveys have demonstrated a big fall in willow warbler numbers (30% over 25 years) since the late 1980s, particularly in the south of England. Numbers have held up well in Scotland and in the north of England, suggesting that climatic change may well be

behind their overall decrease. The willow warbler is at the most southerly point of its breeding range in the south of England and global warming could be pushing these migrants northwards. Laying dates have become earlier, coinciding with an increase in nest failure rates at the chick stage. This all suggests that as a result of recent climatic change and resultant earlier nesting, sufficient food is not always available for the chicks following late cold snaps.

Decrease

Woodcock

As both a naturalist and a sportsman I have always had a particular fascination for the woodcock. It is a woodland wader that roosts during the day in dry deciduous woodland and flights out at dusk to feed in adjacent damp areas where it probes for earthworms with its long beak. In the spring, dominant males undertake a bat-like territorial display flight in the twilight. The purpose of this roding flight is to attract females on the ground below and it is accompanied by both deep croaking calls and sharp squeaky cries.

The woodcock is a beautiful bird with large, dark 'spaniel eyes' that ensures all-round vision. Its heavily streaked, russet plumage provides superb camouflage when nesting amongst bracken and dead leaves. It has the unique, endearing habit of 'airlifting' its young. If disturbed at its nest the female will move the brood by flying them to a more secure spot, held tightly between her thighs.

The woodcock's sudden appearance when flushed at roost and its jinking flight make it an exciting game bird. Its dark flesh is strong yet delicious, particularly when eaten cold. Countrymen wait in anticipation for the first full moon in November when woodcock migrate in numbers from continental Europe to our more temperate shores. Most birds move south to Ireland, always keeping in front of the cold weather. If the woodcock's long beak is unable to penetrate the frozen soil it will starve.

Few woodcock seen in Britain over the winter months actually breed on our shores. In fact CBC monitoring has demonstrated that native woodcock have declined steeply over the past 25 years although it must be remembered their research is heavily biased

towards the southern half of the country. There were limited breeding records in Britain during the 18th century yet by the end of the 19th century the woodcock was breeding in every county, no doubt aided by the planting of pheasant coverts and associated gamekeepering. Woods with rides for easy access and immature trees are preferred habitat. The period from 1950-1975 saw a major expansion of afforestation in Britain. During the 1980s many of the woods reached the thicket stage and woodcock numbers started to fall.

It is interesting to note that other woodland birds have declined over recent years. Many of our natural woodlands have been drained and the recent series of dry springs is likely to have reduced both breeding success and the overall numbers of nesting birds. Modern chemicals used to dose cattle and sheep have reduced the availability of invertebrate food. Furthermore it should not be forgotten that the woodcock is a shy bird that requires undisturbed roosting grounds during the daylight hours. The enormous increase in the numbers of deer and reared pheasants over the last two decades has lowered the quality of the woodcock's natural habitat.

Decrease

Woodpigeon

Many countrymen consider the woodpigeon the worst avian pest in Britain. Not being an arable farmer I have a more tolerant view. When seen close to, such as in a London park where it becomes surprisingly tame, the woodpigeon is a handsome bird with smooth blue-grey plumage and a pink flush on its breast. It performs a delightful court-ship flight when a steep climb is climaxed by a bout of wing clapping terminating in a downward glide. Above all it entertains us with a lovely lazy, soothing, cooing song, evocative of hot, hazy high summer days. I will not allow the woodpigeon to be shot at anywhere near my house or garden.

The woodpigeon is our largest pigeon. It is wary of man and difficult to approach in the countryside. Historically it was a bird of the woods until it started to breed in isolated trees, hedgerows and villages around 200 years ago. It is the enemy of every farmer, foraging on clover early in the year, arable fields in early spring, ripening grain in summer, stubbles in the autumn and green root crops like kale in hard weather. There was an explosion in the population during the 19th century with an expansion of arable farming which included the provision of green crops such as clover and tur-nips to feed livestock in the winter months.

The winter months were always perilous for the woodpigeon and their numbers were decimated by the severe weather of 1962-63. The introduction of a new crop in the form of oilseed rape in the 1980s changed the woodpigeon's fortunes; winter starvation ceased overnight. Additional varieties of oilseed rape have allowed this crop to be grown further north and as a result pigeon numbers in northern England and Scotland have risen.

After the war the pigeon survived the winter as best it could by feeding on clover and weeds. Organised shoots in February made little differ-ence to numbers as many of these birds would have died from starvation. The woodpigeon population dropped in the 1960s as more and more land was put into cereal production. The introduction of herbicides and a switch to autumn-sown corn resulted in less fallow land and reduced availability of weeds as a winter food source. Before the agricultural revolution the pigeon relied on natural foods such as acorns and beech mast to help them through the winter but some years the crop failed completely. Ivy berries and weed seeds on their own did not support a large pigeon population.

The woodpigeon breeding season is now a long one with eggs having been recorded in the nest every month of the year. The farmers' preference for autumn sown corn has resulted in earlier crop ripening, which in turn encourages an extended breeding season. Nesting now begins as early as May whereas previously the woodpigeon tended to raise its family from July to September.

Substantial Increase

 *Wren*

A series of mild winters guarantees that the tiny unobtrusive wren becomes Britain's commonest bird, comprising some ten million pairs. The wren's song is remarkably powerful for a bird of its size. It can be heard singing in virtually any habitat and in any month of the year.

If it was not for its lusty song the wren would be easily overlooked as it spends most of its life foraging for insects and spiders in the undergrowth. There are four species of wren. I have sat on a boat several hundred yards from the shore in Village Bay and listened to the St Kildan variety. The high-pitched trill was clearly audible above the cries of seabirds. Hudson thought the wren's song was its greatest charm: *'it is unlike that of any other British melodist – a loud, bright lyric, the fine, clear, high pitched notes and trills issuing in a continuous rapid stream from beginning to end.'* Grey was most impressed by the contrast between the size of the body and the strength of the song and writes of *'that shattering wren'*. As with the robin he was particularly grateful that the song could be heard in every month of the year.

Others claim the wren's charm lies with its architectural abilities, for the male is a compulsive nest-builder. He builds a number of snug dome-shaped 'cock-nests' constructed of leaves and moss. The favoured nest is then chosen by the female and lined with feathers. One of the discarded nests is often used as a communal roost in the winter as these little birds suffer terribly in harsh winter conditions.

Winter weather is the major determinant of the wren population as they face the difficulties of a high rate of heat loss and a poor capacity to store winter fat. The wren population was decimated during the cold winters of the 1960s and then witnessed a rapid increase in the mid-seventies. Woodland represents the preferred habitat and, following recovery from the severe winter of 1962-3, gardens and farmland were the last habitats to be recolonised.

Thankfully the population has been stable over the last decade following a series of mild winters. A more recent concern centres on global warming, which can give rise to earlier nesting attempts. This leaves the wren susceptible not only to higher predation as a result of a lack of vegetation in which to conceal its nest, but also exposed to a late cold snap which might well cause brood failure.

Stable

Yellowhammer

The yellowhammer ranks as one of Britain's best-loved birds yet tragically its numbers have crashed over the last ten years. The bright yellow cock bird is strikingly beautiful and his song, often likened to '*a little bit of bread and no cheese*', is familiar to most country-men.

I have two abiding memories of this handsome bunting. In the late 1980s we spent New Year in the Borders of Scotland when a light covering of snow carpeted the open rolling countryside. While driving down a small country lane we came across a stubble field deco-rated in a patchwork of colour. A huge flock of finches and buntings, including yellow-hammers, greenfinches and linnets, was foraging for seeds. A rare sight indeed today.

One of the joys of the yellowhammer is that he sings late into August when other birds are silent. My parents-in-law used to live near Winchester, and the yellowhammer was so evocative of those high summer Hampshire days. On drowsy hot afternoons the only sound emanating from the hedgerows on the edge of the downs was the repetitive, wheezy ditty of the yellowhammer. WH Hudson describes the song in *British Birds*:

'*it is composed of half a dozen or more short, reedy notes, all exactly alike, and shaken out, as it were, in a hurry, followed by a long, thin note, or by two notes, slightly melodious in character. It may be described as a trivial or monotonous song, but it is a summer sound which most people hear with pleasure.*'

Over the last 25 years yellowhammer numbers have fallen by over 60% on a steepening curve, following a period of relative stability. A substantial recovery was noted by CBC surveys following the severe winter of 1962-1963. Prior to this date there was little evidence of any long-term change in yellowhammer populations except a sharp decline in the 1950s, most noticeably in eastern England.

The yellowhammer is a farmland bird and, being one of the larger seed-eaters with a more powerful bill, it exploits bulkier seeds such as cereal grains. Its initial decline coin-cided with the introduction of toxic chemicals for seed dressings. Coupled with the loss of hedgerows over this period and general urbanisation, the effects on the yellowhammer population were predictable.

But why the catastrophic crash in numbers over the last decade? Returning to my Border country experience there is no doubt that the loss of winter stubbles has taken a terrible toll. The switch from spring-sown corn to autumn planting has resulted in a damaging re-duction in winter food for the yellowhammer. Tidier farmyards and more efficient methods of grain storage have also played their part.

The loss of rough grass field margins, hedges and ditches to intensive agriculture has meant fewer nesting opportunities for yellowhammers. The Game Conservancy has undertaken some recent research demonstrating the potential that game management offers for the conservation of the yellowhammer. Game management practices such as winter feeding with wheat, the maintenance of hedgerows, the establishment of conservation headlands and predation control, all greatly assist yellowhammers. They prefer to nest low down in a bank, hedge or in grassy vegetation. Maintaining wide field margin strips of perennial grasses provides an important nesting habitat for yellowhammers. The Game Conservancy has also shown that predation of these birds by crows is much lower in herbaceous field boundary vegetation than in the shrubby vegetation of the hedge itself.

In the nesting season the yellowhammer needs invertebrate food such as spiders, beetles and caterpillars on which to feed their chicks. This is available not only in herbaceous vegetation around field boundaries but also in game crops. Insects that feed on weeds are a vital source of protein for young chicks and, without such a resource close to the nest, young yellowhammers, like grey partridge chicks, simply perish. With the application of widespread modern herbicides and insecticides, this is precisely what has happened. Hence the vital importance of well-run shooting estates for British songbirds.

A gleam of hope for the future lies with the introduction of set-aside, albeit designed as a production control measure. Rotational set-aside, where a field is left as stubble for one year with a naturally regenerated vegetation cover, has provided foraging habitat for a wide range of seed-eating species, including the yellowhammer.

Dangerous Decrease

Yellow wagtail

The yellow wagtail is a most attractive, canary yellow, summer visitor. It is not as such a rare wagtail but rather one of patchy distribution. It is a bird of open grassy places. It is associated with damp meadows along river valleys, freshwater marshland, the edges of lakes and sewage farms. It has a brief warbling song punctuated with a sharp wag-tail-like *'tsweep'* call-note. The yellow wagtail is part of a family group that sports different varieties of head pattern and is replaced by the blue-headed wagtail on the Continent. Britain holds almost the entire population of the distinctive race *flavissima* and as such any population changes are of significance.

   The yellow wagtail is a social bird and in late summer I have seen it in small flocks on the reclaimed water meadows behind Sandwich Bay in Kent preparing for the long journey to west Africa. It is often confused with its close cousin the grey wagtail but the yellow wagtail is not a true 'water person' and is therefore not affected by changes in river management.

   Yellow wagtail numbers have been falling since the turn of the century and have declined by nearly 30% in the last 25 years. The early 20th century saw big declines in Ireland and a contraction in the south-west of England and in the north. In Scotland it retreated to the Clyde valley. The general intensification of agriculture was probably behind the decline with a loss of breeding habitat due to drainage and the conversion of much pasture to arable land. Today it occurs more frequently in coastal south-east England.

   The yellow wagtail nests in both wet grassland and increasingly in tangled crops such as peas or potatoes. Its favoured habitat, fields with a varied sward containing a high proportion of bare earth and perhaps surrounded by wet ditches, is becoming rarer and rarer. The wagtail will nest in the taller tussocks and forage for invertebrates in the bare areas and around water. The yellow wagtail is often found in close association with cattle as it catches insects disturbed by the animal's hoofs. Intensively managed grassland where silage is taken results in dense vegetation and prevents access to

insect food. On arable land early nests tend to be in cereals and later nests in potato and pea fields where cover is insufficient to provide the necessary concealment. Unfortunately many of the latter are harvested too early for the birds to complete raising their young.

   The yellow wagtail is a trans-Saharan migrant and as such could be vulnerable to habitat and climate changes in its winter quarters. There is no evidence that it has been adversely affected by drought.

Decrease

Postscript
by Rt. Hon. Lord Lamont of Lerwick

Even the tabloid press has become increasingly aware of the decline or disappearance of many once familiar British birds. We now regularly see articles about how there are many fewer song thrushes, skylarks, tree sparrows, and even starlings. Many Londoners are aware that the cheeky, noisy house sparrow has almost disappeared in our capital city. Why this has happened in London but not in Paris or Milan is a mystery. It would be good to have an answer.

It is for this reason Michael Waterhouse's book *The Strange Death of British Birdsong* is so timely. This beautifully illustrated book charts the fortunes of around 140 birds in the English countryside. With the decline of each species also goes the disappearance of their song. Our woodlands and grasslands become quieter. The word 'song' is not restricted to the mellifluous outpourings of warblers, but includes countryside sounds like the rasping call of the corncrake. For each species in decline Michael covers the reasons for their demise; sometimes there is no clear-cut evidence; he can only speculate.

Many of the birds that have experienced the sharpest drops in numbers in recent years are farmland birds. This would suggest that changes in agricultural methods are among the reasons for the disappearance of many birds such as cirl or corn buntings. The greatest declines of ground nesting birds have been in grassland areas. Modern grassland is increasingly barren, and in addition a lot of wet grassland has been drained. Permanent grasslands are now virtually all ploughed and reseeded with the result that flowers, bugs, insects and food have declined.

The revolution in herbicides has led to the extinction of weeds on arable land. There has been a dramatic change in the season of cultivation with the advent of autumn sowing resulting in the loss of winter stubble and tilled ground in the spring. For skylarks and lapwings nesting in tall dense winter cereals is almost impossible. In particular, come June, crops are far too tall when second and third breeding attempts are made.

It is not, of course, possible to turn the clock back in a futile attempt to return to some mythical golden age. But it should be possible even at this late date to reverse some of the catastrophic errors that have been made in the Common Agricultural Policy (CAP).

Most people are aware of the waste of the CAP, its food mountains and the harm to third world economies. They are less conscious of the harm done to the countryside. Yet it is difficult to overstate the environmental damage. A paper for the Royal Society concluded that 'agricultural intensification has had deleterious and measurable effects on farmland bird populations. Our results suggest that such effects are detectable at a continental level, making them comparable in scale with deforestation and global climate change as major anthropogenic threats to biodiversity. Rapid progress is required in adapting EU agricultural policy...' *

The most harmful aspect of the CAP is that the subsidies were based directly on how much the farmer produced. It was this that caused the hugely wasteful surpluses. For more than thirty

300

years EU subsidies have encouraged farmers to cultivate every square inch of land. Producing for subsidy rather than for a market has also led to needlessly and massively intensive farming with the heavy use of fertilizers.

What has happened in much of Western Europe could also happen in Eastern Europe. Many of the species that are less common in Western Europe like the corncrake, the yellowhammer, the corn bunting and the red-backed shrike are more numerous in Eastern Europe where agricultural methods are less intensive. The same paper for the Royal Society quoted above has shown that farmland bird population declines between 1970 and 1990 were significantly greater in Western European countries than in former communist countries. The study demonstrated that cereal yields, milk yields, fertilizer use, and tractor use were significant predictors of bird population trends. Cereal yield explained the greatest variation in populations.

It has never been the purpose of agriculture to preserve a particular landscape. It would be unrealistic to expect farmers to go back to spring sowing. Planting crops in the autumn gives the plants longer to grow and thus generates more income. We need to look at ways of adapting winter planting that does not destroy the farmers' already thin margins.

RSPB research has been directed at ways to make winter cereal fields more attractive to skylarks and lapwings by creating spaces between the crops. Skylarks feed chicks mainly on insects but weed seeds become the main food in winter.

We need more funding tied to the farmer's activities, which reflect the public needs. That means including wildlife in farming's overall aims and directing part of the subsidy towards the environment.

But what is needed most of all is root and branch reform of the CAP. The Government does appear to have made a breakthrough although I have seen many so-called reforms of the CAP come to nothing. In June 2003 Agricultural Ministers agreed sweeping reforms that will continue subsidies for the time being, but in return for greater environmental sensitivity.

Instead of a single policy applied across Europe the reforms set minimum requirements for member states to decouple the link between subsidies and the quantity of crops they grow or the livestock they keep.

The Government has decided that provided farmers keep land in 'agricultural order' they will be paid a fixed single farm payment no matter how little food they produce. This is to be warmly welcomed.

The decoupling of subsidy payments from production should have positive implications for the environment and our bird populations. Measures to help the environment will become more attractive because conservation interests will no longer be competing with production. Lower prices will reduce the incentive for overproduction where there is no market, and with lower prices intensive producers will need to cut costs.

Let us hope the promised reform of the CAP will in time bring back some of the birdsong that has disappeared from our countryside. It is comfort to remember that bird populations have declined in the past and then witnessed an improvement in their fortunes. Once organochlorine pesticides like DDT were banned species that had suffered, particularly birds of prey, subsequently recovered. Right and timely action can still help to save endangered birds.

* Agricultural intensification and the collapse of Europe's farmland bird populations by P.E. Donald, R.E. Green and M.F. Heath

Index

Index

Bibliography

Including but not limited to:-

Breeding Birds in the Wider Countryside. BTO Research Report

The New Atlas of Breeding Birds in Britain & Ireland 1988-91. T & AD Poyser

The Breeding Bird Survey. BTO Research

The Wetland Bird Survey 1999-2000. Wildfowl & Wetlands Trust and others

The State of the UK's Birds. RSPB/BTO and others

The Population Status of Birds in the UK. Birds of Conservation Concern 2002-2007. RSBP/BTO research

Red Data Birds in Britain. T & AD Poyser

The Atlas of Breeding Birds in Britain & Ireland. T & AD Poyser

The Historical Atlas of Breeding Birds in Britain & Ireland 1875-1900. T & AD Poyser

The State of the Nation's Birds. Chris Mead

Population Trends in British Breeding Birds. BTO research

The Charm of Birds. Grey of Fallodon

British Birds. WH Hudson